Don't Ask, Don't Tell

Don't Ask, Don't Tell:

Homosexuality, Chaplaincy, and the Modern Military

Edited by
John D. Laing
and
Page M. Brooks

RESOURCE *Publications* · Eugene, Oregon

DON'T ASK, DON'T TELL
Homosexuality, Chaplaincy, and the Modern Military

Resource Publications
An Imprint of Wipf and Stock Publishers
199 W. 8th Ave., Suite 3
Eugene, OR 97401
www.wipfandstock.com

ISBN 13: 978-1-62032-606-0
Manufactured in the U.S.A.

Dedicated to
the Lord Jesus Christ
who died to grant us forgiveness and rose to give us life
and to
the chaplains of the armed forces
who serve God by ministering His Word
and country by loving service persons

Contents

List of Contributors ix
Acknowledgments xi
Foreword—by Douglas L. Carver xiii
Preface—by John D. Laing xvii

1 Introduction: Don't Ask, Don't Tell! (Don't Care?) / 1
Homosexual Service in the Military
—Douglas Lee and the Editors

Part One Understanding Homosexuality

2 "A Gay Gene?" / 15
Homosexuality, Biology, and Philosophy of Science
—J. Alan Branch

3 "Rainbow Rights?" / 54
Homosexuality, Political Activity, and the Law
—John D. Laing

Part Two Responding to Homosexuality

4 "An Abomination?" / 103
Homosexuality, the Bible, and Christian Theology
—Page Matthew Brooks

5 "Virtue or Obedience?" / 125
Homosexuality, Repeal of DADT, and Chaplains
—John D. Laing

6 "Hate the Sin, Love the Sinner?" / 160
Chaplain Ministry to Homosexual Service Members and their Families
—Scott N. Callaham

7 Afterword / 182
The Questions Surrounding Homosexuality and Military Service
—John D. Laing

Commonly Asked Questions about the Bible and Homosexuality / 197
—Page Matthew Brooks

Bibliography / 203

Contributors

John D. Laing, Ph.D., Southern Baptist Theological Seminary, 2000, is Associate Professor of Theology & Philosophy at Southwestern Baptist Theological Seminary's Havard School for Theological Studies in Houston, Texas, and Director of the seminary's Chaplaincy programs. He is also a chaplain (Lieutenant Colonel) in the Texas Army National Guard, serving as Division Chaplain for the 36th Infantry Division (HVY), headquartered in Austin, Texas. His mobilizations/deployments include Noble Eagle (ONE), 2001-2002; Kosovo Force 7 (2005-2006); and Iraqi Freedom (2009-2010).

Page Matthew Brooks, Ph.D., New Orleans Baptist Theological Seminary, 2008, is Assistant Professor of Theology & Islamic Studies at New Orleans Baptist Theological Seminary and Book Review Editor for *The Journal of Baptist Theology and Ministry*. He also serves as a Brigade Chaplain (Major) in the Louisiana Army National Guard. His deployments include Operation Iraqi Freedom/New Dawn, 2010.

Douglas E. Lee is the Executive Director of the Presbyterian and Reformed Joint Commission for Chaplain and Military Personnel (PRJC), a chaplaincy endorsing agency servicing six denominations. He assumed this position after retiring from a 31-year career as a chaplain in the United States Army Reserves. He attained the rank of Brigadier General, serving as the Army Chief of Chaplains Director, Reserve Components Integration (2004-2005), and as the Assistant Chief of Chaplains for Mobilizations and Readiness (2005-2006).

J. Alan Branch, Ph.D., Southeastern Baptist Theological Seminary, 2001, is Professor of Christian Ethics at Midwestern Baptist Theological Seminary in Kansas City, Missouri. He also served as a chaplain

(Captain) in the United States Army Reserves. His deployments include Operation New Dawn (2010-2011).

Scott Nelson Callaham, Ph.D., Southwestern Baptist Theological Seminary, 2006, has served as a visiting professor at both Malaysia Baptist Theological Seminary and Singapore Baptist Theological Seminary. He also was a reserve and active duty Navy Chaplain for nine years (2002-2011), completing his service as a Lieutenant Commander. His most recent assignments included tours on U.S.S. John C. Stennis (CVN-74) and as a Battalion Chaplain at the United States Naval Academy at Annapolis, Maryland (2008-2011).

Acknowledgments

THE EDITORS AND CONTRIBUTORS wish to thank all who have supported their ministries and work on this volume. Our families, employers, churches, friends, and colleagues have provided invaluable service through prayer, feedback, editorial assistance, and encouragement.

We would like to offer specific thanksgiving, first, to our Lord and Savior, Jesus Christ, through whom God's infinite grace has been granted to us and works in us. Second, we would like to thank each of our wives: Stefana Dan Laing, Ashley Nalls Brooks, Nancy Lee, Lisa Branch, and Chingman Callaham. Ladies, we want to publicly express our love for you, thank you for your patient endurance through the writing of this work and through multiple mobilizations and deployments, and acknowledge your value as wives and mothers of noble character—Proverbs 31 women. You are far more valuable than gold or precious stones. We are each truly blessed to have found you (v. 10), have lacked nothing good because of it (v. 11), and our ministries and stature(s) were only enriched by our associations with you (v. 23). We love you.

Foreword

by Douglas L. Carver

IN JANUARY 2009, I received a sobering phone call from my senior non-commissioned officer responsible for the strategic leadership and management of the Army's 2900 chaplain assistants. He said, "Get ready, sir. The Sergeants Major of the Army have just advised the Army's senior leadership that we're prepared to support the potential repeal of the Department of Defense's 'Don't Ask, Don't Tell' (DADT) policy. We agreed that we should not pass this cultural challenge on to the next generation of NCOs, even though we're currently engaged in wars in Iraq and Afghanistan." He ended with these prophetic words, "Get your chaplains ready, sir. It's coming."

Like many others in the military and religious communities, I am surprised by the speed with which unforeseen events have taken place since the repeal of DADT, and the manner in which the media and special interest groups have shaped the public mind regarding the issue of homosexuality. The American culture, including a growing number of Christian churches and organizations, accepts and celebrates the homosexual lifestyle to be as normal and legitimate as that of heterosexuals. In retrospect, a resource like this book you are presently reading would have been, and will prove to be, an invaluable reference point to navigate the uncharted waters of the post-DADT military environment, the potential repeal of the Defense of Marriage Act, and a cultural worldview that embraces homosexual lifestyles and conduct. Let me offer a few recommendations on how this volume will assist chaplains, pastors, lay leaders, churches, and religious organizations.

First of all, consider this resource as a kind of playbook to fully understand the grand strategy of the gay agenda that was developed and implemented in the United States to effect cultural change well over 25 years ago. Second, absorb the contents and conclusions of this book with the compassionate heart of a pastor and the love of Jesus Christ. On numerous occasions in his earthly ministry, Jesus taught His disciples that He had come to seek out and to save the lost, regardless of their sinful behavior or lifestyle. Far too often Christians and local churches have failed to reach out to the homosexual community with the same merciful love that has been shown to us in our sinful state. The writers of this book provoke us to serve as agents of reconciliation to all people, regardless of their sexual orientation.

Finally, this book contains a strong and timeless prophetic message. We must remain true and uncompromising in obedience to the Word of God. As Christians, we are subject to the authority of Almighty God as revealed in the Holy Scriptures in all matters of life. Read this book with the words of Jeremiah 6:16 in mind, "Thus says the LORD, 'Stand by the [cross]roads, and look, and ask for the ancient paths, where the good way is; and walk in it, and find rest for your souls.'" (ESV).

The American church stands at the crossroads today perhaps unlike any other generation of Christians in recent history. An increasing tension exists between the church and the culture. Not only do we live in an era that denies absolute truth, but we also live in an age of increasing hostility directed towards those who claim the existence of authoritative truth as recorded in the sacred Scripture. Renowned theologian, D. A. Carson, in his book *The Intolerance of Tolerance*, writes that today's world labels people as intolerable who would simply "question or contradict the view that all opinions are equal in value, that all worldviews have equal worth, that all stances are equally valid."[1]

The writers of this book challenge us personally to choose the right course as we stand at the crossroad of human sexuality issues, and that we faithfully instruct and guide those under our God-anointed pastoral leadership as well. The Bible clearly defines God's perfect design for man and woman, holy matrimony, and the family. I commend the writers of this book for their courage, candor, conviction, and commitment to keep us faithful to the sacred Scripture that has formed and guided

1. Carson, *Intolerance of Tolerance*, 12.

the Christian church and all of humanity for thousands of years. I pray that this volume convicts all who read its contents to remain under the authority of God regarding all aspects of our lives. Only then can we find rest from the plethora of cultural issues that plague our souls.

Douglas L. Carver
Chaplain (Major General) Doug Carver
United States Army, Retired
22nd Army Chief of Chaplains

Preface

by John D. Laing

Paul Tillich has correctly noted that experience is essential to theological development, because "experience is the medium" though which theologians receive and interpret the sources of theology.[1] Evangelicals have often bristled at existentialist theologies, largely because they tend to accord experience too great a role in theological method, and to displace or minimize the status of Scripture as revelation. Still, it cannot be denied that experience impacts scriptural interpretation, especially with regard to the application of its truth in one's life. Therefore, we should not eschew consideration of our experiences when engaging in theological reflection, even while giving the biblical text as interpreted through sound hermeneutical principles and responsible exegesis, the place of primacy.

My own experience was one of growing up in rural North Carolina, just outside a relatively small city in the foothills of the Appalachian Mountains. Since we lived across the county line, I attended high school approximately 20 miles away, down winding country roads which passed many farms and lakes. The community exuded Southern charm, and the people were genuinely friendly and hard-working, salt-of-the-earth types. Although I was born in Canada, I still consider myself today something of a Southern country-boy. I loved my childhood there, love the area, and always enjoy it when I can get back for a visit.

As with most things in life, though, it had its negative aspects. When my family moved there in 1978, overt racism was still prevalent, and some persons expressed continued disappointment and anger over the results of the American Civil War (or as I was informed, *War Between*

1. Tillich, *Systematic Theology* 1:40.

the States, or *War of Northern Aggression*). In fact, I got into my first fight in school when a boy attacked me for no reason, other than he thought I was a "Yankee" (and perhaps figured he could take me because I was in the academic classes). All of this is just to say that there were some folks (certainly not all or even the majority!) in the community who were not only *traditional* in their beliefs, but downright hostile to those different from them. If racism was something of a problem, then what has come to be known as "homophobia" was epidemic! Toleration of homosexuality was not even a consideration, much less an expectation, and it would not have been surprising if a cross were burned in the yard of a homosexual couple, had one been discovered.

That is why I was so shocked to find out that one of my junior high teachers was gay. My parents had run into this teacher and his partner at an art event in the city, and as they all conversed, they discovered the connection. When my parents first shared their newfound knowledge with me, I must admit that I had an immediate sense of revulsion, but after the initial shock, I began to think about the man himself. He was somewhat soft-spoken, clean-cut, kind, and fair, a generally all-around nice guy. He wasn't my favorite teacher, but certainly not the worst I had ever had. I liked him, and I found myself fighting the urge to think about him in labels or stereotypes, or in terms of his sexuality. Rather, I worked hard at simply viewing him as a human being, rather than as a gay or homosexual man (or worse, a "faggot"). I never told anyone what I knew and never mentioned it publicly until now. At least I don't remember doing so, and I do recall feeling a sense of responsibility to protect his secret for the sake of his job and perhaps, his personal safety.

As I have contributed to this work and edited its chapters, I have earnestly sought to think about that teacher and whether he would be hurt by its words. At one level, of course, I should expect that he would be, as it is always somewhat hurtful when others express disapproval of your actions or lifestyle. At another level, though, it is my hope (and the hope of the other contributors) that each of the chapters has conveyed not mere disapproval of the homosexual lifestyle, but also compassion and love, and a desire to gain understanding of those in the homosexual community. My experience of knowing that teacher so many years ago transformed my own thinking about homosexuals and homosexuality. It brought a human face to the issue. Suddenly, homosexuals were not objects of scorn or derision, but were people with feelings, hopes, and aspirations, and who had families who care for and love them. They were worthy of my compassion, concern, and respect. That experience did not change my perspective on the normalcy of homosexuality—I thought it contrary to nature, though I did not take a moral stand against it (I was brought up in a very open-minded, liberal, and basically secular home)—but it did give me pause when joining with others in joking about the topic. Regrettably, I did not always refrain from such juvenile antics; I was a typical boy, after all. Nevertheless, after becoming a Christian and having a religious basis for my objections to homosexuality, I have retained my view that homosexual persons are worthy of love and respect (and in point of fact, it has been heightened). It is in this spirit that this work has been offered.

With this in mind, there is one issue not so clearly addressed which many readers may have expected to comprise a large portion of the book's material and which deserves mention at the outset: the question of the rights of conservative chaplains in the military (or working for any other organization, governmental or private) to preach and counsel in accordance with their personal beliefs and with the dictates of their ecclesiastical endorsers. To be sure, concerns over the possibility of forced homogeneity and/or persecution of those who hold fast to their moral and religious convictions regarding the sinfulness of homosexual conduct abound and are valid, and the topic is woven into the fabric of almost every chapter of the book. Lee's introductory essay highlights many cases where those fears were borne out through a variety of situations and scenarios. Branch also expresses concern that the use of science in the courts and by governmental entities may eventually serve as the basis for limiting speech that is critical of homosexuality. I discuss the issue briefly in both of my chapters, noting that we ought not let it consume our energies and that we have a strong legal basis upon which to stand, if ever the time comes when religious speech on the topic of homosexuality is curtailed in favor of so-called "politically correct" speech. However, the question was intentionally left a minor point in the volume.

What is of greatest concern here is that there is a fundamental flaw at the heart of the whole discussion surrounding the place of homosexuals and homosexuality in American society and culture. All parties involved seem to place too much emphasis on their own rights, to the detriment of civil discourse about personhood, morality, and the Good. Homosexuals demand their right to live as they choose, regardless of how their exercise of that right may affect others. If it causes others harm, if it disrupts social harmony, if it infringes on the rights of others, so be it, for they have their rights! Similarly, socially conservative chaplains (in particular evangelicals) demand their right to express their opposition to and beliefs about homosexuality, with little concern about how doing so may hurt others. If it causes emotional distress to those who struggle with homosexual tendencies, if it drives families of homosexuals from the church, so be it, for we have our free exercise rights! In both cases, it seems, greater concern for self than compassion for the other is being exhibited.

I would like to suggest that while rights are vitally important to both our national identity and sense of our own humanity, they should not be exalted above another, equally important aspect of those two fundamental bases of our being: community. The idea of community sits at the very heart of the concept of the nation-state, and if it means anything for one to call himself an "American," it is that he belongs to a people with a proud heritage grounded in ideals of not only freedom, but also hard work, cooperation, and unity. Community is even more fundamental to the *being* (*ontos*) of humanity, for it is an essential component or aspect of what it means to say humans are made in the image of God.

The concept of the *imago dei* has received a significant amount of attention by systematic and biblical theologians in recent years. The doctrine has historically been approached in one of two ways: either by asking how humans are unique in the created order (i.e., different from animals), or by considering how humans are like God. The former approach has enjoyed a long tenure, with suggestions ranging from physical oddities like opposable thumbs or an upright gait, to more cerebral traits like rationality or abstract thought, to speculation regarding the spirit or soul. The current discussion has tended to follow the latter method, with a number of thinkers reflecting on the possibilities Trinitarian theology offers for understanding the image, along with consideration of the biblical text.

Perhaps the most obvious biblical passage related to the meaning of the *imago dei* is that of humanity's creation recorded in Genesis (Gen 1:24-31, esp. 26-27). In this passage, three aspects of the image can be seen: dominion, relationality, and similarity. With respect to dominion, it is clear that God tasks humanity with a responsibility to care for the creation; humans are God's representatives and are told to care for the Garden, to "subdue" the creation, and to "rule" over the creatures of the air, land, and sea. Concepts of similarity underlie the language of image and likeness, as noted by the Hebrew terms, *tselem* and *damah*. While there is some controversy over the relationship of the terms one to another, it is abundantly clear that they are often used with regard to pagan idols, which were supposed to represent the god/gods.

Of concern here, though, is the concept of relationality in the image. In the verses following the introduction of God's intent to make humans in His image, the Genesis record states: "So God created man in His own image; He created him in the image of God; He created them male and female. God blessed them, and God said to them, 'Be fruitful, multiply, fill the earth, . . .'" (Gen 1:27–28). Interestingly, the passage goes on to again affirm man's unique rulership over the created order. Several indications point to a relational understanding of the image in this passage. First, the more personal deliberative introductory statement to the creation of humanity points to relationality ("Let Us make man . . ." vs. "Let there be . . ."). Second, the gender distinction (male and female) associated with the statement that humans are made in the image of God points to this relationality. Third, the point is strengthened when the command to increase through sexual relations is considered. Fourth, and more importantly, the account of woman's creation points to the need for relationality beyond rulership over the beasts ("It is not good for the man to be alone" 2:18). Fifth, the image is directly tied to the sonship of those who are image-bearers. Adam has a son who is after his image and likeness (Gen 5:3), and it is this son (i.e., Seth) who perpetuates the *imago dei*. Thus, the biblical text clearly supports a relational understanding of the image of God in humanity.

The relatively recent revival of Trinitarian theology has yielded a treasure-trove of thought on its significance for understanding the *imago dei*. One of the most creative thinkers on this front has been Colin Gunton, who worked on the topic for well over twenty years. His Bampton Lectures, published under the title, *The One, the Three, and the Many*, along with his later works on Trinitarian theology, have reshaped the way Western theologians have approached the subject. Gunton claims that relationality is constitutive of the created order, whose subsistence depends upon the work of humans in it, as they represent God's rule over all. Relationality is so fundamental that, he contends, "the world is what it is by virtue of its relation to those who bear the image of God."[2] By this, he means that the human representation of God in space and time

2. Gunton, *One, Three and Many*, 216. Similarly, Hefner suggests that *imago dei* means that humans portray or represent God to the rest of the creation, but he does not take this to mean dominion. Instead, he sees it as something of a mediatorial role born out of relationship and possibility. See Hefner, "Imago Dei," 88-89.

as the *imago dei* enables the created order to be what it is. Humans bring morality, aesthetics, and intimacy (all fundamental aspects of the created order) into what would be an otherwise brutish world. Drawing on the orthodox conception of Trinitarian theology wherein God is seen as a communion of persons, Gunton argues that both otherness and relationality are necessary for human flourishing: "Only where both are given due stress is personhood fully enabled. Their co-presence will rule out both the kind of egalitarianism which is the denial of particularity, and leads to collectivism, and forms of individualism which in effect deny humanity to those unable to 'stand on their own feet.'"[3] He notes that modernity's focus on individualism and individual rights has emphasized the otherness aspect, with disastrous results to man, for it manifests itself in either anarchy or its seeming opposite, forced homogeneity. Gunton therefore places emphasis on the countervailing notion of a relationality that is grounded in love of the other and mutual constitutiveness. The point, of course, is that if Gunton and others who have argued similarly are correct in their assertion that relationality is fundamental to the being of God and is therefore, an aspect of the *imago dei*, then at least a part of what it means to be human is to be in relation, over against the assertion of individuality.

However, the tenor of much of the current discussion regarding the roles homosexuals play in American society takes almost none of this into consideration because of the overdeveloped sense of entitlement and the exaggerated focus upon rights by the parties involved. Individual concerns have generally taken precedence over communal concerns or concern for the other. The discussion is cast in oppositional terms, with language of "war" being more typical than language of brotherhood or community.

To be sure, we are involved in something of a broad cultural war, what George has called a *clash of orthodoxies*, and the stakes arguably couldn't be higher.[4] The very impetus behind this work's compilation was the combination of a profound love for our nation and its military and a sincere concern for their future. Nevertheless, in what follows, we hope that it is not only a battle-cry which is heard; indeed, we hope that such a cry is overshadowed by a call to love, even while the former is still present. As Christians, we seek to honor God by upholding His Word and the

3. Gunton, *Promise of Trinitarian Theology*, 117. See also Schwöbel and Gunton, *Persons, Divine and Human*.

4. George, *Clash of Orthodoxies*.

standards it sets forth regarding morality, interactions with others, and our dispositions toward Him. Out of our love for God, we have sought to balance our proclamation of what we take to be the truth of Scripture with a clear communication of our love for others. We have sought to maintain humble attitudes, submitted to God and selfless in our interactions with others. We have not sought to assert our own rights, but to defend God's Word and the rights of others to hear that Word, while also respecting the rights and honoring the lives of homosexuals. If we have fallen short in any of these goals, the blame belongs squarely on our shoulders, for we are frail, limited, and prone to sin.

In this spirit, we offer the present volume in the hope that it proves helpful to those in chaplaincy or in military service who struggle with how to respond to open service of homosexuals. We also hope it can serve as a basis for understanding among those within and without the homosexual community, especially for those serving in the armed forces. Finally, we hope the work can foster thoughtful and respectful dialog about the issues related to homosexuality in the broader culture. In all of this, we desire the work to honor the Lord.

John D. Laing
Houston, TX
2013

1

Introduction: "Don't Ask, Don't Tell! (Don't Care?)"

Homosexual Service in the Military

—Douglas Lee and the Editors

Religious liberty is under attack in America today. Federal mandates to provide abortion services, litigation from people "offended" by Christian references, university students being discriminated against for their personal religious convictions, virulent attacks via many kinds of media . . . all point to a dramatic changing moral climate in the United States and a hostility to conservative Christian sensibilities in some quarters.

Many American groups have been concerned about religious liberty issues from the beginning of America. For example, Baptists were in the forefront of these issues during the formation of this fragile republic, as were other minority religious groups (e.g., Jewish, Unitarian, etc.). Baptist writer, blogger, historian, and teacher Don Boys declares, "The fact is, we would not have the First Amendment (and probably the other nine) if it were not for the Baptists, especially those in Virginia and Massachusetts . . . They wrote in part: 'When the Constitution first made its appearance in Virginia, we, as a society, feared that the liberty of conscience, dearer to us than property or life, was not sufficiently secured. Perhaps our jealousies were heightened by the usage we received in Virginia, under the regal government, when mobs, fines, bonds and prisons were our frequent repast . . .'"[1]

1. Boys, "Washington, Jefferson, Madison, Baptists, and the Constitution!"

Don't Ask, Don't Tell

Anyone interested in the preservation of America's founding principles ought to be just as concerned about religious conscience or liberty today at those Founders were then, not only for our military personnel, but for our society in general. It seems that the efforts of homosexual (aka Gay, Lesbian, Bisexual, Transgender or GLBT) lobbyists are focused on weakening religious freedom. For example, consider the astounding comment which came from the lips of the Commissioner of the Equal Employment Opportunity Commission, Chai Feldblum, in 2006. In addressing the potential conflict between religious liberty and homosexual conduct, she said, "I'm having a hard time coming up with any case in which religious liberty should win." She made similar arguments in her law review article on that topic, stating that the conflict was a "zero-sum game" where "society should come down on the side of protecting" homosexual conduct.[2]

As chaplains, we prefer to speak and write about the joys of the chaplaincy with titles such as "The Excitement of the Chaplaincy!" or "Do you want High Adventure? Become a chaplain!" We much prefer talking about how chaplains "nurture the living, care for the wounded and honor the dead" or how chaplains "professionally operate in a religiously diverse environment," to discussing the potential difficulties faced by this unique ministry. But the so-called "Don't Ask; Don't Tell" repeal has become something of a fixture in America's landscape today, and needs to be addressed biblically, theologically, philosophically, and perhaps most importantly, ministerially.

The policy was first enacted during the presidential administration of Bill Clinton, as an attempted compromise between those who wished to lift the ban on homosexual service in the military, and those who wished to maintain current policy of ensuring the ban through actions in the recruitment process. It was officially announced by President Clinton on July 19, 1993 at Fort McNair's National Defense University in Washington as "Don't Ask, Don't Tell, Don't Pursue." As with most compromise situations, no parties were satisfied, and many feared it would prove disastrous to their respective concerns. Supporters of gay rights felt betrayed by the President, who had promised to lift the ban during his campaign, and expressed disappointment with the policy because it appeared to change nothing. In fact, many have since claimed that DADT actually led to more discharges of homosexuals because it created a false

2. Feldblum, "Employment Commissioner."

sense of security for gay and lesbian service members and because many commanders failed to follow the third dictate, "Don't Pursue." The result, they argue, was much government waste in time, resources, and talent (not to mention the investment of training in thousands of personnel eventually discharged), and a breakdown, rather than strengthening, of unit cohesion. For example, Frank writes, "'Don't ask, don't tell' has invaded the privacy of all service members—gay, straight, and everything in between—by casting a cloud of suspicion and uncertainty over the intimate lives of everyone in the armed forces. Straight service members have been investigated, threatened, and even discharged . . . The resulting atmosphere was, at times, akin to a witch hunt, accompanied by inevitable fear and uncertainty . . ."[3] Opponents of homosexual service saw DADT as just the initial step in an all-out assault upon traditional values, and were concerned that it would eventuate in open service of homosexuals. Even prior to the implementation of DADT, James Dobson predicted that the ban would be lifted, if not through executive order or direct legislation, then through the liberal courts. Commenting on Secretary of Defense Les Aspin's comments to that effect, he said, "He's really right . . . We're checkmated . . . the president is going to appoint at least a hundred new federal judges . . . and those guys are out of reach and ultimately they'll be the ones that implement his liberal agenda, and they'll do it for years."[4] Clearly the latter concern was justified.

Still, the ambiguity regarding the status of homosexuals in the United States Armed Services under DADT was nothing new. Many have argued that the U.S. military has a history of selective enforcement of its anti-gay rules and regulations. Haggerty contends that military policies toward gays "have been selectively enacted, enforced, rationalized, ignored, and repealed."[5] Enforcement has generally been tied to draw down in personnel needs, as Shilts and others have shown.[6] As Mezey puts it, "laxity in wartime demonstrates that the military's position on gays in service is often governed by expediency."[7] A brief survey of only a few cases will make the point.

3. Frank, *Unfriendly Fire*, 167. For a thorough argument against the continuance of DADT from a homosexual perspective, see Frank, chapters 7 and 8.

4. Dobson, "Homosexuals in the Military," quoted in Loveland, *American Evangelicals*, 335.

5. Haggerty, "History Repeating Itself," 10.

6. Shilts, *Conduct Unbecoming*.

7. Mezey, *Queers in Court*, 136. See also Shilts, *Conduct Unbecoming*, chapter 6.

Mary Roseann Saal sued the Navy when she was discharged and barred from reenlistment for engaging in homosexual acts. Saal's complaint was that she was deprived due process in her removal from service. California District Court Judge Schwarzer agreed, ruling in her favor, but it was a short-lived victory. The ruling was overturned on appeal by the Ninth Circuit Court, along with two other similar cases.[8] Judge (now Justice) Anthony Kennedy wrote the majority opinion, which relied upon the War Powers clause to give deference to the Navy's opinion in matters pertaining to these issues. Similarly, the Navy discharged James Dronenberg for homosexual acts in the Navy barracks. Dronenberg argued that his rights to privacy and equal protection were violated. District of Columbia Disctrict Court Judge Easch awarded the Navy summary judgment. On appeal, District of Columbia Circuit Court Judge Bork argued that equal protection does not apply and *Griswold* (v. Connecticut) does not extend privacy rights to homosexual conduct. Judge Bork found that the Navy can rationally conclude that homosexual conduct has a harmful effect on morale and discipline and ruled that "the Navy is not required to produce social science data or the results of controlled experiments to prove what common sense and common experience demonstrate."[9]

The tumultuous career of Army Staff Sergeant Perry Watkins is perhaps the most clear example of the military's selective enforcement of these policies. When he was drafted in 1967, Watkins was very open about his homosexual tendencies, but was nevertheless enlisted. In fact, he sought discharge when he discovered that another recruit was removed from service for being gay, but his request was denied. Despite being aware of Watkins's homosexuality, military officials allowed him to re-enlist on several occasions, until 1975, when his commanding officer began discharge proceedings against him due to his homosexuality. Over the next 15 years, Watkins battled the Army in the courts, first for trying to remove him involuntarily from service, and then for denying

8. *Matlovich v. Secretary of the Air Force* (1976) and *Berg v. Claytor* (1977). Interestingly, these two cases were combined on appeal, and the government lost! *Beller v. Middendorf* 632 F. 2d 788 (1977).

9. *Dronenberg v. Zech* 741 f. 2d 1388 (1984), 1398. The important point to note is that the courts have generally deferred tot eh military leadership with regard to limitations upon service members' individual rights for the good of the military (readiness, effectiveness, etc.), and arguments against homosexual service—whether tied to perceived security risks or to detrimental effects upon unit cohesion and morale—have always been available.

his security clearance. Watkins eventually won his cases, gained back pay for the time he was out of the service, and granted retirement benefits.[10]

Many wonder what the effect of the repeal is having on the armed services, in particular with respect to military chaplaincy. A brief survey of some recent homosexual lobbying efforts and legal challenges can give a good idea of how an unchecked repeal could impact behavior, medical issues, education and religious freedom of service members and chaplains. These lobbying and legal efforts have touched Christians in virtually every aspect of society, from business and commerce, to educational institutions, to governmental agencies.[11]

Some homosexual legal efforts have adversely affected Christian employees and business owners. For example, in *Walden v. Center for Disease Control*, a Christian counselor was fired by her private employer, based in part on pressure from a federal government entity, because she declined to provide counseling that would have facilitated a same-sex sexual relationship, even though she promptly and professionally referred the client to another counselor who addressed the client's concerns.[12] Similarly, in *Elane Photography*, A small New Mexico photography business owned and operated by a young Christian couple was fined over $6,000 for refusing to photograph a same-sex commitment ceremony, even though same-sex "marriage" and civil unions are illegal in the state.[13] Even religiously-affiliated businesses are not immune from attack. In New Jersey, a United Methodist church campground had its tax exempt status revoked for failing to allow its facilities to be used for same-sex commitment ceremonies.[14]

Christian students at public institutes of higher learning have been censured or in some cases, even persecuted, because of their ethical positions on homosexuality among other issues. In one case, a Christian student group was denied recognition by state university because the group

10. See www.answers.com/topic/perry-watkins, accessed March 7, 2014. See also, Mezey, 144–48.

11. All examples are from "Letter to President Obama and Secretary of Defense Robert Gates," April 10, 2010 from 33 Chaplain Endorsers.

12. *Walden v. Center for Disease Control* Case No. 1:08-CV-02278-JEC (N.D. Ga. 2008).

13. *Elane Photography v. Willock* HRD No. 06-12-20-0685 (N.M. Human Rights Common 2008).

14. *Bernstein v. Ocean Grove Camp Meeting Assoc. N.J.* Div. on Civ. Rights, No. PN34XB-03008 (2008).

requires its officers to affirm Christian beliefs and live by Christian moral norms.[15] In a similar move, a Christian society at a public law school was discriminated against by the school because the society required its leadership to abide by certain religious beliefs, including a prohibition on extra-marital sexual conduct like homosexual behavior. The school based its discriminatory action on its "non-discrimination" policy that protected homosexual behavior.[16] It should be noted that other universities are following suit.[17] In what is perhaps the most shocking and disturbing occurrence, a counseling student was expelled by a state university for refusing to compromise her Christian beliefs and instead "see the error of her ways" and change her "belief system" regarding homosexuality's immorality.[18]

Of particular concern to military chaplains are cases where a governmental entity has punished chaplaincy personnel or forced conformity due to the issues surrounding the acceptance of homosexuality. For example, in the case of *Akridge v. Wilkinson,* the 6th Circuit Court upheld the punishment of a prison chaplain who refused to allow an openly homosexual prisoner to lead a worship service.[19] In another case, a volunteer prison chaplain was allowed to be sued for refusing to permit an openly homosexual prison inmate to take a leadership role in chapel services.[20]

Two other examples should be mentioned, if only due to their direct applicability to military chaplaincy and concerns over the repeal of DADT. In one case, a United States military chaplain on an exchange program in Canada counseled a lesbian in accordance with his Christian beliefs. He had explained he would do so prior to the counseling, and had received permission from the service member to do so. Nevertheless, the chaplain was counseled by a senior chaplain, and advised that if he had

15. *Alpha Delta Chi v. Reed.*

16. *Christian Legal Society v. Martinez* 130 S.Ct. 795 (2009).

17. Vanderbilt University recently applied a similar policy for all registered student groups. A number of Christian student organizations protested, and some have decided to be unregistered in the future in order to preserve their right to have like-minded persons in leadership. A simple web search will turn up numerous articles on the subject. See, for example, http://www.huffingtonpost.com/2012/04/10/vanderbilt-religious-groups_n_1416561.html, or http://radio.foxnews.com/toddstarnes/top-stories/vanderbilt-tells-group-leaders-can't-be-followers-of-christ.html.

18. *Ward v. Wilbanks* 2009 WL 4730457 (E.D. Mich. 2009).

19. *Akridge v. Wilkinson* 178 Fed. Appx. 474 6th Cir. 2006).

20. *Phelps v. Dunn* 965 F.2d 93 (6th Cir. 1992).

been a Canadian chaplain, he would have been brought up on charges of violating federal hate speech regulations. The other issue of concern has to do with the *Defense of Marriage Act* (DOMA). A key goal of the GLBT lobby is to rid the U.S. of this law. The homosexual lobby is desperate to seek federal approval of their partnerships and DOMA is the biggest hurdle in that process. President Obama has already indicated that his administration will not seek to prosecute anyone for violating DOMA, and has already allowed military chapels to be used for homosexual unions.

These are but a few of the scores of issues being battled out in courts across America. Will the repeal of DADT impact the military? The homosexual strategy hints, and current litigation strongly suggests that it will in some significant ways, and there is serious cause for concern. Many of the same issues raised today, as a result of the removal of DADT, were raised by evangelical and other conservative religious leaders before the compromise of DADT was brokered. That is, concerns over the freedoms of religious service members are nothing new.[21]

The evangelical theologian and philosopher Frances Schaeffer once asked, "How should we then live?" Dr. Schaeffer served as a mentor, coach, philosopher and missionary in the 60's and 70's. His question is critical in this new millennium. In light of his question consider these 3 non-negotiables for any Christian:

The first non-negotiable is that "it is all about the Bible." Francis Schaeffer warned the Church that America would follow in Europe's footsteps insofar as ignoring God's Word was concerned. Like Europe, America's citizens are becoming woefully ignorant of the Bible. The Bible must be the basis for our worldview in all areas of life. It informs us of who God is, who God says we are, and what God says our purpose is. The Bible also informs us of how God designed our sexuality and the best way to practice that sexuality, within a monogamous relationship between male and female.

Second non-negotiable is "it is all about sin…and forgiveness." Sin is anything contrary to God's perfect design for the world and His holy character. The Southern Baptist Convention declared several years ago that "homosexuality is not a valid alternative lifestyle. The Bible condemns it

21. For an account of evangelical reactions and strategies for responding to the possible lifting of the homosexual ban by President Clinton, see Loveland, chapter 21, "The Confrontation over Homosexuals in the Military," 322–41.

as sin." [22] The Roman Catholic Catechism of the Catholic Church, § 2357, reads: "Basing itself on Sacred Scripture, which presents homosexual acts as acts of grave depravity, tradition has always declared that homosexual acts are intrinsically disordered."[23] Homosexuality is not the only sin.... but it is a sin with far-ranging ramifications. Its continued practice strikes at the heart of our Judeo-Christian view of morality.

The third non-negotiable is "it is all about Jesus . . . and hope, love, mercy, forgiveness, and grace." Christians must be bold, loving and clear that no matter what sin besets people, there is forgiveness in Christ. Repentance and faith brings forgiveness, restoration, wholeness, mercy and help. He repairs "God's good design." There is no sin so awful that Jesus blood cannot cover it.

We do wonder what the effect of the DADT repeal will have on the military. Nevertheless, a larger question is, How can biblically faithful chaplains be equipped to serve men and women in the military given the current conditions? How can Christians in general have an impact on culture rather than culture having an impact on them? Only God knows what the implications of the repeal of DADT will be. In the meantime we can be encouraged by the Apostle Paul's words to the Philippians from prison, where he was placed partly due to freedom of conscience issues in his culture:

> *Now I want you to know, brothers, that what has happened to me has actually resulted in the advance of the gospel, so that it has become known throughout the whole imperial guard, and to everyone else, that my imprisonment is in the cause of Christ. Most of the brothers in the Lord have gained confidence from my imprisonment and dare even more to speak the message fearlessly. To be sure, some preach Christ out of envy and strife, but others out of good will. These do so out of love, knowing that I am appointed for the defense of the gospel; the others proclaim Christ out of rivalry, not sincerely, seeking to cause me anxiety in my imprisonment. What does it matter? Just that in every way, whether out of false motives or true, Christ is proclaimed. And in this I rejoice. Yes, and I will rejoice because I know this will lead to my deliverance through your prayers and help from the Spirit of Jesus Christ. My eager expectation and hope is that I will not be ashamed about anything, but that now as always, with all boldness, Christ will be highly honored in my body, whether by*

22. Southern Baptist Convention, "Homosexuality not valid lifestyle."
23. Catechism of the Catholic Church, § 2357.

> *life or by death. For me, living is Christ and dying is gain. Now if I live on in the flesh, this means fruitful work for me; and I don't know which one I should choose. I am pressured by both. I have the desire to depart and be with Christ—which is far better— but to remain in the flesh is more necessary for you. Since I am persuaded of this, I know that I will remain and continue with all of you for your progress and joy in the faith, so that, because of me, your confidence may grow in Christ Jesus when I come to you again. Just one thing: Live your life in a manner worthy of the gospel of Christ. Then, whether I come and see you or am absent, I will hear about you that you are standing firm in one spirit, with one mind, working side by side for the faith that comes from the gospel, not being frightened in any way by your opponents. This is a sign of destruction for them, but of your deliverance—and this is from God.* (Philippians 1:12–18, HCSB)

The hope of the chapters to follow is that they may equip chaplains to continue to be effective ministers in the military. Our goal is to offer a biblical worldview that is faithful to the witness of the Scriptures, loving in approach but non-compromising on beliefs, and informative in various areas of this complex issue. The book is divided into two main sections, one informational, and the other prescriptive. Part one, consisting of chapters one and two, will present the current scholarly discussion of homosexuality in American culture. Part two, comprised of chapters three, four, and five, will offer Christian responses to homosexuality in the military. These responses will be specific to the U.S. military, but will also be applicable to the wider culture.

Christians have long questioned the validity of the supposed evidence for the genetic and/or biological evidence for the origins of homosexual feelings. In chapter two, Alan Branch examines the continuing controversies over biological testing and medical experimentation regarding homosexual tendencies. The infamous reports from twin studies is presented, with the most recent (Bailey & Pillard; Hamer et al.) receiving the greater scrutiny. The ongoing research regarding the connection between the hypothalamus and homosexuality is critically examined, with the work of Swaab and Hoffman, along with that of LeVay being compared with that of Byne, Tobet et al., among others. Finally Branch will offer a theological interpretation of the data, noting that while a connection between homosexuality and genetics has yet to be proven, a robust hamartiology that is consistent with Scripture could account for any such claim.

Chapter three is authored by John Laing, and offers an overview of the homosexual agenda. It begins with an examination of the much-publicized, "Gay Manifesto," written by Michael Swift for the *Gay Community News* in 1987 and read into the Congressional record in 1989. Laing then sets forth a brief survey of homosexual lobbying activities, highlighting significant legal and political victories for both those in favor and those opposed. The chapter closes with a discussion of hate crimes legislation, its impact upon free speech, and prospects for the future with particular attention to effects on military chaplaincy.

Many liberal denominations have long affirmed open homosexuality as a viable lifestyle for Christians. In 2005, the United Church of Christ offered official support for marriage of same-sex couples, and in 2003, the Episcopal Church ignited a firestorm of controversy when it elected Gene Robinson its first openly gay bishop. Still, most evangelical and mainline Protestant denominations, along with the Catholic and Orthodox churches, have continued to officially condemn homosexual practices as being antithetical to the teachings of Scripture and the historic Christian faith. However, in recent years, a number of more conservative and evangelical groups have questioned this reading of the Scripture and have instead seen some room for alternate interpretations. For example, some have argued that the prohibitions against homosexuality in the Torah are properly understood as condemnations of the homosexual practices which were part of the pagan religions of the Ancient Near East. Similarly, some have claimed that there are examples of righteous homosexual couples in the Bible (e.g., David and Jonathan, Jesus and John, etc.), and that therefore, homosexuality is not the issue: promiscuity and/or paganism is really the problem. This is the topic of the fourth chapter by Page Brooks. Brooks presents the biblical arguments against homosexuality, and will respond to the biblical arguments in support of homosexuality by means of sound theological and exegetical work.

When Congress and the President announced their intention to repeal DADT and to thereby allow open homosexual service in the armed services of the United States, complaints poured in from a number of sources, but the most vocal opponents among service members and retirees were chaplains. Many chaplains and their endorsing agencies have expressed particular concern over the effect that the repeal will have on the free speech and free exercise rights of conservative religious service members, including chaplains. In the fifth chapter, John Laing offers a response that evangelical chaplains can use which will allow them to retain their prophetic voice while avoiding court-martial or accusation of harassment and/or intimidation.

There are several avenues that conservative chaplains can take in response to the repeal. First, they can combat implementation of the repeal on the grounds of the sinful or unbiblical nature of homosexuality. Second, they can argue that open homosexual service will be detrimental to unit morale or will lead to increased problems with sexual harassment or even violence among service members. While both approaches have attractive features, they are ultimately unhelpful and will thus prove ineffective or counter-productive to the chaplain's public cause. It may seem that chaplains' only alternative is to support homosexual service. After all, this approach will preserve the important concept of freedom of choice/conscience, so central to the legal justification for military chaplaincy; however, it has the unsavory consequence of the chaplain arguing for something he/she deems ultimately at odds with God's Word. There is, however, another approach available which retains the chaplain's prophetic voice, preserves the principle of freedom of conscience/choice, and also allows for limits on the range of appropriate beliefs/choices: he can appeal to universal morality, natural law and virtue theory. Such an appeal stands at the heart of decency legislation, which has withstood strict judicial scrutiny, and seems to naturally apply here as it has applied to pornography, prostitution, and the adult entertainment industry. In this way, the chaplain can uphold the philosophical concept of freedom of choice while refusing to advocate an "anything goes" or relativistic approach to ethics. We argue that this is the best approach for the thoughtful conservative, Evangelical chaplain to take.

The goal is to offer sound advice to those Christians who wish to continue to serve in the military after the repeal of DADT is placed into effect. In chapter six, Scott Callaham addresses how Christian chaplains can minister to the homosexual community within the armed forces without compromising their convictions. "Love the sinner and hate the sin" is a slogan often voiced in evangelical circles, but all too often, the hatred of sin is indistinguishable from hatred of the sinner. Chaplains called upon to counsel homosexual service members have the right to refer those cases to others, but they may find the opportunity to counsel invaluable.

The final chapter serves to tie it all together. Whether open service of homosexuals in the military will stand remains to be seen. However, the fact of the matter is that we live in a culture where homosexuality exists and we need to understand those in that community if we are going to be effective in ministering to them. As ministers serving in a governmental agency within that cultural context, chaplains especially need to be aware of the intricate legal issues at stake. Ultimately, we wish to honor the Lord with our service to country. If we are not doing this, then we must reconsider our motives and effectiveness, perhaps even our service.

Part One

Understanding Homosexuality

2

"A Gay Gene?"

Homosexuality, Biology, and Philosophy of Science

—J. Alan Branch

Introduction

THE POP MUSIC SENSATION Lady Gaga (Stefani Angelina Germanotta) released a song in 2011 that has become an anthem for many people in the homosexual community. Titled *Born This Way,* the lyrics articulate a crude sort of biological/genetic justification for various forms of behavior. In many ways the song reflects the spirit of a culture infatuated with a sexually libertine ethic:

> No matter gay, straight or bi
> Lesbian, transgendered life
> I'm on the right track, baby
> I was born to survive
> No matter black, white, or beige
> Chola or orient made
> I'm on the right track baby
> I was born to be brave
> I'm beautiful in my way
> 'Cause God makes no mistakes
> I'm on the right track, baby
> I was born this way[1]

1. Germanotta, *Born This Way.* http://www.azlyrics.com/lyrics/ladygaga/bornthisway.html. The term "chola" is apparently used by Germanotta as a reference to

Germanotta's lyrics reflect a moral reasoning common among many young people including young soldiers. She moves casually between the issues of sexual morality and ethnic heritage, asserting that the two are morally equivalent because each person is "born this way." To add greater strength to the argument, God Himself is credited with being the author of both racial distinctions and sexual preferences. The obvious inference is that sexual preference, like race, is hard-wired into who we are from birth. Since these sexual preferences are innate, they must be from God. Therefore, no moral criticism should be leveled at people involved in the homosexual lifestyle. After all, homosexuals are "born this way."

The moral argumentation of *Born This Way* reflects the way scientific research into human sexuality is communicated on a street level. In the last forty years, an intense effort has been underway to establish in the public mind that science confirms a biological/genetic connection to homosexual behavior and thus remove moral stigma associated with homosexual acts. When the popular press reports on scientific research regarding homosexuality, it often does so with headlines trumpeting a genetic cause for homosexual behavior. Sadly, in our day of sound-bite moral reflection, most people have not thought deeply or seriously about the relationship between biology, genetics and moral accountability. Instead of rigorously examining the topic, it is easier to engage in crude moral argumentation and say, "If there's a genetic component, then people must be born that way. It's not fair to judge people for the way they are born." The assumption is that if any biological or genetic aspect of homosexuality is discovered, then it is prejudicial to form a negative moral opinion about homosexual behavior.

How should Christians respond to the "born this way" moral argument? It is not enough for us to mourn the societal slide towards Gomorrah. We must attempt to interact with, evaluate, and respond to the research associated with homosexuality. As we do so, several questions emerge: To what degree, if any, does biology or genetics contribute to homosexuality? If there is a biological/genetic aspect of homosexual behavior at any level, then should people be held morally accountable for homosexual acts? If a biological/genetic component exists, then how do we reconcile this with the clear denunciations of homosexual behavior in Scripture? In what follows, I hope to offer a brief answer to these and other questions associated with the relationship between scientific research

people of Mexican or Mexican-American ethnic heritage.

and the moral status of homosexuality. A review of the research will show that, while there are some genetic or biological factors that correlate with a higher incidence of same-sex attraction and homosexual behavior, there is no proof of genetic or biological causation for homosexuality. Beginning with the work of Alfred Kinsey, I will address issues chronologically, focusing on some of the most significant research produced in relation to homosexuality and brain structure, twin studies, and genetics. I will conclude with several remarks concerning scientific research regarding homosexuality and Christian moral reflection with focus on the Christian doctrines of sin and humanity. Also, since male homosexuality has consistently been found to occur more frequently than female homosexuality, male homosexuality has been researched more extensively. In fact, claims about male homosexuality made by Alfred Kinsey serve as a good starting point for our survey.

Alfred Kinsey

During the Twentieth Century, no one individual did more to bring homosexuality into the public forum than Alfred Charles Kinsey (1894–1956). A professor at the Indiana University, Kinsey was a zoologist by training and spent the early years of his career studying gall wasps, collecting thousands of specimens of the insects. Kinsey then transferred his obsessive and taxonomic approach of research to the study of human sexuality. Much like he collected gall wasps, Kinsey and his colleagues collected thousands of "interviews" in which he or his researchers asked detailed questions about the sexual backgrounds of research participants. Kinsey compiled the findings from these interviews into two books that were the opening salvos of the sexual revolution that soon swept the United States: *Sexual Behavior in the Human Male* (1948) and *Sexual Behavior in the Human Female* (1953). Both works contain many sweeping assertions and often move quickly from tables full of data to moral speculation about the repressed sexual ethics of America.

Kinsey's research was carried out under the auspices of the Institute for Sex Research at the Indiana University. Now known simply as The Kinsey Institute, the center was founded in 1947. Kinsey actually began research in 1941 with the help of funds from the Rockefeller Foundation and with the assistance of the National Research Council. What has become clearer in the years since the publication of the Kinsey reports is that he was not merely gathering information about other people's sexual experiences, but was also engaging in assorted sexual practices with various members of the research team. Instead of the staid atmosphere most people associate with academia, the Institute for Sex Research became a kind of sexual utopia for the gratification of the appetites of Kinsey and his team. According to one biographer, "Kinsey decreed that within the inner circle men could have sex with each other; wives would be swapped freely, and wives too, would be free to embrace whichever sexual partners they liked."[2] Kinsey himself engaged in various forms of sexual behavior, including filming various sexual acts in the attic of his home. My purpose here is not to engage in *ad hominem* attacks on Kinsey, but to emphasize that Kinsey was not a dispassionate scientist seeking truth; he was an agenda-driven reformer bent on changing the sexual ethics of a nation.

As Kinsey and his colleagues tabulated the data, they used a novel approach to defining human sexuality and employed a graded scale to define a person's sexuality. Prior to Kinsey, people were generally considered to be either heterosexual or homosexual. Instead of this binary approach, Kinsey saw sexual behavior on a continuum which could rarely describe individuals as either strictly homosexual or heterosexual. The Kinsey Scale is as follows:

0—Exclusively heterosexual with no homosexual

1—Predominantly heterosexual, only incidentally homosexual

2—Predominantly heterosexual, but more than incidentally homosexual

3—Equally heterosexual and homosexual

4—Predominantly homosexual, but more than incidentally heterosexual

5—Predominantly homosexual, only incidentally heterosexual

6—Exclusively homosexual[3]

On the Kinsey scale, six out of the possible seven scores could be interpreted as indicating some level of homosexual attraction. In this way, the Kinsey scale normalized homosexuality and helped contribute

2. Jones, *Alfred Kinsey*, 83. I have borrowed the phrase "sexual utopia" from Jones.

3. The Kinsey scale is found at Kinsey et al., *Sexual Behavior in the Human Male*, 638. Notice that while a score of "0" is defined as "heterosexual with no homosexual," a score of 6 simply says "homosexual," without a corresponding "with no heterosexual."

to inflated percentages in some findings. The Kinsey scale has since been widely used in numerous research projects related to sexuality.

When *Sexual Behavior in the Human Male* was released in 1948, it sold thousands of copies. The report asserted that nearly 69% of men in the United States had sex with prostitutes,[4] and that between 30% and 45% of husbands had adulterous affairs. Most surprising were the claims about the incidence of homosexuality among American men. Kinsey claimed 37% of males had homosexual physical contact to the point of orgasm at least once. Furthermore, he claimed 10% of all males are exclusively homosexual for at least three years between the ages of 16–55, and 4% of males are exclusively homosexual throughout the entirety of their lives.[5] In *Sexual Behavior in the Human Female,* Kinsey further asserted between 2–6% of unmarried females are exclusively homosexual between the ages of twenty and thirty-five.[6] While there was significant criticism of Kinsey's claims, Bayer notes that for "homosexuals who were just beginning their efforts at organization and the struggle for social acceptance and legal rights, the findings were emboldening."[7]

Reflecting on the public morality of the day, Kinsey suggested that American society's moral revulsion toward many of the sexual acts he described originated in "ignorance and superstition" and not in "scientific examinations of objectively gathered data."[8] After dismissing traditional morality as superstition, Kinsey then argued, "While this problem [ethics based on superstition] will be met again in other places, the present discussion of frequencies of total sexual outlet provides a good opportunity for understanding the futility of classifying individuals as normal or abnormal, or well-adjusted or poorly adjusted, when in reality they may be nothing more than frequent or rare, or conformists or non-conformists with the socially pretended custom."[9] In this way, Kinsey argues much like other sexually libertine propagandists of the second half of the

4. Kinsey et al., *Sexual Behavior in the Human Male*, 597. Kinsey's claim refers to white males only.

5. Ibid., 651.

6. Kinsey et al., *Sexual Behavior in the Human Female*, 473–74. See also the statistical chart on page 488.

7. Bayer, *Homosexuality and American Psychiatry*, 44.

8. Kinsey, et al., *Sexual Behavior in the Human Male*, 203.

9. Ibid., 203. For Kinsey, the term "total sexual outlet" meant the number of orgasms an individual had during a particular period regardless of the way the orgasm was achieved.

Twentieth Century: we should no longer look at sexual behavior in the categories of right versus wrong, but instead in the categories of more common versus less common.

A closer look at Kinsey's research reveals many problems with his findings. The most obvious problem with his data is the source of his sample. While the sample for *Sexual Behavior in the Human Male* numbered over 5,000, a disproportionate number came from prison inmates, many of whom were sex offenders.[10] The Kinsey team interviewed some African Americans, but their data was not included in the tabulations. Furthermore, Kinsey over-sampled people recruited via homosexual-friendly organizations or magazines. College students also represented a disproportionate number of his sample. Jones and Yarhouse rightly critique these problems with Kinsey's sample: "This is obviously not the type of methodology a person would implement if he or she were trying to get a representative outlook on the sexual behavior of the general population."[11] In many ways, Kinsey's sample insured that he found what he was hoping to find: statistical confirmation of sexually adventurous behavior.

Another glaring problem in Kinsey's report is the phenomenon of volunteer bias. Survey participants who volunteered to be questioned about their sexual experience were more likely to be sexually adventurous and out of the mainstream.[12] Volunteer bias may have been especially prominent considering that most of Kinsey's research was done prior to 1950, an era of much more conservative ethics. Many people simply would not have discussed the intimate details of their sexual lives, and those who were willing to do so were more prone to have a sexually libertine ethic. Kinsey himself seems to have been aware of this problem and acknowledged that the people who answered his questions may have been "less inhibited sexually."[13] Just as was seen in the problems with his sample, the problem of "volunteer bias" skewed Kinsey's data toward the conclusions he wanted.

The most disturbing and hotly debated part of Kinsey's research is chapter 5 of *Sexual Behavior in the Human Male* titled, "Early Sexual Growth and Activity." Kinsey gathered data from people who can only

10. It is difficult to determine exactly what percentage of Kinsey's sample came from prisoners.

11. Jones and Yarhouse, *Homosexuality*, 37.

12. Westfall, "Kinsey Report," 221.

13. Kinsey, *Sexual Behavior in the Human Male*, 99.

rightly be called *child molesters*. Describing the source of some of his data on small children he said, "Better data on pre-adolescent climax come from the histories of adult males who have had sexual contacts with younger boys and who, with their adult backgrounds, are able to recognize and interpret the boys' experiences."[14] Kinsey then goes on to say that "9 of our adult subjects have observed such [pre-adolescent] orgasm. Some of these adults are technically trained persons who have kept diaries or other records which have been put at our disposal; and from them we have secured information on 317 pre-adolescents who were either observed in self masturbation, or who were observed in contacts with other boys or older adults."[15] This disturbing description of child molestation is accompanied by a statistical chart that documents the observation of pre-adolescent experiences in orgasm for children between the ages of *2 months and 15 years old*. Later on in the book, Kinsey discusses masturbation and says, "Of course, there are cases of infants under a year of age who have learned the advantage of specific manipulation, sometimes as a result of being so manipulated by older persons; and there are some boys who masturbate quite specifically and with some frequency from the age of two or three."[16] Another chart in the male report records the length of time it took for children to reach climax and includes the notation, "Duration of stimulation before climax; observations timed with a second hand or stop watch. Ages range from five months to adolescence."[17] Perhaps the most painful reading in the male report is the description of children who supposedly orgasm, a description supplied from adults who had sex with children, describing the children "groaning, sobbing, or more violent cries, sometimes with an abundance of tears (especially among younger children)" and also children who "will fight away from the partner."[18] This final description sounds like a terrified child being molested.[19]

14. Ibid., 176–77.

15. Ibid., 177.

16. Ibid., 501.

17. Ibid., 178.

18. Ibid., 161.

19. Judith A. Reisman has strongly suggested that Kinsey's researchers were the ones guilty of perpetrating the violence on the children; cf. Reisman and Eichel, *Kinsey, Sex and Fraud*. Reisman's claims have been quite controversial and The Kinsey Institute itself categorically denies that Kinsey or his researchers participated in experiments on children. John Bancroft, director of the Kinsey Institute from 1995

What do we make of the data on children in *Sexual Behavior in the Human Male?* If Bancroft is correct, then Kinsey is *at least* guilty of lying in his research by asserting the data came from several people when in actuality it came from one man who can only be described as a serial child molester. Furthermore, Bancroft's protest that Kinsey did not encourage child molestation seems to be a weak defense. Recently, Joe Paterno was fired from Penn State because he did not report a child molester to the police, which is the same thing Kinsey failed to do. What is most disturbing is Kinsey's refusal to make any moral judgment concerning the "data" he obtained about children. Notice the terms he uses for child molestation: the observers were "technically trained," the molesters are called "adult observers," and the molesters are actually called the child's sexual "partner." Perhaps Kinsey's own distorted view of child sexuality is best found in *Sexual Behavior in the Human Female* in which he says, "It is difficult to understand why a child, except for its cultural conditioning, should be disturbed at having its genitalia touched, or disturbed at seeing the genitalia of other persons, or disturbed at even more specific sexual contacts."[20] Kinsey could not sympathize with the reaction of the children to being molested. The inability to sympathize with victims is a character trait associated with a person whose conscience is seared and non-functional.

Two aspects of Kinsey's research have had the most enduring impact in relation to homosexuality: the Kinsey Scale and the "10%" myth. As noted above, the Kinsey Scale is weighted to find any level of homosexual attraction and it is still used in research today. By using the Kinsey Scale, some assessments may have a built-in bias. Giving exclusive heterosexual attraction a score of "0" significantly skews the conclusions

---

to 2004, contends all the data in Kinsey's statistical tables regarding pre-adolescent orgasm came from one man who had sex with many adults and children beginning in 1917 until the time Kinsey interviewed him in the mid-1940s. Since Kinsey mentions gathering data from nine people who molested children, Bancroft says he does not know why Kinsey did not want to admit all the data came from one person, but suggests Kinsey "did not want to draw attention to this one man, or alternatively because he was particularly interested in this evidence and did not want to diminish its possible scientific credibility by revealing its single source." Bancroft further argues that Kinsey did not promote child molestation, did not train people to molest children, and was not in any sense a pedophile. Bancroft, "Alfred C. Kinsey Politics of Sex Research," 16–17. At a bare minimum one would expect Bancroft to concede the lack of informed consent on the part of the children, but he does not do so.

20. Kinsey, *Sexual Behavior in the Human Female*, 121.

about the prevalence of homosexuality.[21] But perhaps the most enduring element of Kinsey's report is the 10% myth—the idea that 10% of people are homosexual. The true number of people who are homosexual is much lower than Kinsey suggests. The pro-homosexual Williams Institute at UCLA's School of Law reported in 2011 that about 3.5% of American adults self-identify as lesbian, gay, or bisexual and that a further .03% identify as transgender. Among the 3.5% who identify as gay, lesbian, or bisexual, bisexuals comprise a slight majority of 1.8% as opposed to 1.7% who identify as gay or lesbian. About 1.1% of women and 2.2% of men self-identify as exclusively homosexual.[22] Although Kinsey's data and conclusions are flawed, his work opened the door for public discussion of homosexuality and helped set the stage for one of the most defining moments in the Gay Rights movement: the removal of homosexuality as a mental disorder from DSM-II in 1973.

American Psychiatric Association

The American Psychiatric Association (APA) is the world's largest professional organization for psychiatrists. It publishes the *Diagnostic and Statistical Manual of Mental Disorders* (DSM), the standard professional reference work used by psychiatrists and mental health professionals for determining a diagnosis. The DSM's first edition was published in 1952 with subsequent revisions following in 1968 (DSM II), 1980 (DSM III), 1994 (DSM IV), and a new revision due in May of 2013 (DSM V).

Both DSM I and II listed homosexuality as a mental disorder, but soon after the publication of DSM II, homosexual activists began exerting strong pressure to remove homosexuality as a mental disorder. At a 1970 meeting of the APA held in San Francisco, homosexual activists used tactics similar to anti-war protests of the era and interrupted the

21. Anne Fausto-Sterling comments, "In studies that search for a genetic link to homosexuality . . . the middle of the Kinsey scale disappears; researchers seek to compare the extreme ends of the spectrum in hopes of maximizing the chance that they will find something of interest." Fausto-Sterling, *Sexing the Body*, 10.

22. Gates, "How Many People are Lesbian, Gay, Bisexual, and Transgender?" http://williamsinstitute.law.ucla.edu/wp-content/uploads/Gates-How-Many-People-LGBT-Apr-2011.pdf. One is left to wonder why the Kinsey Institute can claim, "Interestingly, most statistics, such as homosexual behavior, did not change significantly from the original reports." Kinsey Institute, "Facts About *Kinsey* The Film." www.kinseyinstitute.org/about/Movie-facts.html). This statement is plainly inaccurate and self-serving.

meetings, yelling at psychiatrists and shouting down different program speakers. In particular, Irving Bieber (1911–1991), a noted psychotherapist working at New York Medical College, was presenting a paper on homosexuality and transsexualism when he was interrupted by protesters, one of whom shouted, "I've read your book, Dr. Bieber, and if that book talked about black people the way it talks about homosexuals, you'd be drawn and quartered and you'd deserve it."[23] The homosexual activists were even more animated during a panel discussion addressing issues in sexuality and asked one speaker, "Where did you take your residency, Auschwitz?"[24]

Caught off guard by the fierce protests, the APA responded to the pressure, and at the 1971 annual meeting held in Washington, DC, the APA sponsored a special panel discussion composed of homosexuals themselves. At this meeting, homosexual activists associated with the Gay Liberation Front stormed into the building and interrupted the meeting, demanding the APA change its stance on homosexuality. Change quickly followed, and on December 15, 1973, the board of trustees of the APA voted to remove homosexuality as a mental disorder from DSM II. In 1974, the membership at large of the APA was asked to vote to sustain or deny the change to the DSM II. Ten thousand psychiatrists participated in the referendum and approved the change by a 58% margin. Thus, via political pressure and protests, homosexual activists were able to force a change in the DSM. The revised seventh printing DSM II now only mentioned "sexual orientation disturbance," but in 1980 this was changed to "ego-dystonic homosexuality," a classification that was reserved for homosexuals who were distressed about their orientation.[25] The revised language essentially allowed psychiatrists to treat homosexuals who were uncomfortable with their lifestyle. But the language of "ego-dystonic homosexuality" was removed from the DSM-III in 1987. The APA went further in 1998 and rejected any attempt to help people change their sexual orientation, saying, "The American Psychiatric Association opposes any psychiatric treatment, such as 'reparative' or 'conversion' therapy, which is based upon the assumption that homosexuality *per se*

23. Bayer, *Homosexuality and American Psychiatry*, 103.

24. Ibid. The question was directed at Australian psychiatrist Nathaniel McConaghy.

25. Latham, "Scientific Homophobia." http://www.psychologytoday.com/blog/therapy-matters/201104/scientific-homophobia.

is a mental disorder, or based upon a prior assumption that the patient should change his/her homosexual orientation."[26]

Much of the conflict over homosexuality in the APA reflects a larger debate within the psychiatric community about psychoanalytic theory versus theories that see a biological basis for mental health disorders. The current trend in psychiatry and mental health is toward neurobehavioral or neurobiological solutions.[27] As a result, the psychoanalytic approach to treatment, with its origins in the work of Freud, has been largely replaced by a pharmacological approach. These battles within psychiatry were fueled by many new findings in the late Twentieth Century, including new discoveries in brain research as well as a general fall from favor of many Freudian concepts regarding sexuality. Several breakthroughs in our understanding of the brain resulted in new directions for scientific research and homosexuality.

Homosexuality and Brain Research

The change in the stance of the APA towards homosexuality was paralleled by rapid advances in brain research occurring at the same time. Initially, researchers discovered differences between the male and female brains in certain animals. This led scientists to ask the next logical question, "If there are differences in the brains of male and female animals, are there differences in the brains of male and female humans?" During the 1970s and 1980s, the conclusion was reached that human brains are somewhat sexually dimorphic, meaning the brains of males and females exist in two somewhat distinct forms. Then, some researchers began to speculate that homosexuals may also have brain differences which separate them from heterosexuals in a similar way to how male and female brains are distinguishable. The claims and counter-claims regarding

26. The American Psychiatric Association, "LGBT-Sexual Orientation." http://www.psychiatry.org/mental-health/people/lgbt-sexual-orientation. This stance of the APA is reflected in a recent California law banning therapy to help minors overcome homosexual temptation and become heterosexual. As of this writing, implementation of the law is awaiting review by the Ninth Circuit Court of Appeals.

27. "Neurobehavioral" refers to the action of the nervous system and behavior. A "neurobiological" disorder is an illness of the nervous system caused by genetic or other biological factors. For example, bi-polar disorders and obsessive compulsive disorders are considered neurobiological disorders.

findings in this area have often been controversial with significant implications in political arguments for homosexual rights.

Initial research into the differences between the brains of male and female rodents sparked the concept of sexually dimorphic brains. In 1971, two Oxford University scientists, Geoffrey Raisman and Pauline Field, discovered differences between male and female rat brains. They found that female rats had more synapse connections between brain cells in the hypothalamus than male rats.[28] In a subsequent study published in 1973, Raisman and Field demonstrated that neonatal exposure to testosterone organizes the male typical features in the rat brain.[29] Other studies soon followed confirming and expanding on Raisman and Field's findings.[30] A team of neurobiologists led by Roger Gorski of UCLA identified differences between the hypothalamus in male and female rats. They observed a small cluster of cells (or a "nucleus" of cells) in the hypothalamus that was five times larger in the brains of male rats than in female rats. The difference between the male and female rat brains in this area was so pronounced that Gorski found he could determine the sex of rat brains using only the naked eye with near 100% accuracy.[31] The researchers named this observable area of difference in rat brains the "sexually dimorphic nucleus of the preoptic area" (SDN-POA). Hence, by the end of the 1970s, sexually dimorphic differences had been discovered between the male and female brains in rodents, confirming they were sexually dimorphic. The research in rodent brains set the trajectory for the following decades concerning scientific inquiry into gender-specific differences in the human brain.

Building on the rapid advances in understanding animal brains, research now focused on an area in human brains corresponding to the SDN-POA discovered in rats. A 1985 study by Swaab and Fliers claimed to find an area of the human hypothalamus that corresponded to the SDN-POA in rats, and claimed it is larger in males than in females.[32] However, these findings were refuted in 1989 when Laura Allen, a postdoctoral assistant in Gorski's lab, identified four cell groups in the preoptic area of

28. Raisman and Field, "Sexual Dimorphism in the Preoptic," 731–33.

29. Raisman and Field, "Sexual Dimorphism in the Neuropil," 1–29.

30. In 1977, researchers observed differences in the shape of the stimulus-receiving ends of the nerve fibers (dendrites) between the male and female hamsters. Cf. Greenough et al., "Sex Differences in Dentritic Patterns," 63–72.

31. Gorski et al., "Evidence for a Morphological Sex Difference," 333–46.

32. Swaab and Fliers, "A Sexually Dimorphic Nucleus," 1112–15.

the hypothalamus in the brains of humans. These four cell groups were named the "Interstitial Nuclei of the Anterior Hypothalamus" (INAH 1–4). Allen, Gorski and their team were not able to verify that humans have a SDN-POA similar to rats. In fact, what Swaab and Fliers called a "Sexually Dimorphic Nucleus" is now known as INAH 1. However, Allen and Gorski did claim that INAH 2 was twice as large in men as in women and that INAH 3 was 2.8 times as large in men as in women.[33]

Around the same time other researchers began to search for dimorphism in one of the most popular subjects of brain research—the corpus callosum, a thick bundle of nerves that connects the left and right brain. For a number of years, researchers asserted a significant difference between the thickness of the corpus callosum in males and females, typically asserting that the Corpus Callosum was thicker in females. In 2005 one group of researchers from Japan used magnetic resonance imaging (MRI) to view the corpus callosum across what is known as the "midsagittal plane"—a view of a brain which has been sliced between the left and right hemispheres. They claimed the corpus callosum was measurably different between males and females. Furthermore, they asserted that their subjects with gender identity disorder were more likely to have a corpus callosum more similar to the sex with which they identified than the sex with which they were born. In other words, males who identified as females were more likely to have a corpus callosum similar to females than males. Likewise, females who identified as males were more likely to have a corpus callosum similar to males than females. The researchers went so far as to conclude that their data "can be utilized for diagnosis of GID [Gender Identity Disorder] as an objective and quantitative criteria."[34]

Caution should be urged when forming opinions about homosexuality based on studies of the corpus callosum since several factors can affect the measurement of the corpus callosum or its individual areas. Zaidel and Lacoboni note that "sex differences in any proportion measure[d] . . . must be interpreted with caution, since any association with sex and age and the ratio's denominator can create a substantial effect. As a result, significant sex differences in ratio measures have often been found to disappear when analysis of covariance is used on the same

33. Allen et al., "Two Sexually Dimorphic Cell Groups," 497–506. This study compared the brains of the cadavers of twenty-two adult men and women. The area Swaab and Fliers called the "SDN-POA" is now called the INAH1.

34. Yokota et at., "Callosal Shapes at the Midsagittal Plane," 3058.

data."[35] Gorski and his colleagues attempted to find sexual dimorphism in the corpus callosum, but found "no conclusive evidence of sexual dimorphism in the area of the corpus callosum or its subdivisions."[36] Contradictory opinions abound concerning purported gender-specific differences in the corpus callosum, making inferences about sexual preference based on dimorphism in the corpus callosum even more speculative.

Before moving forward, it is important to connect the study of gender-specific brain studies and research into biological causes of homosexuality. The argumentation of some homosexual activists is as follows: (1) Brains of males and females are sexually dimorphic; (2) In a similar way, brains of homosexuals are also sexually dimorphic; (3) Since our society says it is wrong to discriminate against someone because of their innate gender differences, it is also wrong to discriminate against homosexuals because they too have scientifically proven innate differences in sexual orientation.

There are several problems with this line of thinking, but I will mention four. First, attempts to find sexual dimorphism in human brains as clear as that found in animals has produced inconclusive results. Second, due to the wide variety of people on earth, a certain amount of deviation should be expected when measuring the sizes of various parts of the human brain any time two different groups are studied. This leads to the third criticism, which is that differences between male and female brains have sometimes been exaggerated. Males and females, both homosexual and heterosexual, have the same components and structures in their brains. Differences which have been identified are usually differences in volume or shape. One author goes so far as to say, "During the past century, numerous researchers have tried to find anatomic factors differentiating the male and female brain. To date, only one reliable difference has been found—regardless of sexual orientation, men have slightly larger brains than women."[37] In what follows we will see that while there seems to be some minor gender associated differences in the

35. Thompson et al., "Mapping Structural Alterations," 98.

36. Allen et al., "Sex Differences in the Corpus Callosum," 933. Even more amazingly, some people are actually born without a corpus callosum, a condition known as agenesis of the corpus callosum. As an example of contradictory evidence, in 2003 John Allen and his colleagues performed MRI measurements of male and female brains and actually found the volume of males to be greater than females; cf. Allen et al., "Sexual dimorphism and Asymmetries," 880–94.

37. Cohler and Galatzer-Levy, *The Course of Gay and Lesbian Lives*, 83.

hypothalamus, the brains of men and women are basically identical. The fourth problem with the way brain studies have been used relates to brain plasticity. "Plasticity" of the brain, or neuroplasticity, is a way of describing the remarkable way in which the human brain can form new neural pathways, strengthen existing neural pathways by repetitious use, or bypass damaged pathways. This is important for moral debates because these pathways can be strengthened, discarded, or by-passed based on volitional choices. In other words, some differences in the measurements of human brains are definitely the result of our response to the environment in which we live.

On occasion one may encounter a person struggling with issues of sexual temptation or gender identity who claims to have a "female brain in a male body" or a "male brain in a female body." In this way, brain research is used in a crude manner to validate transgender or homosexual behavior. This assertion is made on flawed assumptions about the differences between male and female brains. Evangelical preachers sometimes add to this confusion by over-emphasizing the differences between male and female brains in well-intended efforts to affirm healthy distinctions between the genders. Beyond the differences in brain volume mentioned above, two small areas of the hypothalamus have consistently shown some minor differences between men and women: The preoptic area of the hypothalamus tends to be larger in males than in females (this is related to the INAH 1 – 4) and the Suprachiasmatic Nucleus of the Hypothalamus is shaped differently in males and females.[38] Since the hypothalamus is the area of the brain where some differences between male and female brains have been identified, it also has been the focus of research concerning the possible difference in brain structures between homosexuals and heterosexuals. Because the hypothalamus connects the nervous system to the endocrine system by producing hormones, the hypothalamus affects the human sex drive. This relationship between the sex-drive and the hypothalamus further explains why it has been the focus of research concerning a biological origin for homosexuality. Two studies have been the focus of interest in particular: Swaab and Hofman on the Suprachiasmatic Nucleus and Simon LeVay on the Interstitial Nucleus of the Anterior Hypothalamus.

38. University of Washington, "Neuroscience for Kids." http://faculty.washington.edu/chudler/heshe.html. The hypothalamus is a highly complex area of the brain below the thalamus that regulates any number of physiological processes and autonomic activities of the human body.

SCN

Swaab and Hofman—the Suprachiasmatic Nucleus

One of the most influential researchers in the area of homosexuality and brain research has been Dutch scientist Dick F. Swaab. From 1978–2005, he served as the director of the Netherlands Institute for Brain Research. Swaab has published hundreds of articles and is widely quoted in literature concerning homosexuality and brain structure. Swaab's most frequently cited study was published in 1990 in the journal *Brain Research*. Co-written with Michael Hofman, the article was titled "An Enlarged Suprachiasmatic Nucleus in Homosexual Men." The Suprachiasmatic Nucleus (SCN) is a collection of nerve cell bodies on either side of the hypothalamus. It is thought to have an involvement in sexual desire because of the varying body rhythms associated with sexual desire as well as the sexual changes that come with aging.[39] Swaab and Hofman studied the SCN in thirty-four cadavers. Of these thirty-four cadavers, eighteen were a reference group of males who died of various causes, ten were homosexual men who died of AIDS, and six were heterosexuals who died of AIDS (two males, four females). Swaab and Hofman claimed to observe a larger SCN in the cadavers of homosexual men than those in the heterosexual reference group: "The SCN volume in homosexual males was 1.73 times larger than male subjects from the reference group . . . and contained 2.09 times as many cells."[40] They went on to say that this size difference means that homosexuals have a more elongated SCN than heterosexuals. Furthermore, they suggested this enlargement of the SCN might be a cause of homosexuality: "An association was found . . . between sexual orientation in men and SCN size, from which the functional implications are momentarily not clear."[41] It is important to reiterate that Swaab and Hofman were building on previous research which asserted differences between the male and female brains. Just as some suggested males and females have sexually dimorphic brains, Swaab and Hofman suggested homosexuals also have a dimorphic brain structure based on sexual orientation.

However, Swaab and Hofman's research on the Suprachiasmatic Nucleus was plagued by several problems. First, the findings about the SCN have not been replicated to date.[42] Second, this study was very

39. Feinberg and Feinberg, *Ethics for a Brave New World*, 368.

40. Swaab and Hofman, "An Enlarged Suprachiasmatic Nucleus," 145.

41. Ibid., 146. It should also be noted that Swaab and Hofman claimed their research refuted the idea that male homosexuals have a "female brain" (ibid., 145).

42. LeVay, *Gay, Straight, and The Reason Why*, 200.

small, consisting of only thirty-four cadavers, and of these only ten were homosexuals. Third, the reference group identified as heterosexuals may not serve as a reliable comparison, since, as Swaab and Hofman state themselves, "Sexual preference of the subjects of the reference group was generally not known."[43] In other words, the researchers *assumed* the members of reference group were heterosexuals or arbitrarily assigned them the designation. In either case, if the reference group is not confirmed, all the data comes into question. Finally, the connection between the SCN and sex has been questioned.[44] If the SCN is not associated with sex, then it is difficult to see how it can be associated with same-sex desire.

Simon LeVay—Interstitial Nucleus of the Anterior Hypothalamus

Simon LeVay is a neuroscientist who worked for the prestigious Salk Institute for Biological Studies from 1984 to 1993. A practicing homosexual, LeVay was the co-founder of The Institute of Gay and Lesbian Education located in West Hollywood, CA, and served as the Institute's chairman of board of directors from 1992 to 1996.[45] Building on the earlier findings of Gorski and his colleagues that the INAH 2 & 3 are larger in males than in females, LeVay also focused on the INAH 1–4 to see if there were any corresponding differences based on sexual preference. Studying 41 cadavers, LeVay identified 19 of the subjects as homosexual men (including one man who self-identified as bisexual, but was placed in the category of "homosexual"), all of whom died of complications from AIDS; 16 as heterosexual men, 6 of whom died of AIDS-related illnesses; and 6 as heterosexual women, 1 of whom died of AIDS. LeVay's findings were published in the August, 1991 issue of *Science,* and were widely reported as evidence for a biological cause for homosexuality. LeVay could not replicate Allen and Gorski's claim that INAH 2 is larger in males than in females. But he did find that the INAH 3 is larger in males than females. Furthermore, he claimed the INAH 3 cell group was more than twice as large in heterosexual men as opposed to homosexual men.

43. Swaab and Hofman, "An Enlarged Suprachiasmatic Nucleus," 141.

44. LeVay, *Gay, Straight, and the Reason Why*, 200. Readers should note that Swaab and LeVay each argue for competing theories concerning the biological origin of homosexuality. LeVay promotes his own hypothesis while rejecting Swaab's.

45. LeVay, "My Resume." http://www.simonlevay.com/my-resume.

LeVay's claims were profound not only because he claimed to replicate the finding that a certain amount of sexual dimorphism existed at INAH 3, but he was claiming that homosexual men have an INAH 3 closer in size to women than to heterosexual men.[46] While LeVay did assert that further interpretation of the results of his study must be considered speculative, he concluded by saying that it is more likely "the size of the INAH 3 is established early in life and later influences sexual behavior than that the reverse is true."[47] Hence, LeVay was saying that the size of the INAH 3—smaller in homosexual males—affects sexual orientation, and he was rejecting the idea that sexual behavior affects the size of the INAH 3.

LeVay's research was greeted with quite a bit of fanfare, but it is also plagued by some significant problems. First, much like Swaab and Hofman's research, LeVay's sample was very small, consisting of only 41 subjects. It is imprudent to make global assumptions about same-sex attraction based on a study consisting of such a small number. But a larger problem with LeVay's research is related to the manner in which he classified his research subjects as either heterosexual or homosexual. Satinover notes that LeVay's definitions for each were very imprecise, nor was there any way of verifying sexual orientation since the subjects being studied were dead.[48] Writing in *Technology Review*, Paul Billings and Jonathan Beckwith commented on Levay's study, emphasizing that LeVay's "research design and subject sample did not allow others to determine whether it was sexual behavior, drug use, or disease history that was correlated with the observed differences among the subjects' brains."[49] The effect of AIDS on the subjects of LeVay's study is also not clear. Could AIDS have affected the area of the brain LeVay was studying, thus accounting for the differences? In 2000, Jones and Yarhouse asserted that AIDS and medications used to treat the HIV infection can affect the very part of the brain LeVay was studying. Jones and Yarhouse thus conclude, "We do not know whether his [LeVay's] findings are related to

46. Van Wyk and Geist noted that the one subject listed as "bisexual" had an INAH 3 that resembled heterosexual men rather than the other homosexual men in Van Wyk and Geist, "Biology of Bisexuality," 359. They apparently base their comments on LeVay's "Figure 2" in his article; cf. LeVay, "A Difference in Hypothalamic Structure," 1036.

47. LeVay, "A Difference in Hypothalamic Structure," 1036.

48. Satinover, *Homosexuality and the Politics of Truth*, 78–79.

49. Billings and Beckwith, "Born Gay?," 60.

homosexuality or to the medications used to treat HIV." Compounding these difficulties are more fundamental questions regarding the degree to which the hypothalamus does or does not affect sexual orientation. Cohler and Galatzer-Levy go so far as to say "there is little evidence that the hypothalamus plays any role in human sexual orientation."[50]

Further investigation into the INAH-3 has challenged LeVay's conclusions. In 2001, William Byne, director of the Neuroanatomy and Morphometrics Laboratory at the Icahn School of Medicine at Mount Sinai Hospital, led a research team that examined the INAH 1–4 and its connection to sexual orientation. This particular study measured via autopsy the INAH from 34 men presumed to be heterosexual (10 of whom were HIV positive at death), 34 presumed heterosexual women (9 of whom were HIV positive at death), and 14 homosexual men, all of whom were HIV positive at death. Byne and his colleagues asserted that there does seem to be evidence that INAH-3 occupies a larger volume and contains more neurons in heterosexual men than in women, but there was no differentiation in the number of neurons between heterosexual men and homosexual men. The researchers stated, "The present study provides further evidence that INAH-3 occupies a larger volume and contains more neurons in presumed heterosexual men than women. The primary sexually dimorphic cellular characteristic of INAH-3, neuronal number, did not vary as a function of sexual orientation."[51]

Two specific findings from Byne's research are worth noting concerning the relationship of the INAH-3 to homosexuality. First, while there was no difference in the number of neurons in INAH-3 between heterosexual and homosexual men, the INAH-3 of homosexual men did tend to occupy a smaller volume in homosexual males than in heterosexual males. Basically, the gay men and straight men had the same number of neurons in this region of the brain, but the neurons were packed more densely in gay men. Another finding of interest in the Byne study was that they found "no evidence for an influence of HIV on INAH3, lending credence to LeVay's (1991) contention that HIV infection did not account for the disparity of INAH3 volume he observed between homosexual and heterosexual men."[52] This is significant because, as noted

50. Cohler and Galatzer-Levy, *The Course of Gay and Lesbian Lives*, 82.

51. Byne et al., "The Interstitial Nuclei," 89.

52. Ibid., 91.

earlier, some had questioned whether LeVay's initial findings were flawed because of the influence of AIDS on the brains of the men he studied.[53]

So what does the Byne study tell us about LeVay's claim that the INAH-3 is different in heterosexual male and homosexual males? First, one of the more robust findings of brain research is that men tend to have more neurons in INAH-3 than women. However, there is no difference in the number of neurons in the INAH-3 of heterosexual males as compared to homosexual males. The neurons in INAH-3 seem to be more densely packed in homosexual males than in heterosexual males, thus leading to the finding that the "volume" of the INAH-3 is smaller in gay men than in straight men. Thus, the researchers say, "Based on the results of the present study as well as those of LeVay, sexual orientation cannot be reliably predicted on the basis of INAH3 volume alone."[54] LeVay himself offers a nuanced response to Byne and says, "Byne's findings were in no way a refutation of the findings of my study, but neither were they a clear-cut confirmation."[55] In other words, LeVay admits that his claims have not been confirmed.

The comments of Byne, et al are even more fascinating because they actually discuss the relationship of environment to brain structure. To understand the importance of their comments, it is helpful to understand some basic concepts about the growth and development of the human brain. The basic building block of the brain and the central nervous system is the neuron, a highly specialized brain cell that communicates information throughout the body. When babies are born, they have just about all the neurons they will ever have, close to 100 billion. Unlike most other cells, neurons generally do not grow or repair after damage. One source explains, "Brain development, or learning, is actually the process of creating, strengthening, and discarding connections among the neurons; these connections are called synapses. Synapses organize the brain by forming pathways that connect the parts of the brain governing everything we do—from breathing and sleeping to thinking and feeling."[56] Closely related to the growth of a child's brain is the concept of

53. For example, Jones and Yarhouse, *Homosexuality: The Use of Scientific Research*, 70.

54. Byne, et al., "The Interstitial Nuclei," 91.

55. LeVay, *Gay, Straight, and the Reason Why*, 199.

56. U.S. Department for Health and Human Services, "Understanding the Effects" https://www.childwelfare.gov/pubs/issue_briefs/brain_development/how.cfm.

brain plasticity introduced earlier. The human brain has greater plasticity at younger ages and less plasticity when older.

Some researchers have suggested that people develop an orientation towards same-sex attraction based on hormones to which they are exposed pre-natally. Byne suggests that "sex related differences may also emerge later in development as the neurons that survive become part of the functional circuits."[57] The upshot of the research is that these differences between the INAH-3 of heterosexual males and homosexual males are not proof of prenatal, biological determination of sexual orientation. Instead, these differences could be the result of postnatal experience. Jones and Kwee explain the importance of Byne's findings and say, "In other words, if there are brain structure differences between homosexuals and heterosexuals, they could well be the result rather than the cause of sexual behavior and preference."[58]

Allen and Gorski (1992)

In 1992, Laura Allen and Roger Gorski published an article in the *Proceedings of the National Academy of Sciences,* arguing the anterior commissure (AC) of the brain is larger in homosexual men than in either heterosexual men or women. The AC is a bundle of nerve fibers connecting the two temporal lobes, and is quite a bit smaller than the corpus callosum. In this study, a postmortem comparison was made between the anterior commissure of 30 homosexual males, 30 heterosexual males, and 30 heterosexual females. The researchers reported there was a significant difference in the area of the [Anterior Commissure] between the three groups: The AC of homosexual men was 18.0% larger than that of heterosexual women and 34% greater than that of heterosexual men.[59]

Though this Allen and Gorski study is still widely quoted as evidence for a biological aspect of homosexuality, there are several reasons this claim should be taken with caution. First, in the 20 years since it was published, the findings have not been replicated. Secondly, when one examines the graph in which Allen and Gorski plotted the average size of the AC in the three groups, it becomes clear that there is significant

57. Byne, et al., "The Interstitial Nuclei," 91.

58. Jones and Kwee, "Scientific Research, Homosexuality," 307.

59. Allen and Gorski, "Sexual Orientation and the Size of the Anterior Commissure," 7200.

overlap in the size of the AC of many of the subjects that they studied. In other words, several homosexual men, heterosexual men, and heterosexual women had ACs very similar in size.[60] Not *every* homosexual subject had an AC that was 34% larger than *every* heterosexual male: the data reflects the average of all the subjects studied, and thus shows a *trend* and not an absolute reality in every case. Neither did the study prove causation, but Allen and Gorski only argued for a "correlation between sexual orientation and the midsaggital area of the AC," adding that their research "clearly argues against the notion that a single brain structure causes or results from a homosexual orientation."[61] In other words, Allen and Gorski seemed more cautious in their article while subsequent reporting of their findings amplified the idea of *causation*.

Savic and Lindstom (2008)

Ivanka Savic-Berglund is a neurologist at the Karolinska Institute in Stockholm. She led a team of researchers who investigated the degree of brain asymmetry in homosexuals compared to heterosexuals. Brain asymmetry refers to the differences in all humans between the two hemispheres of the brain.[62] Savic and her colleagues compared the asymmetry of the brains of 25 heterosexual men, 25 heterosexual women, 20 homosexual men and 20 homosexual women. Using both MRI and PET imaging to evaluate their sample, they made several important claims. First, they asserted that in heterosexual men the right hemisphere of the brain is slightly larger than the left, while in heterosexual women the two hemispheres were about equal in size. Second, they claimed that the brains of homosexual men looked more like heterosexual women with both hemispheres being equal in size, and the brains of homosexual women looked more like heterosexual men with the right hemisphere being slightly larger. Finally, the researchers examined the amygdalae, the two almond-shaped structures in the brain that are closely connected to our emotions, such as fear and anger. They claimed to find that heterosexual men and women have somewhat different connections between

60. It is of some interest to note that two outliers in the data were two homosexual men who died of AIDs and whose anterior commissures were unusually large. Allen and Gorski acknowledged these two outliers.

61. Ibid., 7202.

62. For example, in most people the right hemisphere is often larger and heavier than the left.

the amygdalae and the rest of the brain. Again, the homosexual men in their study showed connections between the amygdalae and the rest of the brain more similar to heterosexual females, and homosexual females had connections more similar to heterosexual males.[63]

Savic's findings were greeted with great fanfare, leading Qazi Rahman of the University of London to announce, "As far as I'm concerned there is no argument any more—if you are gay, you are born gay."[64] Savic and Lindstrom were more restrained and acknowledged that their findings need to be confirmed by additional research.[65] What should be kept in mind is that fundamental to their claims about homosexuality are claims about differences in brain asymmetry between men and women. While their research may be replicated, other claims about the differences between the brains of males and females were also greeted with initial enthusiasm only to be found less compelling in later research.

Homosexuality and Twin Studies

When addressing the degree to which homosexuality is affected by genetic or environmental factors, it is easy to see why researchers would be drawn to twin studies since identical twins share a virtually identical genetic identity. If homosexuality does have a genetic component, then research focusing on the degree to which twins do or do not share a homosexual orientation should be quite informative. Put most simply, a twin study is a genetic study performed to determine the heritability of specific traits. Since identical twins (also known as "monozygotic twins") share the same DNA, the assumption is that any major differences between the twins must be the result of their environments.

Bailey and Pillard (1991, 1993)

Michael Bailey is a psychologist and professor at Northwestern University and Michael Pillard is a professor of psychiatry at Boston University. Together, Bailey and Pillard researched the concordance rate for

63. Savic and Lindstrom, "PET and MRI Show Differences," 9403–408.

64. BBC News, "Scans See Brain Differences." https://news.bbc.co.uk/2/hi/health/7456588.stm.

65. Stein, "Brain Study Shows Differences," http://www.washingtonpost.com/wp-dyn/content/story/2008/06/22/ST2008062202006.html.

homosexuality among male twins hoping to discern a genetic linkage to homosexuality. They published their findings in 1991 and have been often-quoted since then. To develop their sample base, Bailey and Pillard recruited male participants via advertisements in gay-friendly magazines and publications, specifically searching for people in the homosexual community who had a twin. Their goal was to discover what percentage of the siblings were also homosexual males. Based on their research, Bailey and Pillard claimed that 52% of identical twins of homosexual men were also homosexual. Among homosexual males with a non-identical twin brother, 22% of their brothers were also homosexual. They also found that non-twin biological brothers in the sample had a 9.2% concordance rate compared to an 11% concordance rate for non-twin adoptive brothers.[66]

In 1993, Bailey and Pillard performed a follow-on study of homosexual women with a twin. Again recruiting their sample from gay-friendly publications, they reported a concordance rate of 48% for identical twins and 16% for non-identical (fraternal) twins. Bailey and Pillard concluded their report on female twins by saying, "How do the findings of the present study compare with those of Bailey and Pillard's genetic study of male sexual orientation, which employed a similar method? The most important similarity is that both male and female sexual orientation appeared to be influenced by genetic factors. However, in neither study was an indicator of genetic loading found."[67]

What are we to make of the Bailey and Pillard studies? First, while the studies indicate a genetic component to homosexuality, neither study produced 100% concordance rates. Thus, if there is a genetic aspect to homosexual orientation, it is not equal to causation. Satinover rightly says, "If 'homosexuality is genetic,' as activists and their media supporters repeatedly claim, the concordance rate between identical twins—that is, the incidence of the two twins either both being homosexual or both being heterosexual—will be 100 percent. There would *never* be a *discordant pair*—a pair with one homosexual twin and one heterosexual twin."[68] The

66. Bailey and Pillard, "A Genetic Study," 1081–96.

67. Bailey et al., "Heritable Factors," 223. In genetic research, the term "genetic loading" is often used to describe harmful genes that are carried in the genome and transmitted to descendants causing disease or morbidity. In this study, the term merely describes the heritability of homosexuality.

68. Satinover, *Homosexuality and the Politics of Truth*, 83. Another study claimed to find a 2/3 concordance rate for homosexuality in monozygotic twins, but no other

weakness of the genetic argument suggested by Bailey and Pillard is further demonstrated by close examination of their data. Bailey and Pillard claimed that there was a 22% concordance rate between non-identical twin brothers while non-twin biological brothers had a 9.2% concordance rate for homosexuality. Remembering that non-identical twins and their non-twin biological brothers share the same amount of genetic material, one would expect to see a similar concordance rate between the two groups, yet we do not. This led Byne and Parsons to conclude, "If we rely only on the data presented in their [Bailey and Pillard's] study, we must at least consider the possibility that the higher concordance rate for homosexuality in [non-identical] twins compared with non-twin biological brothers is due to increased similarity of the trait-relevant environment in the former."[69] Finally, the method in which Bailey and Pillard's sample was obtained by seeking respondents from gay-friendly publications poses another problem for this study. It is not hard to imagine that homosexuals with a twin who was also a homosexual would be more motivated to respond to such advertisements and participate in the study, thus skewing the sample.

Bailey, Dunne, and Martin (2000)

Bailey and Pillard acknowledged that the method by which they obtained their samples for their 1991 and 1993 studies was problematic. In 1993 they stated, "Future studies of sexual orientation that avoid this bias, for example through the use of twin registries, are clearly desirable."[70] Bailey was able to do just such research and in 2000 published findings using a large population-based sample of twins recruited from the Australian National Health and Medical Research Council Twin Registry, ultimately gathering data from 4,901 participants. Using a much larger and more representative sample provided strikingly lower percentages of concordance rates for homosexuality among twins. Among identical twins, the Australian data revealed that if a male was homosexual, there was a 20% concordance rate for homosexuality and among female homosexuals

study has found a concordance rate nearly this high indicating there were errors in the way the sample was chosen. Cf. Whitman et al., "Homosexual Orientation in Twins," 187–206.

69. Byne and Parsons, "Human Sexual Orientation," 229.

70. Bailey and Pillard, "Heritable Factors," 222.

with an identical twin, there was a 24% concordance rate. Commenting on the much lower concordance rate in the Australian study, the authors addressed the sample bias in the previous studies and said, "In those studies, twins deciding whether to participate in a study clearly related to homosexuality probably considered the sexual orientation of their co-twins before agreeing to participate."[71]

The significance of the Australian twin studies should not be underestimated. The suspected sample bias of the previous studies was proven to be true. Furthermore, the genetic correlation towards homosexuality is much weaker than initially suggested.[72] In 2010, the results were published of a study focusing on homosexuality among twins in Sweden. The Swedish study found concordance rates for homosexuality among twins very similar to the Australian research.[73]

Homosexuality and Genetic Marker Studies

While twin studies have attempted to trace the heritability of homosexuality via family histories, other studies have examined DNA itself in an attempt to prove genetic etiology for homosexual behavior.

Dean Hamer, et al. (1993)

Dean Hamer is an American geneticist who earned his Ph.D. from Harvard and subsequently worked as a researcher for the National Institutes of Health for thirty-five years. Hamer led a team of researchers whose goal was to determine whether or not male sexual orientation is genetically influenced.[74] To determine the answer, Hamer and his colleagues investigated 114 families of homosexual men. Seventy-six of the families were recruited from two Washington, DC area sources: an HIV outpatient center operated by the National Institutes of Health Clinical Center in Washington, DC, and local pro-homosexual organizations

71. Bailey et al., "Genetic and Environmental Influences," 533.

72. The findings of another twin study based on data gathered from the United States was also published in 2000 which produced results similar to the earlier Bailey and Pillard studies, but the sample was smaller than the Australian one with strong evidence of sample bias similar to Bailey and Pillard. Cf. Kendler et al., "Sexual Orientation in a U.S. National Sample," 1843–46.

73. Langström et al., "Genetic and Environmental Effects," 75–80.

74. Hamer et al., "A Linkage Between DNA Markers," 321.

in the Washington, DC area. The other 38 families were recruited via advertisements in pro-homosexual publications.

To understand the Hamer study, it is helpful to note some basic tenets of genetics. Human DNA consists of 23 pairs of chromosomes and the sex chromosomes are one of these pairs, with women having two X chromosomes and men having one X chromosome (from the mother) and one Y chromosome (from the father). Based on preliminary research into the family histories of homosexual men, Hamer and colleagues suspected there might be a gene inherited from mothers that predisposed their sons to homosexuality. Hamer and his colleagues were curious to know if any genetic markers consistent with male homosexuality were common in homosexuals via the X chromosome inherited from their mothers. Their findings were published with much fanfare in the July 16, 1993 edition of *Science*. When the average person mentions that researchers have found a "gay gene," this is the study they usually have in mind.

What did the Hamer study conclude? From their original sample of 114 families, the researchers selected a sub-group of 40 families in which there were two gay brothers and no indication of paternal transmission of homosexuality. From this select population, Hamer claimed 33 of 40 pairs of homosexual brothers had co-inherited genetic information in the X-chromosome in a region called "Xq28." Hamer concluded, "We have now produced evidence that one form of male homosexuality is preferentially transmitted through the maternal side and is genetically linked to chromosomal region Xq28."[75] A follow-on study by Hamer's team in1995 found similar results, but at a much lower level of statistical significance. This second report was interesting because it reported some non-homosexual men who shared the Xq28 marker with a homosexual brother. In other words, both brothers shared the marker, but only one of them was homosexual.[76]

Understanding what Hamer claimed can be confusing. When the average person reads the popular reports of Hamer's study, they assume all 66 men from the 33 pairs of gay brothers had exactly the same DNA sequence at chromosome Xq28. This is not what Hamer claimed. As noted in *The Hastings Center Report*, "In fact, all he showed was that each member of the thirty-three concordant pairs shared his Xq28 region with his brother but not with any of the other sixty-four men. No single

75. Ibid., 325.

76. Hu et al., "Linkage Between Sexual Orientation and Chromosome Xq28," 248–56.

specific Xq28 sequence was common to all sixty-six men."[77] In other words, the sequence at Xq28 was different among each of the 33 pairs of brothers. What was common was the *location* of the sequences.

There are many problems with Hamer's research. In fact, the issue of *Science* following the publication of Hamer's work included an article critical of his findings.[78] But the most significant problem is that his findings have not been consistently replicated in the 20 years since his study was published. In 1999, Bailey and his colleagues reported no definitive linkage between Xq28 and male homosexuality.[79] Also in 1999, Canadian researchers failed to replicate Hamer's findings and were unable to find a link between Xq28 and male homosexuality, asserting that homosexual brothers are no more likely than their heterosexual brother to have the marker at Xq28[80] Even Simon LeVay says, "Unfortunately, Hamer's report has not been robustly confirmed."[81] Evangelical authors Jones and Yarhouse point out that Hamer's research, even if considered accurate, did not prove that a chromosomal pattern at Xq28 is either necessary or sufficient to cause homosexuality. They say:

> If [Xq28] was necessary to the homosexual condition, then they would not have found the 7 out of 40 homosexual brother pairs who did not share this characteristic (these 7 brothers did not have the chromosomal pattern but were gay anyway). If it was sufficient to cause homosexuality, then they would not have found, in their second study, nonhomosexual brothers who shared the genetic characteristic but not the sexual orientation. Having the genetic marker does not mean you are a homosexual (not sufficient), and not having the genetic marker does not mean you are a homosexual (not necessary).[82]

In spite of these weaknesses in Hamer's research, the idea of a "gay gene" has taken on a life of its own and is now commonly accepted by many people.

77. Schüklenk et al., "The Ethics of Genetic Research," 7.
78. Risch et al., "Male Sexual Orientation," 2063–65.
79. Bailey et al., "A Family History Study," 79–86.
80. Rice et al., "Male Homosexuality: Absence of Linkage," 248–56.
81. LeVay, *Gay, Straight, and the Reason Why,* 171.
82. Jones and Yarhouse, *Homosexuality*, 81.

Mustanski, et al. (2005)

In 2005, a group of researchers associated with Dean Hamer published another study on homosexuality in men. The sample for this study was drawn from 73 families previously studied in Hamer's 1993 and 1995 reports along with 73 new families which had never been researched. When all the families were taken together, it resulted in a sample of 456 individuals from 146 unrelated families, of which 137 families had 2 gay brothers and 9 families had 3 gay brothers. Instead of focusing only on the Xq28 region, this study was a genome-wide scan, meaning all the chromosomes were examined. Studying the entire sample of 146 families, no evidence was found of linkage to homosexuality at Xq28. When the researchers did not find a linkage at Xq28, they divided their sample and separated the old participants from the new participants and then examined the Xq28 region for each group individually. By doing so they did find a linkage for Xq28 among the 73 families that participated in the original studies, but they did not find an Xq28 linkage among the 73 new families in the study. This undermines Hamer's earlier assertions concerning Xq28 and reinforces suspicions that either his earlier sample was flawed or some other problem exists. The important finding is this: when the sample was taken as a whole, there was no statistical significance associated with chromosome Xq28, thus Hamer's earlier findings were not confirmed.

The 2005 study did report three new regions of genetic interest concerning male homosexuality on chromosomes 7, 8, and 10. But a careful reading of the report shows a weak linkage between male homosexuality and these chromosomes. The researchers' strongest finding was on chromosome 7 at 7q36. However, Mustanski and colleagues admitted that the connection they found falls just short of "criteria for genomewide significance."[83] They went on to say that certain regions on chromosomes 8 and 10 "approached criteria for suggestive linkage."[84] Their report shows that none of the new data met professionally accepted criteria for statistical significance. Simon LeVay summarizes this study thus: "The statistical power of these findings was low, however, and the findings should be thought of as pointers for future research rather than as actual identifications of regions containing 'gay genes.'"[85]

83. Mustanski et al., "A Genomewide Scan," 276.

84. Ibid.

85. LeVay, *Gay, Straight, and the Reason Why*, 172.

Homosexuality and Other Factors

Several other issues are often mentioned in relation to scientific research and homosexuality. I will briefly summarize some of the most common ones.

Prenatal Hormones and Homosexuality

A standard argument related to the origin of homosexuality is that exposure to certain hormones in the womb can cause children to have a homosexual orientation. As is well known, estrogen and testosterone are closely related to human sexuality. In males, testosterone levels peak at three different times. During the early part of pre-natal development—from around weeks 6 to 20—in male babies, testosterone drives the development of male genitalia. A second rise in testosterone levels occurs soon after birth and continues until around 6 to12 months. A final rise in testosterone in males occurs at puberty and continues throughout life, though the levels decrease with age. Some suggest that if a male's testosterone levels are negatively affected in either phase 1 or phase 2, then the child may subsequently be homosexual. In recent years, Gorski has argued that the brain is basically female during early prenatal development. For a male to develop structural and functional characteristics typical of his species, his brain must be exposed to testicular hormones during a critical period, or critical phases, of development.[86] Research ethics prevent researchers from proving whether this same effect is observable in humans, but a common assertion is that a person's sexual identity is affected by the timing and amount hormones released either prenatally or postnatally.

A syndrome called Congenital Adrenal Hyperplasia (CAH) occurs once out of every 10,000 to 18,000 births and has also provided some evidence that prenatal hormone levels may affect a child's sexuality. CAH can occur in both males and females and is caused when a pre-born child has an enzyme defect that makes it impossible for the baby's adrenal gland to make cortisol, a hormone that is vital for proper pre-natal development. At the same time, in a baby with CAH, the body produces more androgen, a male sex hormone. For males, CAH often results in an early on-set of puberty. In females, the symptoms seem to be more

Interesting.

86. Gorski, "Hypothalamic imprinting," 57–70.

pronounced. In some cases, females are born with abnormal genitals at birth, presenting aspects of both male and female genitalia.[87]

CAH is often cited as evidence that abnormal hormone levels affect not only genitalia but also the brain. Why so? Research indicates that as a group, CAH females are more likely to be sexually attracted to women than are their unaffected sisters, with up to one-third self-identifying as homosexual or bisexual. Nevertheless, a majority of women with CAH report themselves to be exclusively heterosexual, and it is unclear what differentiates them from others who are not. In contrast, males with CAH have generally been found to be similar to their unaffected brothers. Specifically, they do not seem to differ in sexual orientation.[88] Based on the higher incidence of homosexuality among girls with CAH, some have argued that prenatal hormone levels affect the development of sexual identity. At the same time, other researchers argue that the effect of pre-natal hormones on a predisposition towards homosexuality is weak in both males and females, with Louis J. Gooren going so far as to say, "So we are far away from any comprehensive understanding of hormonal imprinting on gender identity formation."[89] Competing opinions abound regarding the pre- or postnatal effect of hormones on gender identity.

Fraternal Birth Order Effect

The "Fraternal Birth Order Effect" refers to the claim that males with multiple older brothers are more likely to be homosexual. To state it differently, homosexual males tend to be born later in their families than their heterosexual brothers. This idea is most closely associated with an article published by Ray Blanchard and Anthony Bogaert in 1996 in *The American Journal of Psychiatry*, where the authors claimed each

87. Medline Plus, "Congenital Adrenal Hyperplasia," http://www.nlm.nih.gov/medlineplus/ency/article/000411.htm.

88. Cohen-Bendahan et al., "Prenatal Sex Hormone Effects," 359.

89. Gooren, "The Biology of Human Psychosexual Differentiation," 589–601. In a more recent article in *The New England Journal of Medicine*, Gooren says the causes of gender-identity disorder are unknown, but he does seem to grant some weight to the idea that male-to-female transsexuals have a more female pattern of sexual differentiation in the brain. He plainly rejects the ideas that gender identity disorders are rooted in hormonal abnormalities, chromosomal patterns (genetics), or in particular family dynamics. Gooren would disagree with the moral stance I take with regard to homosexuality or transsexuality. Cf. Gooren, "Care of Transsexual Persons," 1251–57.

additional older brother increases the odds of homosexuality by 33%.[90] Blanchard and his colleagues suggest that the connection between birth order and homosexuality may reflect a maternal immune reaction. The argument is that in some cases the mother's immune system may react to H-Y antigens in a male fetus. When this happens, H-Y antibodies from the mother may cross the placental barrier and enter the brain of the baby boy. Blanchard explains, "When that happens, these antibodies partly prevent the fetal brain from developing in the male-typical pattern, so that the individual will later be attracted to men rather than women."[91] In a later study led by Blanchard, researchers claimed the birth order effect only applies if the younger brother is right-handed.[92]

As with some of the studies mentioned earlier, Blanchard and Bogaert's research is plagued by sample problems. For example, they clearly state that homosexuals were recruited for their research at homosexual community organizations and at the 1994 Toronto Lesbian and Gay Pride Day parade.[93] Jones and Kwee suggest a negative effect on the sample because later born gay men were perhaps more apt to be "out and proud."[94] At the same time, Kwee and Jones add, "Despite various methodological problems with the fraternal birth order research, we concede that the evidence as a whole points to some sort of relationship between the number of older brothers and homosexuality."[95]

Blanchard and Bogaert's research has been challenged in two other ways. First, their maternal immunosensitization hypothesis is just that—a hypothesis and has not been proven. Second, at least three studies have claimed that a fraternal birth order effect is at work to some degree in certain sexual offenders.[96] If this correlation is confirmed, certainly no one would then suggest the sexual offenders are, through no fault of their own, pre-disposed to act in such a way and thus should be excused from moral censure. But perhaps the strongest critique of the fraternal birth order effect is the fact that half or more of all homosexual men have zero

90. Blanchard and Bogaert, "Homosexuality in Men" 27–31.

91. Blanchard, "Fraternal Birth Order," 109–10.

92. Blanchard et al., "Interaction of Fraternal Birth Order," 405–14.

93. Blanchard and Bogaert, "Homosexuality in Men," 28.

94. Jones and Kwee, "Scientific Research, Homosexuality," 309.

95. Ibid., 310.

96. Lalumière, "Sexual Deviance and Number," 5–15; Côté et al., "Birth order, Birth Interval, and Deviant," 67–81; MacCulloch et al., "Birth Order in Sex-Offending," 467–74.

older brothers, a fact that Blanchard himself admits and comments, "The maternal immune hypothesis was never intended to account for the sexual orientation of all homosexual men." [97]

Various and Assorted Assertions About Homosexuality

Several other biological or genetic traits among homosexuals are often mentioned. There are frequent claims that handedness—being left-handed versus right-handed—correlates with homosexuality, the assertion being that homosexual men have a higher incidence of being left-handed. Some say that right-handed men with older brothers and left-handed men without older brothers have a higher chance of being homosexual.[98] Another common claim relates to the ratio of length between the ring finger and the index finger with an increased propensity for homosexuality. In males, the ring finger is usually longer than the index finger. In females, the ring finger and the index finger are typically about the same length. One group of researchers reported that lesbians have finger lengths more similar to men than to women and suggested this was due to prenatal exposure to androgens.[99] In 2005, researchers associated with the Karolinska Institute in Stockholm claimed homosexual men reacted to male pheromones in a manner similar to heterosexual women.[100] Another study even attempted to find a connection between scalp hair rotation patterns and male homosexuality.[101] Other claims abound and more will certainly emerge in the near future.[102]

Conclusion

Several scientific studies were initiated in recent decades to substantiate the pro-homosexual argument that homosexuals are not just different in their sexual behavior, but they are constitutionally different from

97. Blanchard, "Controversies in Sexual Medicine," 3248.

98. Blanchard et al., "Interaction of fraternal birth order," 405–14.

99. Kraemer et al., "Finger Length Ratio," 210–14.

100. Savic et al., "Brain Response to Putative Pheromones," 7356–61.

101. Klar, "Excess of Counterclockwise," 2027–30.

102. Though I have mentioned CAH earlier, I have not extensively addressed incidences of children born without clearly differentiated genitalia, but these cases are sometimes brought to bear in debates about homosexuality.

heterosexuals. Pro-homosexual advocates hope these studies will remove moral stigma associated with homosexuality by proving it is not really a "choice," but an expression of their innate nature. Their goal is to convince others that if homosexuals are constitutionally "born this way," then they should not receive moral censure for their sexual lifestyle. Furthermore, homosexuality should be viewed as an innate characteristic as immutable as one's race. Since it is wrong to discriminate against someone because of race, it is equally wrong to discriminate against someone because he or she is homosexual. Yes but we still need to account for the Pedophiles.

Contrary to popular opinion, scientific research has not found a "gay gene." No genetic marker has been found that conclusively links homosexuality with any specific genetic sequence. Despite the common myth that a gay gene has been found, the claim of a genetic marker for homosexuality at Xq28 has not been replicated or substantiated. No genetic marker rises to the level of statistical importance when searching for a gay gene. Some twin studies do indicate correlation for a genetic component to some forms of homosexuality, but even in these studies, the correlation is weak and is neither necessary nor sufficient for homosexuality.[103] Earlier twin studies claiming a much stronger correlation have not been replicated. The fraternal birth order effect seems to show a weak correlation between some forms of male homosexuality and maternal inheritance. Explanations of this phenomenon are speculative at present.

There is no conclusive evidence that homosexuals have a substantially different brain structure than heterosexuals. Claims that homosexuals have a brain structure that differs from their gender (males have "female" brains or females have "male" brains) find their origin in overstated claims about the differences in male and female brains. The only difference between heterosexual and homosexual brain structures that has any real weight is LeVay's claim that INAH-3 is smaller in homosexual males than in heterosexual males. Yet, even this claim is based on very limited research and Byne, et al have stressed that the difference is not in the number of neurons, but in the density of the neurons of the INAH-3 in homosexuals. Again, this finding shows a weak correlation and the difference in INAH-3 is neither necessary nor sufficient for homosexuality.

103. Several times in my conclusion, I will mention that no factor has been found that is necessary or sufficient for homosexuality. My thinking here is influenced by Jones and Yarhouse, *Homosexuality*, 81.

Other factors show a weak correspondence to homosexuality and none of them are sufficient or necessary for homosexuality. Hormones obviously affect the development of children in the womb, but it is unclear exactly how pre-natal or post-natal hormones affect one's later gender-identity. Claims that "10% of all people are gay" are based on Kinsey's flawed data and even misrepresent what Kinsey claimed. Approximately 2–3% of the population is either exclusively homosexual or bisexual, and exclusive homosexuality is more common among men than women.

A survey of modern scientific research demonstrates there are some factors that *correlate* with a higher incidence of homosexuality among some populations. However, there are no biological or genetic factors that have been shown to *cause* homosexuality. In moral debate, this vital distinction between correlation and causation is usually lost. Correlation refers to the degree that two different variables are related. When two sets of data are strongly linked together (example: smoking and lung cancer), there is a strong correlation. When two sets of data are not strongly linked together, there is a weak correlation.[104] The research we have surveyed has tried to find out how one variable, homosexuality, is dependent on other variables such as brain structure or genetics. We conclude that no such strong correlation can be established between homosexuality and other genetic or biological variables.

But correlation does not equal causation. To say that one variable *causes* another variable is logically immodest and equally difficult to substantiate. In causation, one event or variable necessarily precedes another event or variable. If the first event does not occur, the second event does not follow. No relationship like this exists between any biological or genetic factors and homosexuality. Furthermore, in a cause-effect relationship, the "effect" is unlikely to have occurred without the previous cause. Again, no relationship like this exists between any biological or genetic factors and homosexuality. When most people think of a genetic link to any form of human behavior, they tend to think of genes like a "light switch": the same-sex attraction is either on or off. Human behavior, especially sexual behavior, is far more complex than that.

One of the more frustrating aspects of public debate about homosexuality is the manner in which the distinction between correlation and causation is blurred, ignored, or knowingly misrepresented. For example,

104. Researchers typically use the terms "no relationship", "positive relationship", and "negative (inverse) relationship." I've used the terms "strong" and "weak" for simplicity and convenience.

when reporting on Dean Hamer's research, the July 26, 1993 cover of *Time Magazine* was emblazoned with the words: "Born Gay: Science Finds a Genetic Link." In fact, Hamer's research at best showed a genetic component to homosexuality, but the *Time* headline pronounced "Born Gay," a statement implying that all argument about the cause of homosexuality should cease. Furthermore, there was no headline on *Time* when Hamer's research was not replicated.[105]

Are there genetic or biological components to homosexuality? Absolutely. Every choice we make while living on earth is affected by biology and genetics. Most temptations have a strong biological component: we are tempted to engage in forbidden pleasure because it initially feels good. We seek pleasure and shun pain, sometimes to destructive ends. The problem is that our very bodies have been affected by the Fall, and even our genetic code is not what it was intended to be. In New Testament terms, we *battle the flesh*. When examined from this New Testament perspective, we begin to see the flawed logic of a "born this way" mentality. Yes, we are born this way: we are born sinners with a rebellious desire to do what God says not to do, but a "natural desire" to participate in an act does not necessarily mean the act in question is approved by God, something Paul goes to great lengths to explain in Romans 1–6. Christians should not be surprised to find some genetic or biological component to homosexuality. Creation, including the human body, is burdened by the weight of the Fall and awaits the second coming of Christ.

An example of the way in which genetics predispose individuals to certain destructive behavioral patterns can be seen in alcoholism. There is increasing evidence of a genetic component for susceptibility to the risk of alcoholism.[106] However, a genetic predisposition to alcoholism does not require the specific behavior of consuming alcohol to excess. In fact, awareness of a genetic predisposition would call for increased vigilance in this area of one's life. Likewise, if one desires to be a fully devoted follower of Jesus Christ, awareness of one's predispositions in different areas of life requires special focus, even if we are discussing sexual temptations.

105. In a similar way, Swaab and Hofman's findings about the SCN were widely reported as proof of a biological cause for homosexuality. But most reports failed to mention that Swaab and Hofman themselves said, "The relationship between a SCN and homosexuality is, of course, not necessarily a causal one." Swaab and Hofman, "An Enlarged Suprachiasmatic Nucleus," 146.

106. Beauvais, "American Indians and Alcohol." http://pubs.niaaa.nih.gov/publications/arh22-4/253.pdf.

What we really are discussing is human sinfulness. One of the tragedies of sin is that while most people know how to begin a particular sin or sinful habit, very rarely do we realize the third and fourth order consequences of sin. One of the most painful results of sin is that it is habit-forming. As was noted earlier, the brain can construct neural pathways and these pathways become reinforced and stronger each time we engage in various sins. In this way, we begin to live out the consequences of Jesus' warning, "Everyone who commits sin is a slave of sin" (John 8:34).

While there is no proof of genetic causation of homosexuality, there is enough of a genetic or biological component that we should show sympathy for those who struggle with this temptation. When some homosexuals claim that they have always struggled with same-sex attraction, even from their youth, I believe they are telling the truth. I suspect that future research will demonstrate that homosexuality is a highly complex combination of many factors, including biology, genetics, family of origin, social environment, and personal choice. Furthermore, male homosexuality and female homosexuality seem to be significantly different in both their occurrence and etiology with men and women apparently arriving at a homosexual orientation via different paths. People are not lying when they describe this as a strong attraction. While not compromising the clear Biblical message, we should demonstrate compassionate pastoral care, just as we would to someone struggling with other temptations.

We should not overlook the worldview conflicts that are inherent in the debate about homosexuality. Pro-homosexual researchers will sometimes point out that homosexual behavior is observed in animals. Thus, from a Naturalistic Darwinian worldview, homosexuality in humans is neither good nor evil but simply a naturally occurring variation of sexual behavior.[107] But this is a form of the naturalistic fallacy, drawing the conclusion homosexuality ought to be affirmed because it is "natural." In this way, a strong overtone of genetic determinism drones on in the background of many pro-homosexual arguments. If one agrees that Darwinian naturalism is the correct meta-narrative and that humans are nothing more than chemicals that have learned to self-reflect, then we are truly the sum of our DNA and doomed to whatever behavioral destiny lies in the millions of base pairs within the double helix of our genetic structure, and therefore not responsible for our deeds. But what if we are more than

107. Some have even argued that homosexuality can be explained via Darwinian as a trait related to high female fecundity within certain groups. Cf. Ciani et al., "Sexually Antagonistic Selection," e2282.

that? What if the Bible is correct when it says each person has a soul that transcends our genetic and biological composition? In that case, we really are morally accountable decision-makers with an ability to move beyond the limits of genetic or biological predisposition.

This worldview war is more intense than most evangelical preachers realize. Modern psychiatry asserts that sexual orientation cannot be changed. Thus, when we call people to repent of their sin, many mental health professionals believe that homosexuality should be excluded from this discipline. Most chaplains may be unaware of how strongly this idea of an "immutable" sexual orientation is embedded within modern mental health doctrine. When someone comes to a pastor and admits homosexual sin, a faithful pastor will encourage confession, repentance, and prayers to God for forgiveness. Furthermore, a pastor will encourage the development of spiritual disciplines such as prayer, scripture memory, fasting, and accountability partners in order to find victory over sin. By contrast, many (most?) mental health professionals would consider this type of spiritual counsel counter-productive to the mental health of someone involved in homosexuality. Instead, many mental health professionals see this type of pastoral care as harmful to the well-being of an individual, and in fact they believe this will push the person more deeply into conflicting feelings about their sexuality. Instead, modern psychiatry argues the healthiest thing a person can do is accept their own sexual orientation, embrace it in a healthy manner, and celebrate who they are.[108]

The worldview collisions associated with homosexuality are clearly seen in the personal examples of many of the researchers attempting to find genetic or biological causes to homosexuality. As was noted, Kinsey was sexually adventurous. Dean Hamer is in a same-sex marriage to Joe Wilson. The two of them produced *Out in Silence*, a film with the stated purpose of changing the way rural communities and small towns view homosexuality. Simon LeVay is an open homosexual and avid activist for gay rights. Richard Pillard was the first openly gay psychiatrist in the United States. Mustanski is the director of the Impact GLBT Health and Development program at Northwestern University. Michael Bailey

108. With this strong animus against the Christian position, it is difficult to believe that the current policy—allowing chaplains to preach within their faith convictions about homosexuality—will be retained for any length of time. To be blunt: in the armed forces, chaplains who tell people to repent of sexual sin will be considered part of the problem and not the solution. More likely, the current policy is a half-step closer to prohibiting chaplains from publicly or privately suggesting that homosexuality is sinful.

generated controversy in 2011 when he let two sexual "exhibitionists" perform sex acts in front of a college class.[109] The idea that these are coldly analytical scientists with no biases is ludicrous: these are agenda-driven activists with a significant emotional investment into the cause of sexually libertine morals and gay rights.

There are genetic and biological aspects to same-sex attraction and homosexual orientation, with some evidence pointing to a correlation between certain variables and same-sex attraction. This should not surprise us. The Christian worldview asserts that we are both body and soul. Because this is so, we are not doomed by a genetic predisposition towards any number of sinful behaviors. The Christian worldview also asserts that the entire creation has been damaged by a historical Fall wherein sin entered the world and distorted everything, including our biological and genetic predispositions. Homosexuality is rooted in multiple factors, and future research will probably address different "homosexualities" as opposed to one form of "homosexuality." A strong inclination towards a particular behavior does not prove that all behavior is necessarily good or that we should suspend moral judgment about the behavior.

109. "NU Cancels Human Sexuality Class." http://chicago.cbslocal.com/2011/05/09/nu-cancels-human-sexuality-class.

3

"Rainbow Rights?"

Homosexuality, Political Activity, and the Law

—John D. Laing

Introduction

WHEN ONE HEARS THE term, "gay rights," a number of things may come to mind, depending largely upon his or her background, social setting, and views on political and/or social issues. While many social and political liberals may think of a struggle for freedom, equality, or independence, their conservative counterparts will most likely have a very different conception. For them, the term may conjure up images of the most flamboyant gay pride parades or worse, the idea of a full-blown political, social and educational agenda designed to undermine the very foundations of Western civilization.[1]

Much controversy surrounds the language of *agenda*, as the terminology has, as one might expect, become politically charged. The terms, "gay agenda" and "homosexual agenda" are rejected by most gay rights

1. Suspicion abounds on both sides of the issue. Many homosexuals believe that religious conservatives have an agenda to subvert the Constitution and take over the country through political action with a view to setting up something of a theocracy. Consider the following quote: "The opposition to gay rights is the advance guard of the religious right's wholesale invasion of the political life of this country . . . They are more careful than they once were to disguise their *broad agenda* . . . Such paranoiac politics represent a grave danger to the Constitution and the society it informs, far graver than the imagined danger represented by constitutional equality for gays and lesbians." Nava and Dawidoff, *Created Equal*, 101–2.

groups as misleading, derogatory, and largely an invention of those whom they perceive to be the *radical right*. As one prominent gay-rights organization puts it, "Notions of a so-called 'homosexual agenda' are rhetorical inventions of anti-gay extremists seeking to create a climate of fear by portraying the pursuit of equal opportunity for LGBT people as sinister."[2] For most gays and lesbians, the words of Texas Municipal Court Judge Steve Russell, in denying the Driskell Hotel's request for a new trial after it lost a 1970 case where it was found to be in violation of Austin's anti-discrimination ordinance because it removed persons found engaging in same-sex dancing, sum up the heart of the issue of gay rights, that it is "one of human dignity, of the right to go about one's daily life without being publicly marked as inferior, less than human."[3] *Agenda* need not be such a negative term, as we all have goals in our activity.

Thus, this chapter is about different perspectives, different perspectives on issues surrounding gay rights which have led to social and political movements, and eventually found their way into the American courts. It will begin with a brief discussion of the homosexual agenda and key events in the gay rights movement, and then move to a summary of landmark legal cases for the ongoing discussion of gay rights in America with particular concern for their impact upon homosexual service in the nation's military. It will close with a brief study of hate crimes legislation and its impact upon life in America and chaplaincy within the United States armed forces.

Homosexual Agenda

Despite claims by homosexual advocate groups that there is no gay agenda to speak of, a number of Americans are convinced that there is a concerted effort by gay and lesbian activists to push their lifestyle on a largely unwilling populace. One purported example of such work is an article that has received perhaps more attention in recent years than it did when originally published in 1987. It was written under the presumably fictitious name, Michael Swift and entitled, "The Gay Revolutionary," though it has come to be known more colloquially as "The Gay Manifesto."[4] The

2. [GLAAD] *Media Reference Guide*, 13.
3. Quoted in Ball, *From the Closet to the Courtroom*, 9.
4. Not to be confused with Whitman's piece by the same name.

section of the article most often quoted, due not doubt to its shock value, follows:

> We shall sodomize your sons, emblems of your feeble masculinity, of your shallow dreams and vulgar lies. We shall seduce them in your schools, in your dormitories, in your gymnasiums, in your locker rooms, in your sports arenas, in your seminaries, in your youth groups, in your movie theater bathrooms, in your army bunkhouses, in your truck stops, in your all male clubs, in your houses of Congress, wherever men are with men together. Your sons shall become our minions and do our bidding. They will be recast in our image. They will come to crave and adore us . . . If you dare to cry faggot, fairy, queer, at us, we will stab you in your cowardly hearts and defile your dead, puny bodies . . . All churches who condemn us will be closed. Our only gods are handsome young men. We adhere to a cult of beauty, moral and esthetic . . . We shall be victorious because we are fueled with the ferocious bitterness of the oppressed who have been forced to play seemingly bit parts in your dumb, heterosexual shows throughout the ages. We too are capable of firing guns and manning the barricades of the ultimate revolution. Tremble, hetero swine, when we appear before you without our masks.[5]

Social and religious conservatives have often seen this as proof, if not of a gay conspiracy, then at least of an unspoken agenda among some within the gay community, an agenda that is frightening in its goals and tactics. Hice's comments are representative: "Although the views expressed by Swift may not represent everyone in the gay lifestyle, it certainly represents a significant number. These shocking words by Michael Swift have been considered part of the 'gay manifesto' by many, and reveal the radical agenda that is currently threatening our nation."[6] Hice continues, "Again, not everyone in the homosexual movement is an extremist like Swift. Many are productive and law-abiding citizens; however, it is abundantly evident that those within the movement who are radical are *really* radical!"[7]

5. Swift, "Gay Revolutionary."

6. Hice, *It's Now or Never*, 70. Hice is not alone. Not only has the article been cited by mainstream evangelicals like James Dobson's *Focus on the Family* group, but it was also supposedly read into the Congressional record by Representative William Dannemeyer (CA), and was cited as evidence in the Supreme Court case, *Lawrence v. Texas* 539 US (2003).

7. Ibid.

Many in the gay community have defended the article, most often by pointing out its satirical nature and excessively antagonistic tone as evidence that it was never meant to be taken seriously. For example, Bull and Gallagher note, "The article is hardly the dire threat the religious right contends. As lesbian social critic Cindy Patton has pointed out, the writer is actually parodying paranoid right-wing conspiracy theories about the gay movement."[8] They go on to dismiss the notion of a gay agenda, arguing that "the gay community is far too disorganized and politically diverse to agree upon a unified 'gay agenda' that the religious right claims to have identified."[9] Other groups highlight the first line of the article as indicative of its satirical goal and accuse religious conservatives of purposely omitting it in an effort to deceive the public. For example, the popular gay-rights group, Rainbow Alliance, states on its website, "But when the religious right cites this text, they always omit the vital first line, which sets the context for the piece. In other words, every

8. Bull and Gallagher, *Perfect Enemies*, 267. Bull and Gallagher are particularly dismissive of the article, claiming that "the vast majority of gays and lesbians have never heard of it, let alone agree with its sentiments." Ibid.

9. Ibid. Bull and Gallagher are surely correct insofar as the entire population of gay and lesbian persons go—all homosexuals are not actively working toward an agenda, there is not secret "gay handshake," and they do not make use of secret code in their communications. Likewise, they are also correct if they mean to say that all homosexual organizations and gay rights groups cannot produce a list of primary goals to which all can agree. Nevertheless, their claim is still at least somewhat disingenuous in that it suggests homosexuals have been ineffective and unsuccessful at organizing for political and social activism, and nothing could be further from the truth. The homosexual community is perhaps the best organized and most well-funded of any group with special interests. The mere existence of public relations, think tanks, and political lobbying groups like GLAAD and the National Gay Task Force, among others, belies the effort in the community for organized public activity. For scholarly treatment of the topic, see Rimmerman, *From Identity to Politics*; or Barclay et al., eds., *Queer Mobilizations*. As early as 1972, a gay rights platform with lists of demands for federal and state legislators was published at the National Coalition of Gay Organizations Convention held in Chicago. Similarly, organizers of the 1993 Lesbian, Gay, Bisexual and Transgender march on Washington, D.C., set forth a platform of demands. Many conservatives have seen the strategy outlined by Kirk and Pill [Madsen] as evidence that an organized, concerted effort by the gay and lesbian community to normalize their lifestyles/sexual orientation is not only possible, but a reality. First published in an article in *Guide Magazine* and further developed in their controversial book, *After the Ball*, it includes seven items: (1) Talk about gays and gayness as loudly and as often as possible; (2) Portray gays as victims, not as aggressive challengers; (3) Give protectors a just cause; (4) Make gays look good; (5) Make the victimizers look bad; (6) Solicit funds; and (7) Gen on air/in the media. Kirk and Pill [Madsen], "The Overhauling of Straight America," 7–14; Kirk and Madsen, *After the Ball*.

other version of this found on the net and in the literature of the religious right political activists is part of the radical right's great lie about gay people."[10] It is true that the opening line of the piece has been omitted in many critical renderings of the piece and it does set the stage for all to follow. It reads, "This essay is an outré, madness, a tragic, cruel fantasy, an eruption of inner rage, on how the oppressed desperately dream of being the oppressor."[11] Surely it is meant to be hyperbolic satire and caricature.

Nevertheless, what the article's defenders fail to recognize is that for most religious and social conservatives, the very topic of pedophilia is so disturbing and so far beyond the realm of propriety, that it is out of bounds for jokes and satire. Similarly, the references to violence and murder of heterosexuals are in bad taste and seem to bear a measure of truth in desire, for some homosexual activist websites seem to advocate violence and the use of armed force in dealing with what it perceives to be an intolerant and even dangerous heterosexual community.[12] In fact, many conservatives see the references to youth groups and schools in the

10. http://www.rainbowallianceopenfaith.homstead.com/GayAgenda.html. Countless other examples of similar argumentation could be given. McEwen writes, "He [Swift] is plainly leading the reader to make assumptions about the gay and lesbian community; assumptions that only someone with a basic ignorance of the community would make." McEwen, *Holy Bullies*, 97.

11. Swift.

12. See, for example, www.thegaymanifesto.com, a homosexual watchdog site of sorts, though it could reasonably be seen as an alarmist site that incites hatred and violence. It includes numerous stories of purported attacks against gays and lesbians, both verbal and physical, and casts the discussion in terms of war. It maintains a list of "Christian Hate Groups," and runs stories with titles such as "Christian Minister Demands Congress Build Concentration Camps, Calls for Genocide Against Gay & Lesbian Americans," and "North Carolina Pastor Sean Harris Directs Christian Congregation to Beat Gay & Lesbian Children—Local School Threatened." Clearly, some of the stories misrepresent the words and intentions of the pastors' sermons and the points being made. However, it is instructive for at least three reasons. First, it should help Christians to see how their words can be misunderstood or in some cases, deliberately mischaracterized to hurt the cause of Christ. Second, it can help reasonable Christians understand why our relatively sedate disagreement with homosexuality can arouse such intense feelings of anger, sadness, and fear in gay and lesbian persons. No distinction is made between hateful, inflammatory rhetoric and reasoned, rational argumentation against homosexuality. Both of these recognitions should lead us to choose our words very carefully and to be particularly sensitive when engaging homosexuals on the issue. Third, we should condemn in no uncertain terms, the words of those pastors who do call for violence against gays and lesbians. It is an embarrassment to our faith and an affront to Christ. See Scott Callaham's chapter on how we can lovingly engage homosexuals in dialogue and minister to them when in need.

Swift article as indicative of a propensity within the homosexual community—even if a minor position—to endorse or defend pedophilia.

Homosexual advocate groups, understandably, have almost universally spurned attempts to link homosexuality to pedophilia and/or child abuse as entirely inaccurate and even defamatory. For example, one popular media reference guide notes, "Being gay, lesbian, bisexual and transgender is neither synonymous with nor indicative of any tendency toward pedophilia, child abuse, sexual abuse, bestiality, bigamy, polygamy, adultery and/or incest. Such claims, innuendos and associations often are used to insinuate that lesbians and gay men pose a threat to society, to families, and to children in particular. Such assertions and insinuations are defamatory and should be avoided, except in direct quotes that clearly reveal the bias of the person quoted."[13] Yet, as Thorstad points out, the gay rights movement included and tolerated *boy-lovers* "from the beginning."[14] He charges that it was not until the issue became a national concern as a result of Anita Bryant's *Save Our Children* campaign that the gay movement distanced itself from pederasty: "The gay movement went into a defensive mode...It didn't occur to gay spokespeople to draw a distinction between being raped or molested and enjoying sex, or to point out that underage males frequently enjoy and seek to have sex, with men and women. No one thought to ask boy-lovers or boys themselves to respond to the accusation."[15]

Sexual conservatives (and in this, I would include the majority of Christians) thus fear that the normalization of homosexuality is the beginnings of a downward spiral in sexual ethics. These concerns have not been assuaged by some homosexual advocates, who have argued for extreme libertarianism, which results in a virtual relativism with respect to sexual ethics. For example, Rubin seems to view pedophilia as just another variation in personal preference that should be condemned no more than one's personal preference for a particular hair color, body shape, or the like. She writes, "Promiscuous homosexuality,

13. [GLAAD] *Media Reference Guide*, 14.

14. He writes, "Pederasty was a secret not to be told. Yet although man/boy love represented a minority phenomenon within the gay subculture, it was far from unusual." Thorstad, "Man/Boy Love," 253. As evidence of the prevalence of pederasty, Thorstad points to the research of Bell and Weinberg, which suggested that approximately 14–25% of homosexual males had a sexual encounter with a minor (16 years old and younger). Bell and Weinberg, *Homosexualities.*

15. Ibid., 253–54.

sadomasochism, fetishism, transsexuality, and *cross-generational encounters* are still viewed as unmodulated horrors incapable of involving affection, love, free choice, kindness, or transcendence. This kind of sexual morality has more in common with ideologies of racism than with true ethics" [emphasis mine].[16] Thorstad argues that complete sexual freedom was a primary goal of the gay rights movement early on, but that it was undermined by the combination of Bryant's *Save Our Children* movement and the radical lesbian penchant to view all male sex in terms of rape and abuse.[17] He points to the debate sparked by an article in the Gay Community News addressing the issue as evidence.[18] The fact that there was debate over the issue of pederasty seems to justify connecting the fight for homosexual rights to concerns about sexual relativism resulting in acceptance of what many believe to be child molestation and endangerment.

16. She continues, "A democratic morality should judge sexual acts by the way partners treat one another, the level of mutual consideration, the presence or absence of coercion, and the quantity and quality of the pleasure they provide. Whether sex acts are gay or straight, coupled or in groups, naked or in underwear, commercial or free, with or without video, should not be ethical concerns." Rubin, "Thinking Sex," 15. That Rubin means pedophilia when she refers to "cross-generational encounters" can be seen in her defense of child pornography and her discussion of what she sees as illegal harassment due to antiquated laws regulating sexuality. She writes, "Like communists and homosexuals in the 1950s, boy-lovers are so stigmatized that it is difficult to find defenders for their civil liberties, let alone for their erotic orientation. Consequently, the police have feasted on them. Local police, the FBI, and watchdog postal inspectors have joined to build a huge apparatus whose sole aim is to wipe out the community of men who love underaged youth. In twenty years or so, when some of the smoke has cleared, it will be much easier to show that these men have been the victims of a savage and undeserved witch hunt. A lot of people will be embarrassed by their collaboration with this persecution, but it will be too late to do much good for those men who have spent their lives in prison." Ibid., 7.

17. He writes, "Many activists shared the view that the state had no business regulating sex between consenting partners, whatever their age." Thorstad, "Man/Boy Love," 253. He continues, "Under pressure from the women's movement and lesbian activists, the gay movement began to internalize straight society's stereotype of pederasty as inherently exploitative, a form of 'sexual abuse,' even when the youth wanted and enjoyed it. Like society at large, the woman's and lesbian/gay movements seemed more concerned about consensual sex between men and boys than about actual physical abuse of children within the family, an epidemic problem. Most activists in these movements, both adult-run, wished the issue of cross-generational sex would just go away." Ibid., 254.

18. Thorstad, "Statement to the Gay Liberation Movement," 5.

These concerns have only been heightened by the on-going scholarly discussion of these issues. For example, a mainstream academic journal which focuses on homosexual concerns, published an extended issue dealing with the *pedophilia debate.*[19] In his article examining sexuality in children, Plummer argues that children give meaning to sexual activity only when adults convey meaning to it, either positive or negative. He further argues that children can have physiological experiences normally associated with sexuality (e.g., erection, orgasm, etc.), but since they are *blank slates* of sorts (my image, not his), children may not view those experiences in sexual ways or feel shame as a result. Meaning, he argues, is a social construct; there is no inherent value in sexual acts and no innate attitudes toward sexuality. The implication of Plummer's analysis is that children may not be as adversely affected by cross-generational sexuality as is often thought.[20]

What Plummer largely leaves to implication, Jones argues explicitly, questioning the assumption that children cannot give consent and that therefore, all adult-child sexual relations *de facto* involve abuse.[21] Rather, he distinguishes *intergenerational intimacy* from child abuse, writing that the key difference has to do with mutuality and control or force. He writes, "Abuse consists of unreasonable, unilateral imposition by the adult of unwanted behavior upon the other person…thereby at least partially denying the younger individual's exercise of choice…These strategies are not typical of intergenerational intimacy, where the ability of both persons to exercise choice is fundamental."[22] Jones then moves to

19. The journal, published by respected academic publisher Taylor & Francis, is *Journal of Homosexuality.* The reference to debate comes from the foreword to the special issue, Schmidt, "Foreword: The Debate on Pedophilia," 1–4.

20. Plummer, "Understanding Childhood Sexualities," 231–49.

21. Jones is critical of the bulk of literature on the subject of adult-child sexuality, seeing it as caving in to political pressure, presumably due to an outdated Puritanical morality. He writes, "Consideration of the full range of possibilities in child-adult interactions often seems to be ignored in favor of more and more discussion about the importance of insulating children from anything even potentially sexual involving adults." Jones, "Intergenerational Intimacy in North America," 276. Jones charges that many of the scientific studies in the scholarly corpus on child-adult sexual interactions are dishonest and manipulate the data. He thus presents his goals in writing: "One purpose of this paper is to show how these trends are reflected as well as abetted in social science literature, and then to outline and encourage alternatives for more accurate, unbiased and comprehensive future research." Ibid., 277.

22. Ibid., 278. Jones claims that abuse, as he has defined it, in seldom at play in homosexual pedophilia: "Even explicitly sexual pedophilia—particularly homosexual

the more startling claim that, not only is sexual contact with adults not harmful to children *in se*, but also may be actually helpful in some cases! He writes,

> A typical assumption of the child sexual abuse literature is that sexual contact with an adult is emotionally traumatic and causes damage that often extends well into adulthood. This is not at all an established conclusion in the empirical literature. Such harm undoubtedly can occur, though a number of authors have pointed out that the trauma may be induced or exacerbated by strong reactions of parents, police, court officials and other adults when they discover that such activity has taken place. Some studies have found benign or even beneficial results in boys who were at the time involved with men and in adults who had been involved in sexual relationships with adult men when they were boys. These findings are significant because the child sexual abuse literature, as it developed in the 1970s, ignored the earlier studies that found no harm due to sexual contact per se, just as today's writers are ignoring more recent literature which discusses intergenerational contact and child sexuality in value-neutral terms.[23]

Jones seems wont to normalize pedophilia, and he utilizes arguments analogous to those used by the gay community to normalize homosexuality. He claims that pedophilia should be seen as a sexual orientation, no different in legitimacy from that of homosexuality or heterosexuality: "The possibility should be considered that intergenerational attraction on the part of some adults could constitute a lifestyle 'orientation,' rather than a pathological maladjustment as is typically assumed. It has been suggested…that some forms of intergenerational contact…are a result

---

(i.e., man-boy) contact—rarely involves the use of force or violence. The few studies done outside institutional settings (e.g., Ingram, 1981, Sandfort, 1981; 1983) suggest that such relationships can exist without the exercise of any manipulative power on the part of the adult." Ibid., 286–87.

23. Ibid., 280. For purposes of the quotation, I omitted the numerous parenthetical references Jones included: Bender and Grugett, "Follow-up Report," 825–37; Ingram, "Participating Victims," 177–87; Landis, "Experiences of 500 Children with Adult Sexual Deviation," 91–109; Lempp, "Psychological Damage to Children," 243–45; Mohr, "A Child Has Been Molested," 43–50; Sandfort, *Het Seksuele Aspekt van Pedofiele Relaties*, later published in English as *The Sexual Aspect of Pedophile Relations*; Sandfort, "Pedophile Relationships in the Netherlands,"164–83; Tindall, "Male Adolescent Involved with a Pederast Becomes an Adult," 373–82; Weeks, "Sexually Exploited Child," 848–50; Wilson and Cox, *The Child-Lovers*.

of an integral, lifelong social/sexual preference...which is analogous to the more familiar lesbian, androphile homosexual, or heterosexual orientations."[24] The conclusion is obvious: if sexual attraction to children is natural to some, then it is natural and should be free for exploration and in no way should be criminalized or even criticized.

In a perhaps the most disturbing article, Li seeks to present the viewpoints of pedophiles which he has gleaned from personal interviews. He argues that we need to hear from pedophiles in order to better understand their sexual lives as experiencing subjects. As he puts it, "The search for a categorical etiology or pathology for pedophilia as an objective entity will mask the rich complexity of the unique life of the individual concerned, and will reify the subjective human experiences involved."[25] One of the particularly disconcerting trends that emerges from Li's study is the attitude many pedophiles have with regard to their own desires; they seem to believe that the innate nature of their desires makes them natural and that therefore, they are within their rights to pursue the fulfillment of those desires through sexual contact with children.

After summarizing the motivations and desires which lead some men to engage in sexual acts with children, Li concludes that dismissing them as pathological or disordered "masks the complexity of human existence."[26] Li attempts to walk a fine line between moral relativism and a tolerance with limits. While not rejecting pedophilic arguments and justifications outright, he also sets limits to acceptable behavior:

> While to a certain extent this discussion seems to be endorsing a relativization of the concept of 'normality,' it is not my intention to defend all types of sexual contact between adults and children. Lust, murder of children and coercive sexual contact must be ruled out as unacceptable no matter how these acts are construed by the adult committing them. But when it comes to the question of consensual adult-child sexual activities, there is much more room for alternative constructions, and hence it is more difficult to arrive at a blanket judgment.[27]

Thus, Li suggests that the widely held principle that children cannot give consent is false, and calls for continued critical engagement of the

24. Ibid, 288.
25. Li, "Main Thing is Being Wanted," 131.
26. Ibid., 140.
27. Ibid., 141.

community with pedophiles in an effort to come to agreement regarding appropriate limits in sexual conduct and interaction: "In dealing with this problem, it must be borne in mind that the viewpoint of mainstream society cannot simply be taken as correct and that of the pedophiles taken as suspect. Instead, each should be analyzed in terms of its historical and ideological roots. Only after such an exercise can we begin to address the more practical questions of ethics, the law, and social policies with regard to sexual contact between adults and children."[28] While it is clear that the perspectives of Rubin, Thorstad, Plummer, Jones, Li, and others like them cannot be taken as representative of the homosexual community, it is equally clear that they use the very arguments set forth to normalize gay and lesbian love.

Homosexuality as Mental Illness

The removal of homosexuality from the list of mental illnesses in 1973 by vote of the American Psychiatric Association (APA) has been a source of contention in gay rights debates because it occurred largely as a result of political activism, and less due to substantial scientific agreement or anything approximating consensus.[29] Social conservatives and gay activists do not disagree significantly on the details or facts, but they do have a fundamental disagreement over the motive behind and goals driving the pressure that was brought to bear on the APA. For example, Satinover represents the view of many in the conservative camp when he argues that the reclassification campaign was part of a larger programme of normalization of homosexuality in the culture. He writes, "In the early years of 'gay liberation,' this reality [a reference to the immense influence exerted in the society/culture by mental health professionals] was used for the fledgling gay activists' advantage. They anticipated that if the influential American Psychiatric Association (APA) could be convinced to redefine homosexuality, the other guilds would follow shortly thereafter and then so would the rest of society."[30] By contrast, homosexual activists contend that the inclusion of homosexuality in the *Diagnostic and Statistical Manual* (DSM) as a psychiatric illness had long been used as

28. Ibid.

29. See Alan Branch's discussion in chapter two of the present volume.

30.. Satinover, *Homosexuality and the Politics of Truth*, 31.

Kinsey

justification for a whole host of laws targeting homosexuals, from state sodomy and crimes-against-nature laws, to federal immigration statutes.

Many identify Kinsey's work as most influential in removing the stigma from homosexuality. While it is true that Kinsey was a pioneer in sexuality study, at least with regards to homosexuality, and that he was sympathetic to the cause, it was largely the work of Evelyn Hooker and Thomas Szasz which gave clinical substantiation to the claims of gay activists that homosexuality should not be construed as a psychological or psychiatric disorder.

Hooker was a professor of psychology who became interested in homosexuality upon discovering that a former student, who appeared well-adjusted, was gay. He, along with a number of his gay friends and acquaintances, convinced her that more research into homosexual psychology was needed. Up until that time (mid-1950's), most research was conducted using homosexuals already seeking treatment for psychological problems and/or disorders. Hooker sought to conduct a study comparing homosexual and heterosexual men in terms of adjustment in life: careers, relationships, etc., and had pairings of homosexual and heterosexual men of comparable age, IQ, and education, take the Rorschach test (a projective test utilizing inkblots which was popular at the time), along with two other projective tests.[31] While Hooker saw the results as tentative and even initially resisted their publication, she nevertheless acquiesced.[32] They suggested that homosexual men *could* be equally well-adjusted as heterosexual males. Judges were often times unable to identify which individual in a given pair was the homosexual and which was the heterosexual. Hooker notes that some judges even showed signs of irritation, complaining of a "forced choice" or having to simply guess[33]. After describing numerous specific cases where judges got the

31. Chapman and Chapman, "Test Results are What You Think," 238–48.

32. The editors of *The Journal of Projective Techniques* prefaced Hooker's article with the following statement: "Editorial Note: It is an uncommon event in these days of compulsive publication to discover an author who has worked diligently and with great detail and who hesitates to published well-substantiated findings until proof is virtually incontrovertible. A study such as Dr. Hooker's challenges several wide-spread and emotional convictions. In view of the importance of her findings it seemed desirable to the editors that they be made public, even in their preliminary form. If some of Dr. Hooker's cautiously presented as they are, seem premature or incompletely documented, the blame must fall on the editors who exercised considerable pressure on her to publish now. –BRF" Hooker, "Adjustment of the Male Homosexual" 18

33. Ibid., 23.

sexual orientation of the subjects wrong or had extreme difficulty in making a determination, Hooker concludes the study by first noting the revolutionary nature of what her results imply. She writes, ". . . what is difficult to accept (for some clinicians) is that some homosexuals may be very ordinary individuals, indistinguishable, except in sexual pattern, from ordinary individuals who are heterosexual. Or—and I do not know whether this would be more or less difficult to accept—that some may be quite superior individuals, not only devoid of pathology (unless one insists that homosexuality itself is a sign of pathology) but also functioning at a superior level."[34] Ultimately, she argues that homosexuality, taken alone, may not necessarily imply psychological pathology, and this, she sees, as leading to three conclusions: "1. Homosexuality as a clinical entity does not exist . . . 2. Homosexuality may be a deviation in sexual pattern which is within the normal range . . . [and] 3. The role of particular forms of sexual desire and expression in personality structure and development may be less important than has frequently been assumed."[35] The upshot and significance of this work, along with Hooker's subsequent work with homosexuals, cannot be overstated.[36] It undermined claims of psychological disorder that had been used to substantiate legislative action against homosexual activity and homosexuals. As Bayer writes, "The implications were clear. What homosexuals needed most was freedom from the crippling effects of exclusion and stigmatization. The elimination of undesirable and 'pathological' traits could only follow a fundamental transformation in the social context of homosexual existence. Social struggle rather than psychotherapy was the appropriate healing tool."[37]

Bayer points to the work of Thomas Szasz as setting up the fundamental philosophical tools necessary for the later confrontation at the APA. Szasz argued against the medicalization of mental disorders and the use of psychology and psychiatry as expert opinion regarding individuals' fitness to live in American society. Specifically with regard

34. Ibid., 29.

35. Ibid., 30.

36. Hooker later argued that signs of mental instability and/or social maladjustment in homosexuals are primarily caused by labeling, stigmatizing, ostracizing, and general hostility by the heterosexual community, rather than as indicators of a problem with homosexuality in se. See Hooker, "Male Homosexuals and Their 'Worlds,'" 83–107.

37. Bayer, *Homosexuality and American Psychiatry*, 53.

to homosexuality, he compared government collusion with the mental health professions in criminalizing homosexuality (viewed as a heterodox or heretical sexuality) to the Inquisition, which criminalized heterodox and heretical religious perspectives and sought to torture their practitioners under the guise of concern for their well-being.[38]

Such rhetorical flourish notwithstanding, the point remains that clinical appraisal has often been used as a tool of the state for substantiating its actions in removing undesirable persons from society. Prior to the removal of homosexuality from the list of disorders, it was used to enact and enforce legislation criminalizing homosexual activity, marginalizing homosexual persons in America, or denying gay and lesbian persons immigrant status.[39]

Gay Rights

The history of gay rights is, arguably, a story of an on-going interplay of the homosexual community's movement from relative obscurity, to persecution or targeting, to defensive posturing, to offensive attack, and back to relative obscurity.[40] In fact, Fetner has argued that the gay rights movement would not have developed as it did if it were not for strong opposition to homosexuality and homosexual rights, as epitomized in that found in religio-political organizations like Falwell's *Moral Majority*, Robetson's *Chirstian Coalition*, or more recently, Dobson's *Focus on the Family Ministries*. She contends that lesbian and gay activism only grew into a large-scale national movement in response to anti-gay activity. She outlines how religious opposition to gay rights helped frame the discussion and direct the strategies of gay-rights organizations.[41] Whether it is

38. Szasz, *Manufacture of Madness*. See especially chapter 10.

39. The cases of George Fleuti, Clive Michael Boutilier, Richard John Longstaff, and Anthony Corbett Sullivan and Richard Frank Adams are just a few of the cases. See *Rosenberg v. Fleuti* 374 US 449 (1963); *Boutilier v. Immigration and Naturalization Service* 387 US 118 (1967); *Longstraff v. Immigration and Naturalization Service* 716 F.2d 1439 (1983); *Adams and Sullivan v. Howerton* 673 F.2d 1036 (1982).

40. Two particularly interesting and helpful books on the topic, due largely to their scope and scholarship are Richards, *The Case for Gay Rights*; and Kranz and Cusik, *Gay Rights: Library in a Book*. Williams and Retter have provided a helpful compilation of primary sources of the gay rights movement and controversies surrounding the push for gay rights. Williams and Retter, eds., *Gay and Lesbian Rights in the United States*.

41. She writes, "It [religious right] has affected lesbian and gay activists' choices

religious opposition or government crackdowns, what cannot be denied is that many homosexual activists became such when they felt that their personal rights had been violated or denied. The case of Frank Kameny, a quiet and reserved astronomer turned outspoken and charismatic gay activist, has become something of an exemplar of this theme.[42]

Gay rights as a movement cannot be separated from the cultural milieu in which it arose. The 1960s and 70s were largely a time of upheaval and questioning of traditional power structures, a time of protest and free love, and these factors clearly had a significant impact on the

---

of which issues to rally around and which issues to put on the back burner. It has blocked or reversed the implementation of policies that would benefit lesbians and gay men. The religious right has changed the rhetoric that lesbian and gay activists use to express their claims. It has also influenced the choice of tactics by the lesbian and gay movement, and even the size and shape of many organizations within the movement. And perhaps most importantly, it has limited the lesbian and gay movement's ability to frame the public debate about gay rights." Fetner, *How the Religious Right Shaped Lesbian and Gay Activism*, xv.

42. When Frank Kameny was fired from the Army Map Service and subsequently barred from further federal employment on suspicion he was homosexual, he filed suit. He was originally arrested because he responded favorably to advances made toward him by an undercover police officer in a San Francisco bathroom. He pled guilty to a reduced charge and served a probationary sentence. His case is most significant because of the arguments he presented in his 60-page request to the U.S. Supreme Court for a hearing. Following Kinsey's work, Kameny asserted that approximately 10 percent of the population is homosexual (though he admitted that Kinsey eschewed such rigid classifications). More importantly, though, Kameny characterized homosexuals as a minority group, and compared their plight to those of traditional minority groups (Negros, Jews, Catholics, etc.), with the exception that homosexuals were being persecuted by the government, rather than protected. In a somewhat overstated claim, he declared that the homosexual minority group had endured "a persecution and discrimination of a harshness and ferocity at least as severe as that directed against these other minorities…a persecution not one whit more warranted or justified than those against Negroes, Jews, Catholics or other minority groups." *Kameny v. Brucker*, petition for *cert.*, quoted in Murchoch and Price, *Courting Justice*, 56. Kameny went on to argue, again following Kinsey, that homosexuals are well-adjusted, psychologically-stable, productive and loyal/patriotic members of society, and that it is the government's duty to protect them. He argued that the government policy against homosexuals is "archaic" and "a relic of the Stone Age," which stands as an offense against proper morality. The heart of Kameny's claim was that disqualifying homosexuals from public service is unlawful discrimination and unreasonable because homosexuality is normal (at least for some) and acceptable. Kameny's request was denied, but he went on to become a leader in the gay rights movement, with a style which was more offense-oriented (as opposed to a defensive posture). He convinced the ACLU to see homosexuals as a persecuted minority group, and was instrumental in the APA's change of position on homosexuality as a mental illness or defect.

thought and ethos of the emerging gay community. That time period saw a flurry of activist groups arise within the homosexual community, often one more radical than the next, but they all built upon the work of earlier, less public groups like the Mattachine Society.

Mattachine Society

In 1948 at a private party for gay men a discussion began about organizing homosexuals to support the presidential campaign of progressive Democrat Henry Wallace. Harry Hay, a communist actor and intellectual, became enthralled with the idea of organized gay social and political action, and after two years of planning and negotiations, he helped form the Mattachine Society. It was the first gay social group in the United States, and styled itself largely an intellectual group. Its primary goal was to argue that homosexuals could integrate appropriately into, and offer significant contributions to society and the "progress of mankind."[43] In addition to its own work, it also helped found other groups, most notably the *Daughters of Bilitis*, a similarly-conceived lesbian organization. The two groups held meetings, supported gay-rights causes (as best they could be done in the 1950s), encouraged homosexual-themed publications (such as ONE and numerous paperback novels), and offered a place of belonging to a displaced group. Reflecting later on the impact of Mattachine, Hay noted, "Mattachine was important because it got us to stop thinking of ourselves in negative terms . . . We believed that as a special people we had made significant contributions for thousands of years, and we were determined that we continue contributing as opening Gay people in present-day society."[44]

Though Mattachine was ground-breaking, by the tumultuous times of the 60's and 70's, it was viewed by many in the gay and lesbian communities as too conservative and passive. It came under sharp criticism for its attempts to portray homosexuals as the same as heterosexuals, rather than embracing homosexuality as a unique identity. There was a growing sense that gays and lesbians should be proud of their sexuality and newer, more radical groups began to spring up, such as the Gay Liberation Front, PRIDE (Personal Rights in Defense and Education) and Vanguard. These

43. MacDonald [pseudonym for Harry Hay], "Preliminary Concepts," quoted in Williams and Retler, eds., 73.

44. Potvin, "Harry Hay Remembers," 14–16.

groups and others like them moved the fight for homosexual rights from the language of *acceptance*, to language of *gay pride*.

Stonewall

Prior to President Barak Obama's January 21, 2013 Inauguration speech, most Americans had probably never heard of the Stonewall Inn, and probably even fewer had any idea of the significance of the events that took place at that small bar for three days in mid-summer, 1969, but for the homosexual community, "Stonewall" has come to mean so much more than the name of an obscure, somewhat seedy bar on Christopher Street in Greenwich Village, New York. At approximately three o'clock in the morning on June 28, 1969, New York city police raided the Stonewall Inn, a known gay bar, for alleged liquor law violations. This was nothing new; police had raided many gay bars and even had something of a routine in place.[45] They would typically pull up two or three paddy wagons and, once in place, begin the raid by rounding up patrons, herding them into the wagons, and transporting them to the precinct headquarters for processing. The charges were normally confined to misdemeanor offenses—loitering and the like—and persons caught would often make bail, pay a fine, and have the charges reduced or dropped, but the names of those arrested were often published in the newspaper and many were thus *outed* as a result. The repercussions of the publication could be worse than a "guilty" verdict on the criminal charges, for the persons could face harassment of varying kinds, including threats of violence or loss of employment.

For reasons still debated in the literature, this time the patrons refused to go quietly.[46] Tensions grew as the raid took longer than expected,

45. A 1967 raid on the known gay bar, *The Black Cat* in Los Angeles, inspired something of a backlash as well, with demonstrations and numerous arrests. It also led to the publication of *The Advocate*, a gay-issues magazine still in print today, and later, to the founding of the Metropolitan Community Church, a largely gay church located in Los Angeles which has grown to become a denomination itself, with 222 congregations in over 35 countries.

46. Some accounts argue that it was a spontaneous reaction to the events when one individual hurled a bottle at police officers when they made their way toward the doors, others suggest that despair over the recent death of Judy Garland, an apparent gay icon, helped spur the patrons to violence. See Mezey, *Queers in Court*, 27–28. Still others have suggested that the beating of a "butch" lesbian who resisted arrest led to the escalation in violence.

and a large crowd grew outside the bar. At some point, clashes broke out between members of the crowd and police, and shortly thereafter, a full-scale riot ensued: bricks were thrown, trash cans were set ablaze, and pandemonium resulted. When the police riot squad arrived, the crowd was quickly dispersed, but they had stood their ground. The next night, an even larger crowd appeared in front of the now destroyed Stonewall Inn, many drawn by the stories printed in the city newspapers. The crowd, numbering in the thousands, was again confronted by the police, but this time, it was able to stand against even the riot squad. Many were injured in the fighting that night, and skirmishes continued for the next several days. Eventually, peace was restored to Greenwich Village.

The effects of Stonewall can surely be overstated, as its importance is largely symbolic. Following the riots, some gay activists pleaded with the mayor's office to stop the war on gays and allow gays free association in their own bars without having to pay protection money. Those requests were not met; the riots did not end persecution of gays, did not even end raids on gay bars in the city of New York, much less across the country. Still, the symbolic power of Stonewall is immense, so much so that in the homosexual community, it stands as the demarcating line for understanding the history of gay rights: Stonewall changed everything; there is a Before Stonewall and an After Stonewall.[47]

Its significance lies in the fact that the men stood up for themselves as a matter of principle, something rarely done at the time. Although the Stonewall Inn is no more, the events of that early morning are memorialized each year in gay pride marches across the country. More significant than throwing bottles or hurling insults at law enforcement personnel was the courage it lent to others to fight for their perceived rights. That fight has largely moved from the streets to the courtroom (and perhaps the airwaves). It is to this that we now turn.

47. These terms are taken from the documentary movies with the same titles. Greta Schiller, dir., John Scagliotti, Robert Rosenberg, and Greta Schiller, prod. Rita Mae Brown, narr., *Before Stonewall: The Making of a Gay and Lesbian Community* (New York: First Run Features, 1985); John Scagliotti, dir., Dan Hunt, prod., Melissa Etheridge, narr., *After Stonewall* (New York: First Run Features, 1999).

Legal Cases, Gay Rights, and Hate

Any attempt to identify and summarize such a wide array of items touching on so many issues will necessarily be limited in scope and decisions regarding which cases to discuss and which to omit will need to be made.[48] Clearly, not everyone will be satisfied with the result. For example, Ball divides case law and personal concern into five areas with one key case as representative of each: Family, *Braschi v. Stahl Associates* (1989), where an appellate court found that two men living together in an intimate relationship may satisfy the legal definition of "family;" Harassment, *Nabozny v. Podilesney* (1996), where school officials were found to have violated a gay student's Constitutional rights to equal protection by ignoring his pleas for protection, failing to punish his attackers, and even laughing at him, over the course of his midde- and high-school years; Discrimination, *Romer v. Evans* (1996), which ruled Unconstitutional an amendment to the Colorado State Constitution preventing any city, town, or county from classifying homosexuals as a protected class; Marriage, *Baehr v. Lewin* (1993, later renamed *Baehr v. Mike*), where the Supreme Court of Hawaii agreed to hear a case arguing that the State Constitution's right to privacy includes a right to same-sex marriage, though it eventually found that it did not, and voters approved an amendment to the Constitution which explicitly allows officials to reserve marriage for opposite-sex couples; and Sex, *Lawrence v. Texas* (2003), where the United States Supreme Court effectively ruled state sodomy laws Unconstitutional.[49] Of the five identified by Ball, only one, *Lawrence*, will be examined here. The cases chosen, though, are representative of those which were victories for gay rights, and those which were victories for its opponents.

Discrimination over the gays + lesbians has opened the door to exposure and acceptance.

ONE, Inc. v. Olesen

Any discussion of the legal issues and concerns involved in gay rights must begin with a little-known Supreme Court case involving the publication and distribution rights of a gay magazine. *ONE* magazine was

48. One illuminating account of the difficulties of gays and lesbians is Mogul et al., *Queer (In)Justice.* Pinello provides scholarly discussion of findings, along with statistical analysis, of cases involving homosexual rights.. Pinello, *Gay Rights and American Law.*

49. Ball, *From the Closet to the Courtroom.*

the first regularly-published magazine dealing with issues of interest to a homosexual audience, begun in January, 1953 by leaders of the Los Angeles chapter of the Mattachine Society. It styled itself as an intellectual publication, designed to present articles relevant to the gay community. *ONE*'s problems with the Postmaster began in the Fall of the first year of publication when its August issue's mailing was held up for three weeks. At the time, there was a law commonly referred to as the *Comstock Law*, after postal inspector and head of the New York Society for the Suppression of Vice (NYSSV), Anthony Comstock, which gave the Postmaster General power to remove from the mail any "obscene book, pamphlet, paper, writing, advertisement, circular, print, picture, drawing or other representation, figure, or image on or of paper or other material, or any cast instrument, or other article of an immoral nature."[50] While the postmaster still had concerns that the magazine was in violation of the law because of its article suggesting the viability of homosexual marriage—a taboo topic to be sure—he eventually cleared it for mailing. The publishers took its release as a sign that its content was within the bounds of the law, and even claimed official approval.[51] Still, *ONE*'s legal advisor, Eric Julber, recommended that the articles and stories remain tame, much to the chagrin of its readership. It would not be long before trouble emerged again.[52]

Almost exactly one year later, the October, 1954 issue was dubbed "unfit to mail." The Postmaster General took particular offense to two items in the issue: an article entitled, "Sappho Remembered," which told of a woman who left her childhood sweetheart to live with another woman in a romantic relationship, and "Lord Samuel and Lord Montagu," a poem about homosexual conduct among British lords. Ironically, it was in that very issue that an article anonymously authored by Julber entitled, "You Can't Print It!," appeared. In it, Julber explained the publishing

50. The Comstock Act 17, Statute 598.

51. The October 1953 cover declared, "...we have been pronounced respectable. The Post Office found that *ONE* is obscene in no way. ...Never before has a government agency of this size admitted that homosexuals not only have legal rights but might have respectable motives as well. This admission is welcome, but it's tardy and far from enough. ...ONE's victory might seem big and historical as you read of it in the comfort of your home (locked in the bathroom? hidden under a stack of other magazines? sealed first class?). But the deviate hearing of our late August issue through jail bars will not be overly impressed. " *ONE* (October 1953): cover.

52. Apparently some of the readership had complained that the magazine was, in the words of early *ONE* columnist Jim Kepner, "so damn tame," and even said they weren't getting their money's worth. Murdoch and Price, 31.

guidelines he had enacted for *ONE* in an effort to prevent it from getting into trouble with the authorities. He noted that the wording of the law was such that the very mention of homosexual feelings, inclinations, desires, or actions could be seen as a violation: "...there is one extreme school of legal thought that would say that *ONE*, merely by its existence, is illegal."[53]

Beginning in the twentieth century, government officials began to display an increasingly tolerant attitude toward sexuality in the media, but appear to have done so at the expense of topics deemed deviant.[54] Prior to the seizure of *ONE*, the Postmaster had begun selectively enforcing the Comstock laws, allowing pinup magazines to ship, while confiscating other, less traditional media. In March, 1947, it prevented the mailing of an issue of *Sunshine and Health*, a popular nudist magazine. Officials argued that delivering the magazines would open the floodgates to unfettered sexuality and pornography, and would "destroy public morals."[55] The issue eventually shipped, but the publisher remained under scrutiny. Eight years later, an issue of each of two nudist magazines were confiscated. The publisher filed suit and lost in federal circuit court. After failing with the Appellate Court, he appealed to the Supreme Court.[56]

When the postmaster refused to ship *ONE*'s issue, the magazine was so insolvent, it could not afford to file suit, but after a year, it did so in federal court, with Julber offering *pro bono* representation. He tried to enlist the help of the American Civil Liberties Union, but was refused, ostensibly because the ACLU was still supportive of sodomy laws and had not yet come to view the cause of homosexuals as one of civil rights.[57] *ONE* lost its initial hearing in federal court, and then lost on appeal before the

53.. Julber, "You Can't Print It," quoted in Murdoch and Price, 31.

54. Hoffman writes, "In the twentieth century, a modern obscenity regime emerged that rejected the moral absolutism of the nineteenth century, but policed the moral boundaries of what John D'Emilio and Estelle Freedman termed 'sexual liberalism.' The growing social, cultural and legal tolerance of heterosexual pleasure in American society, historians have argued, depended on the exclusion of threatening, violent or deviant forms of sex." Hoffman, "A Certain Amount of Prudishness," 708.

55. O'Brien, "Official Transcript of Proceedings before the Post Office Department," 93.

56. *Sunshine Book Co. v. Summerfield* 355 US 372 (1958).

57. Of course, the ACLU is now one of the most ardent supporters of gay rights. It has even published a handbook to inform homosexuals of their rights under the law. Hunter et al., *The Rights of Lesbians, Gay Men, Bisexuals, and Transgender People.*

Ninth Circuit Court.[58] In his *writ of certiorari*, Julber argued that *ONE* was being held to a stricter standard of mailability than other works, and that it was being deprived of equal protection, though he tried to keep the focus primarily on the content of the magazine. Rather than asking the High Court for a referendum on homosexuality or offering a defense of gay lifestyle, Julber instead argued that the magazine was simply "attempting to explain to the layman problems of human life" and insisted that there is no "advocacy of homosexuality as a way of life" in *ONE*, but rather "only a discussion of the problems, social, economic, and personal, which confront those persons possessed of that particular neurosis, or complexion."[59]

ONE's case was eventually considered in the High Court along with the cases of the two nudist magazines published by the Sunshine Book Company because the reasoning behind the seizure of all the literature was essentially the same.[60] The case was never argued before the Court and the justices made their decisions based solely on the arguments presented in the petitions for and arguments against *certiorari* (i.e., petitions for review, arguments against review). No opinion was published; the ruling of the Court was a one-sentence statement referencing an earlier case with no further explanation: "The petition for writ of certiorari is granted and the judgment of the United States Court of Appeals for the Ninth Circuit is reversed. Roth v. United States 354 U.S. 476, 77 S.Ct. 1304, 1 L.Ed.2d 1498."[61]

The case which the ruling referenced, *Roth v. United States*, was a landmark free speech and censorship case, decided along with a similar case, *Alberts v. California* just six months before *ONE*'s case. In its 6–3 decision, the Court upheld the convictions of two men, Samuel Roth and David Alberts, who were book sellers in New York and California, respectively, and were found to be in violation of federal and state obscenity laws. Justice Brennan wrote for the majority. Brennan began by noting the Constitutional questions at issue: primarily the First Amendment

58. The appeals court ruling referred to the Sappho story as "cheap pornography calculated to promote lesbianism."

59. Eric Julber, petition for *writ of certiorari*, quoted in Murdoch and Price, 41.

60. The magazine which was originally seized by postal officials, *Sunshine and Health* and its sister publication, *Sun Magazine* were the targets. The February 1955 and the January-February 1955 issues were deemed undeliverable under postal codes. See

61. *ONE, Inc. v. Olesen* 355 US 371 (1958).

protections of free speech, but also issues related to Fourteenth Amendment protections of due process, given the vague nature of "obscenity." He argued it is demonstrably clear that "the unconditional phrasing of the First Amendment was not intended to protect every utterance."[62] He concluded that "obscenity is not within the area of constitutionally protected speech or press."[63] In addition, he noted that while many courts have argued that obscenity laws are too vague to enforce, the Supreme Court has "consistently held that lack of precision is not itself offensive to the requirements of due process."[64] That is, even if a precise definition of "obscene" cannot be given, a general idea can, and that is sufficient to convict. Most court observers and interpreters have seen the significance of *Roth* not in its decision *per se*, but in how it gave more clarity to the concept of obscenity, as understood by the High Court: an item may be deemed obscene if "to the average person, applying contemporary community standards, the dominant theme of the material taken as a whole appeals to prurient interest."[65] This definition was to stand for almost 20 years.[66]

At the time of the ruling, co-founder and editor of *ONE*, Don Slater, boldly proclaimed, "By winning this decision *ONE* magazine made not only history but law as well and changed the future for all U.S. homosexuals. Never before have homosexuals claimed their rights as citizens… *ONE* magazine no longer asks for the right to be heard; it now exercises that right. It further requires that homosexuals be treated as a proper part of society free to discuss and educate and propagandize their beliefs with

62. *Roth v. United States* 354 US 476 (1957) at 484.

63. Id. at 485.

64. Id. at 491. Justice Brennan's ruling continues, "…we hold that these statutes [California's and Federal statutes outlawing obscene materials], applied according to the proper standard for judging obscenity, do not offend constitutional safeguards against convictions based upon protected material, or fail to give men in acting adequate notice of what is prohibited." Id. at 492.

65. Id. at 489. Justice Brennan appealed to the definition of the A.L.I., Model Penal Code, 207.10: "A thing is obscene if, considered as a whole, its predominant appeal is to prurient interest, i.e., a shameful or morbid interest in nudity, sex, or excretion, and if it goes substantially beyond customary limits of candor in description or representation of such matters." Ibid.

66. The so-called *Roth test* was replaced by the *Miller test*, when the court considered the case of Marvin Miller, convicted of mailing unsolicited pornographic materials under California's obscenity statute. *Miller v.. California* 413 US 15 (1973).

no greater limitations than for any other group."[67] Slater surely saw the victory as one for free speech, thought, and the accessibility of information, and many have agreed with that assessment.[68] Yet, despite Slater's confidence, there was considerable uncertainty about the significance of the ruling, especially given the fact that it was decided concurrently with the case of the nudist magazines. Watson correctly points out, "The message of the court's combined release of the rulings may have been that mere nudity without depictions of explicit sexual conduct was not obscene—or that the Post Office had no legal authority to act as a censor—or that homosexual themes and subject matter, as featured in *ONE*, were not inherently obscene."[69] Since the Court did not hear the case and offered no clear indication of its reasoning, its meaning is left largely to the speculation of court-watchers.

Nevertheless, many homosexual rights groups and historians have since come to view *ONE*'s victory as of significance far beyond the scope of the magazine's readership, which never reached much beyond 5,000. It not only forced the nation and the government to acknowledge the existence of homosexuals among its citizenry, but it also began the discussion of the rights of those persons. Perhaps even more significantly, it opened the door to public discussion of homosexual issues and (at least) denied that the subject is inherently obscene.

Other analysts are not so optimistic. News of the Court's ruling went almost unnoticed by most Americans. It was relegated to page 35 of *The New York Times* and given only brief mention in a column entitled, "Nudist Magazines Win Mail Rights."[70] As Mezey puts it, "Although it eventually ended well for the magazine, this case and others like it reflected society's distaste for material considered deviant and abnormal—out of the mainstream. ...although the litigation benefited the gay community, the Court did not focus on the harm done them; nor did it spend a great deal of time dwelling on the fact that the majority was imposing its view of appropriate reading material on members of a minority group. Rather

67. Slater, "Victory! Supreme Court Upholds Homosexual Rights," 17.

68. For example, see Richlin, "Eros Underground," 421–62. Richlin argues that the story of *ONE*'s victory makes "an especially good symbol of the circulation of knowledge," in that the magazine made knowledge of the homosexual lifestyle and the "forbidden knowledge" of its ancient heritage accessible to a community that was, arguably, far-flung. Ibid., 423.

69. Watson, "Publications of a Dangerous Tendency," 82.

70. Lewis, "Nudist Magazines Win Mail Rights," 35.

the decision in *One* and others like it evolved from the Court's desire to constrain the government's authority to censor the films and books available to the general population."[71]

Lawrence v. Texas

Arguably the most important legal case for homosexual rights in recent years is the Supreme Court case, *Lawrence v. Texas*.[72] It dealt with issues surrounding the Constitutionality of state sodomy laws, long used to harass and arrest homosexuals. On several previous occasions, the Supreme Court had either ruled that such laws pass Constitutional muster, or refused to take cases in which the Appellate court had upheld conviction under state law.[73] The Texas statute in question was specifically directed

71. Mezey, 230.

72. For an engaging and detailed account of the case and the events surrounding it, see Carpenter, *Flagrant Conduct*; see also Carpenter, "The Unknown Past of *Lawrence v. Texas*," 1464–1527.

73. Most notably, the High Court had upheld Georgia's sodomy law, *Bowers v. Hardwick* 478 US 186 (1986), but it had also refused certiorari to other cases dealing with the same topic. The first time a sodomy law was challenged to the Supreme Court was in 1971, and it was the Texas law (different from the law applied in *Lawrence*), which was written very broadly to include a variety of sexual activities, including both homosexual and heterosexual sex acts. The original challenge in federal court before a three-judge panel included a gay man, Alvin Buchanan, who had been arrested for engaging in oral sex in a public restroom stall, a married couple who had not been arrested, and another gay man who also had not been arrested. The hope was to show that the law was too wide and restrictive as to violate the Constitution. The panel ruled that the law cannot outlaw sodomy within marriage, but upheld its application to unmarried couples (something to be rejected by the Supreme Court two years later, *Eisenstadt v. Baird* 405 US 438 (1972)) and to homosexuals. The Supreme Court would only consider Buchanan's challenge because the other litigants lacked standing (a legal term to used to distinguish who has a stake in the outcome; in order to have standing, one must be able to demonstrate harm as a result of a poorly written or unconstitutional law). Ultimately, the Court refused to hear the case and thereby, upheld the Constitutionality of the newly amended Texas law as applied to unmarried sex, specifically in this case, to homosexuals. A variety of challenges to state sodomy laws were raised in both state and federal courts. In 1971, the Florida Supreme Court struck down its state's "crimes against nature" law as vague to the point of meaninglessness, and the finding was upheld and used by a federal judge to free several men in prison as a result of convictions under the law. The Fifth Circuit Court of Appeals agreed in 1972, noting that men of common intelligence would have to guess as to its meaning. Nevertheless, the High Court reversed these decisions and upheld the Florida statute, arguing that the consistent interpretation of the law and its application had made it clear enough that persons convicted under its provisions knew that the activity they engaged in was illegal. *Wainwright v. Stone* 414 US 21 (1973). On the

against homosexual sex and was ruled unconstitutional. More significantly, though, the ruling in *Lawrence* specifically overturned its 1986 ruing in *Bowers v. Hardwick*, which upheld the Georgia state sodomy law, which was more general in nature.[74]

Justice Kennedy delivered the opinion of the Court. He begins by noting the extension of privacy rights—first noted in *Griswold*—to unmarried persons in *Eisenstadt*, because at heart, sexuality is a private matter with which government intrusion is unwarranted. Kennedy questions the historicity of the claim, made in Bowers, that there is a longstanding history of legislation outlawing homosexuality. He admits that there is a history of disapproval of homosexuality, but argues that, since it is mostly religious in character, it cannot serve as a basis for criminal law. As he sees it, the heart of the case has to do with "whether the majority may use the power of the State" to enforce its views of on all persons by means of criminal law.[75] He does not think it should. In addition, Kennedy argues that appeals to the majority view or to the history of Western civilization fall flat because attitudes continue to evolve. In fact, he appeals to precedent in the European Court of Human Rights which ruled that homosexual conduct between consenting adults in private may not be criminalized. This finding is binding on all 45 member nations, and shows that there is not a consensus against the legality of homosexual sex.[76]

Kennedy further claims that *Lawrence* could have simply been decided by appeal to *Romer v. Evans*, which disallowed singling out homosexuals as a group for criminal prosecution. He explains that the Court took the case because it wanted to consider the wider issue of laws regulating private sexual acts of consenting adults by reconsidering *Bowers*.

same day that the Court upheld Florida's law as applied to homosexual conduct, it also dismissed two other cases involving homosexual oral sex due to a lack of a substantial federal question. Many gay rights activists saw this as discriminatory. As Murdoch and Price put it, "Through action and inaction, the justices had created the impression by November 1973 that virtually no law was too vague if homosexuals were being punished by it . . . When laws made no mention of homosexuality, the court allowed prohibitions to be read as anti-homosexual and benefits (such as marriage rights) to be read as excluding homosexuals. By consistently ignoring or ruling against homosexuals' pleas for fair treatment, the court was teetering on the brink of reading homosexuals out of the Constitution." Murdoch and Price, 276.

74. *Bowers v. Hardwick* 478 US 186 (1986).

75. *Lawrence v. Texas* 539 US 558 (2003) at 571.

76. Id at 573.

As noted above, *Bowers* was the case which upheld the Georgia sodomy law that, unlike that of Texas, made no distinction between homosexual and heterosexual sodomy.

Kennedy notes that due process rights are not the only Constitutional considerations in jurisprudence over sodomy laws. Equally important are issues related to proportionality of crime to punishment; the net effect of a conviction under state sodomy laws appears too harsh. Kennedy notes that a stigma is attached to a conviction which extends far beyond the very limited punishment imposed by law (a class-C misdemeanor). The Texas law requires those found guilty to register as sex offenders. Since the finding in *Bowers* appealed to a wider consensus against homosexuality, and such consensus does not exist, the argument cannot hold. Kennedy concludes, "*Bowers* was not correct when it was decided, and it is not correct today. It ought not to remain binding precedent. *Bowers v. Hardwick* should be and now is overruled."[77]

Justice O'Connor wrote a concurring opinion, in which she agreed that the petitioners had made their case, but disagreed with the rationale of the majority opinion and the decision to overturn *Bowers*. She saw the fundamental issue as one of fairness, drawing upon the equal protection clause, rather than the due process clause.[78] O'Connor sees the Texas law as unconstitutional because it appears specifically designed to target homosexuals for persecution.[79] O'Connor maintains that there are significant differences between *Lawrence* and *Bowers*, and argues that *Bowers* withstood scrutiny because the (legitimate) state interest was in promoting morality. *Lawrence* is not the same because, she maintains, there is good reason to question the sincerity of the state's claimed interest in this case as also promoting morality. Rather, O'Connor argues, moral disapproval [of homosexual conduct] is the state's interest, and "moral disapproval of this group [homosexuals], like a bare desire to harm the group, is an interest that is insufficient to satisfy rational basis review

77. Id. at 578.

78. Others have seen the issue this way as well. Peterson, "Right Decision for the Wrong Reason," 653–707.

79. Ironically, the Texas statute was amended by the legislature in 1974 to specifically exclude heterosexual sex after a panel of federal judges ruled it unconstitutional on the grounds that it restricted sexual freedom for married couples, and after the Supreme Court extended the privacy rights afforded married couples in *Griswold* to unmarried heterosexual couples; *Eisenstadt v. Baird* 405 US 438 (1973). See n. 73 above.

under the Equal Protection Clause."[80] O'Connor further rejects the state's claim that its statute only criminalizes *homosexual activity* rather than *being homosexual* by pointing to Texas case law, where it has been held that calling a person "homosexual" is slander because it implies the commission of a crime and where the state has admitted that the sodomy law leads to the conclusion that "*being* homosexual carries the presumption of being a criminal."[81]

Summarizing her argument, O'Connor writes, "But the State cannot single out one identifiable class of citizens for punishment that does not apply to everyone else, with moral disapproval as the only asserted state interest for the law."[82] What is interesting is that, at face value, it seems that the state should be able to criminalize certain activities while allowing others, but at heart here is the *intent* of the law or the *intentions* of lawmakers in passing the law. She then notes that, while she believes sodomy laws can be Constitutional if applied equally to all persons, they would not be tolerated for long if actually enforced.[83]

Justice Scalia penned a dissenting opinion, in which he was joined by Chief Justice Rehnquist and Justice Thomas.[84] Scalia begins by pointing to what he takes to be far too general a position by the Court, noting that the findings will have "far-reaching implications beyond this case."[85] He first expresses concern for the stability of the Court and challenges the consistency of the majority, who appealed to the stayed nature of precedent in order to fend off challenges to *Roe v. Wade*, but who seem all-too-willing to throw out precedent in *Bowers*.

80. *Lawrence v. Texas* 539 US 558 (2003) at 582.

81. Id. at 583. O'Connor referenced *Plumley v. Landmark Chevrolet, Inc* 122 F. 3d 308, 310 (CA5 1997); *State v Morales* 826 S.W. 2d. at 202–3.

82. Id. at 584.

83. Id. at 584–85. As O'Connor states, "A law branding one class of persons as criminal based solely on the State's moral disapproval of that class and the conduct associated with that class runs contrary to the values of the Constitution and the Equal Protection Clause, under any standard of review." Id. at 585.

84. Justice Thomas also wrote his own dissent, in which he expressed his opinion that sodomy laws are "silly," and ought not waste "valuable law enforcement resources." However, he also noted that it is not his job to help petitioners or tell State legislatures which laws to enact, but only to adjudicate the Constitutionality of those challenged before the Court. Since he never agreed with the reasoning in *Griswold* that there is a Constitutionally protected right to privacy, he dissented here as well. Id. at 605–6.

85. He even refers to the approach of the majority as "an unheard –of form of rational-basis review." Id. at 586.

Scalia's greatest concern seems to be with the implications of the ruling upon the State's ability to regulate morality and maintain the rule of law. He argues that the majority's application of the ruling in *Planned Parenthood v. Casey* is inappropriate because it leads to anarchy or is meaningless. Either way, it does not help in adjudicating the question of the Texas statute. He writes,

> And if the Court is referring not to the holding of *Casey*, but to the dictum of its famed sweet-mystery-of-life passage, *ante*, at 574 ('At the heart of liberty is the right to define one's own concept of existence, of meaning, of the universe, and of the mystery of human life'): That "casts some doubt" upon either the totality of our jurisprudence or else (presumably the right answer) nothing at all. I have never heart of a law that attempted to restrict one's "right to define" certain concepts; and if the passage calls into question the government's power to regulate *actions based on* one's self-defined "concept of existence, etc.," it is the passage that ate the rule of law.[86]

Scalia claims that the majority opinion here serves to undermine morality itself, and opens the doors to challenges of every state law regulating sexuality; at a minimum, it leads to a sort of sexual relativism, calling into question all state laws against bigamy, same-sex marriage, adult incest, prostitution, masturbation, adultery, fornication, bestiality, and obscenity.[87] *Bowers* passed Constitutional muster, he notes, precisely because the state has an interest in promoting morality. More than this, though, Scalia makes the philosophical point that the rule of law depends on the state having the power to regulate morality. If it did not, anarchy would ensue. (The reasoning of the majority in following Justice Stevens' *Bowers* dissent here, he argues, "effectively decrees the end of all morals legislation," fundamentally undermines the power of the state to regulate morality, and with it, the rule of law.[88])

86. Id. at 588.

87. Id. at 590. He continues, "The impossibility of distinguishing homosexuality from other traditional 'morals' offenses is precisely why Bowers rejected the rational-basis challenge. 'The law,' it said, 'is constantly based on notions of morality, and if all laws representing essentially moral choices are to be invalidated under the Due Process Clause, the courts will be very busy indeed.' 478 U.S., at 196." Id.

88. Id. at 599. As he states, "If as the Court asserts, the promotion of majoritarian sexual morality is not even a legitimate state interest, none of the above-mentioned laws [criminal laws against fornication, bigamy, adultery, adult incest, bestiality, and obscenity] can survive rational-basis review." Id.

Scalia rejects O'Connor's claim that the Texas law targets homosexuals as a class of persons, and instead claims that it targets behavior. He further argues that her reasoning logically leads to acceptance of same-sex marriage, pointing out that the prohibition against same-gender sex no more violates equal protection than state marriage laws which prohibit same-gender marriages; if equal protection serves to overturn state laws against homosexual sex, then it must overturn state laws prohibiting same-sex marriages. If O'Connor's opinion *suggests* that same-gender marriage is Constitutional, the majority opinion *demands* (by way of logical deduction) the dissolution of the distinction between heterosexual and homosexual marriage. He writes, "Today's opinion dismantles the structure of constitutional law that has permitted a distinction to be made between heterosexual and homosexual unions, insofar as formal recognition in marriage is concerned."[89] Contrary to the claims of the majority, Scalia concludes, the case has everything to do with homosexual marriage: "This case 'does not involve' the issue of homosexual marriage only if one entertains the belief that principle and logic have nothing to do with the decisions of this Court."[90]

As would be expected, the Court's *Lawrence* decision and the various published opinions have generated a vast amount of literature and discussion on a wide array of issues.[91] Gay and lesbian-rights advocates

89. Id. at 604. He writes, "At the end of its opinion—after having laid waste the foundations of our rational-basis jurisprudence—the Court says that the present case 'does not involve whether the government must give formal recognition to any relationship that homosexual persons seek to enter . . . Do not believe it. More illuminating than this bald, unreasoned disclaimer is the progression of thought displayed by an earlier passage in the Court's opinion, which notes the constitutional protections afforded to 'personal decisions relating to *marriage*, procreation, contraception, family relationships, child rearing, and education,' and then declares that '[p]ersons in a homosexual relationship may seek autonomy for these purposes, just as heterosexual persons do.'" Id.

90. Id. at 605.

91. Naeger argues that *Lawrence* has implications for discrimination against gays and lesbians in child custody cases. Naeger, "And Then There Were None," 397–425; Hulstein, "Recognizing and Respecting the Rights of LGBT Youth," 171–97. Greene discusses the application of *Lawrence* to questions of individual privacy rights under the Constitution. Greene, "Beyond *Lawrence*: Metaprivacy and Punishment," 1862–928; see also Crocker, "The Fourth Amendment After *Lawrence*," 1–69. Concomitant to the idea of privacy in sexual relations is the concept of intimacy. Rosenbury questions the assumption in *Lawrence* that sex is only valuable if done in service to intimacy, and instead argues that it should be seen as a right in itself. Rosenbury, "Sex In and Out of Intimacy," 809–68. On the question of the relative punishment of conviction under

have almost universally heralded it as a watershed victory, which has opened the door to full rights for homosexuals under the law. Gay-rights attorney and Harvard law professor Lawrence Tribe referred to *Lawrence* as "the *Brown v. Board of Education* of gay and lesbian America."[92] Similarly, it has been called "the first Supreme Court decision in American history that openly acknowledges" that lesbian and gay men are human beings who have dignity as free persons and who are deserving of respect under the Constitution.[93] Despite such positive assessments, some within the gay and lesbian community have not been so optimistic about *Lawrence*'s far-reaching and long-term prospects.[94] For example, Spindelman has expressed concern that the premises behind *Lawrence* and the cases referred to in its arguments make it less likely that the State will express an interest in prosecuting sexual assault, especially when the parties involved are the same gender.[95]

Court-watchers have noted the unusual and ground-breaking nature of the majority opinion in *Lawrence*, from its broad-based application of rights under the Fourteenth Amendment, to its appeal to foreign legislative thought and judicial ruling.[96] Yet it left many questions un-

---

state sex-crimes statutes when guilty of violating a sodomy law, see Haque, "*Lawrence v. Texas* and Limits of Criminal Law," 1–43. On the issue of the majority's appeal to European courts, see Atkinson, "King Arthur in a Yankee Court," 143–60. On its application to legalization of prostitution in the United States, see "Prostitution and Sex Work," 433–56.

92. See Tribe, "The 'Fundamental Right' That Dare Not Speak Its Name," 1894–95. Others have also compared *Lawrence* to *Brown*; e.g., Graff, "High Court Finally Gets It Right," D11.

93. Spindelman, "Surviving *Lawrence*," 1616–17.

94. Franke argues that the majority opinion created a new kind of liberty that is much more limited in scope than a broad-based conception of freedom. She argues that *Lawrence* only affords a privatized liberty for activity behind closed doors. Thus, *Lawrence* may have a much more limited application than initially thought. Franke, "Domesticated Liberty," 1399–426; By contrast, it has also been argued that the granting of even private sexuality rights to homosexual couples naturally opens the door to expansion of those rights. "Sexual Privacy After *Lawrence v. Texas*," 333–65.

95. Franke, 1615–67. By contrast, Cummings argues that the vagueness in *Lawrence* allows Article 125 of the U.S. Army to stand, which may be used to prosecute all forms of sodomy. In cases where sexual assault is difficult to prove, a conviction for engaging in sodomy may be gained to punish the offender who would otherwise go free. Cummings, "Is Article 125, Sodomy a Dead Letter?," 1–29.

96. Colucci argues that Kennedy's majority opinion was unique because of its appeal to liberty instead of the right to privacy. Ultimately, Colucci argues that in his *Lawrence* decision, Justice Kennedy sought to strike a balance between the progressive approach of the Warren Court and the conservativism of originalists like Justice Scalia.

answered because of its vagueness.[97] Many have argued that *Lawrence* would eventually lead to the undoing of the military's discriminatory polices against homosexual service.[98] Whether it had any bearing upon the actual decision makers at the time of DADT's repeal is doubtful.[99]

Perhaps the most widely-discussed aspect of the *Lawrence* opinion was Justice Scalia's dissent, both with regard to his prognostication of a bleak future for morality-based legislation, and to his reference to the undermining of state marriage laws. Scalia's clam that the majority opinion effectively signaled the end of morals legislation has been accepted by many conservative cultural critics and not a few legal scholars.[100] Still many others have expressed doubts, especially given recent litigation involving a variety of ethical issues.[101] A number of scholars have point-

---

Colucci, "Justice Kennedy's Interpretive Turn." Ruskoia also notes the unique nature of the ruling. Ruskoia, "Gay Rights versus Queer Theory," 235–49. Crocker has discussed the implications of *Lawrence* on Fourth Amendment Jurisprudence. Crocker, "The Fourth Amendment After *Lawrence*," 1–69.

97. Perelman, "A Step in the Right Direction," 217–53.

98. See, for example, Scotti, Jr. "Queer Eye for the Military Guy," 897–931. Scotti argues that DADT cannot survive strict scrutiny in light of *Lawrence*. By contrast, Fugelsang has suggested that DADT should not be evaluated via strict scrutiny, but, using *Cook v. Gates* as a model, should be evaluated by a means somewhere in between strict scrutiny and rational basis review, and if done so, it may survive. Fugelsang, "Reconciling *Lawrence* with 'Don't Ask, Don't Tell,'" 237–78.

99. Hagedorn has convincingly argued that after the *Lawrence* decision, courts were reluctant to read it broadly, especially in the face of public opposition. That is, *Lawrence* was not immediately read as undermining DADT because the public was not ready for its repeal and the decision in *Lawrence* was written sufficiently vague to allow for a more narrow reading and application. Hagedorn, "*Lawrence* the 'Laggard,'" 795–822.

100. For example, see Basiak, Jr. "Dangerous Predictions," 135–74. Park does not accept that *Lawrence* necessarily leads to moral relativism, but does argue that it should result in a more robust conception of individual freedom and liberty. Park, "Defining One's Own Concept of Existence and Meaning," 837–87. Some have seen the majority ruling as an example of judicial activism. For further discussion of the issue, see Rosen, "Kennedy Curse," 15–18; Lund, "*Lawrence v. Texas* and Judicial Hubris," 1555–1614; Kahn, "Originalism, the Living Constitution, and Supreme Court Decision Making," 25–35.

101. Van Camp argues that *Lawrence* does not mean moral relativism or worse (if possible) that morality cannot be considered in legislation. Van Camp, "How Religion Co-opts Morality," 241–51. Others examine specific issues/cases to refute Scalia's bleak outlook. For example, Kamisar considers the impact of *Lawrence* on laws restricting physician-assisted suicide and concludes that it will not serve as a basis, at least as a precedent-setting one, for over-turning them. Kamisar, "Can Glucksberg Survive *Lawrence*?,"1453–78. Curtiss argues that a narrow reading of *Lawrence*, like that applied

ed out that, ironically enough, because *Lawrence* was decided in such a sweeping fashion by appeal to the right to privacy, rather than more narrowly under equal protection concerns (i.e., Justice O'Connor's approach), *Lawrence* has not been applied as broadly to other cases not concerned with privacy rights. That is, if the ruling had been based on equal protection, it would have served to grant equal standing for homosexual concerns to their counterparts among heterosexuals, but because it was founded on the very narrow issue of sexual privacy, it has sometimes been viewed as only applying to those issues involving private, consensual sex among adults.

Scalia's concern that the Court's decision will be used to rule unconstitutional those state marriage laws which prohibit same sex marriage has received widespread consideration. Dubler argues that if the High Court is to remain consistent, it must overturn state marriage laws; *Lawrence* must clear a path to nation-wide legalization of homosexual marriage. She draws an analogy between *Lawrence* and *McLaughlin v. Florida*, which struck down a state law banning interracial sex. *McLaughlin* served as the basis for the ruling in *Loving v. Virginia*, the landmark case which effectively legalized interracial marriage across the country by striking down the Virginia law criminalizing it. Once interracial sex was deemed Constitutionally protected, so also was interracial marriage. In the same way, then, since homosexual sex has been granted Constitutional protections, so also should homosexual marriage.[102]

The issue of same-sex marriage, while certainly of interest to debates about homosexual service and its impact on the military, as well as to the general topic of homosexual rights, is beyond the scope of this work. It is a vast and complicated topic, and touches upon a number of far-reaching issues.[103] Whether *Lawrence* can legitimately be seen as signaling the end

---

in *Williams v. Morgan* (and should have been followed in *Reliable Consultants, Inc. v. Earle*) will not preclude the commercial sale of objects used in sex acts Curtiss, "Unraveling *Lawrence's* Concerns,"1369–98.

102. Dubler, "From *McClaughlin v. Florida* to *Lawrence v. Texas*," 1165–87. See also Karlan, "Loving Lawrence," 1447–63; Others have argued that *Lawrence* at least suggests that same-sex marriages will soon be recognized under the Constitution. See Bluestone, "Going to the Chapel and We're Going to Get Married," 189–221; Reinheimer, "What *Lawrence* Should Have Said," 505–51; Culhane, "Writing On, Around, and Through *Lawrence*," 493–506; Tribe, "Constitutional Inevitability of Same-Sex Marriage," 471–89.

103. There are innumerable resources dedicated to the discussion of same-sex marriage, especially from the more progressive perspective. See, for example,

of the Defense of Marriage Act or state legislation prohibiting same-sex unions, remains to be seen. What is clear, though, is that it was a case that changed the landscape and the discussion surrounding same-sex relationships.

Hate Crimes Legislation

One of the most contentious issues within the discussion of homosexual rights is that of hate crimes legislation.[104] Gay-rights lobbying groups have worked tirelessly to get legislation passed which has special protections for their constituencies (along with variously-defined minority groups) and particularly harsh punishments for violations, commonly known as penalty-enhancement provisions. Many social and religious conservatives have bristled at the idea that some crimes are more heinous simply by the nature of the victim, and argue that provisions already exist in the law for variances in sentencing based upon the details of any given case, but state legislatures and Congress have not agreed. Most states have some form of hate crimes legislation, and federal law has included particularly harsh penalties for racially-motivated crime since the passage of the Civil Rights Act of 1968.[105] There have been constant calls for increased regulation and harsher penalties for crimes involving hatred for a group or class of persons since they include violent crimes and hate speech directed against homosexuals.

Two incidents in particular seemed determinative for Congress raising the issue of the need for changes to federal hate crimes legislation in recent years: the murders of James Byrd in Jasper County, Texas, and of Matthew Shepard in Laramie, Wyoming. Byrd's case led to the removal of language from current law which limited prosecutions to those situations where victims were engaged in federally protected activity at the time of the assault. Although the specifics of Byrd's case were such that the language did not prevent federal involvement, it did demonstrate the

---

Eskridge, Jr., *Equality Practice*. Eskridge argues that, while civil unions are not the same as marriages and could thus be seen as analogous to the despised "separate but equal" doctrine of *Dredd Scott*, they are an important first step toward full equality for homosexual couples under the law. See also Dupuis and Thompson, eds., *Defending Same-Sex Marriage;* Sullivan, ed., *Same-Sex Marriage: Pro and Con, A Reader*.

104. For examination of some issues with hate crimes legislation, see Chorba, "Danger of Federalizing Hate Crimes," 319–80.

105. 18 U.S.C. 245 (b)(2).

value in lending federal investigators and prosecutors the authority to become involved (either through assistance or through direct action) in hate crimes cases, and strengthened the argument for lifting current restrictions.[106] Shepard's case garnered a national outcry and eventuated in the extension of hate crimes protections to sexual orientation.[107] It was probably because Matthew had the look of a typical red-blooded American—the boy next door—that so many were particularly moved by his brutal murder (though of course, no murder is acceptable). As Boulden so wonderfully articulated in a tribute to him,

> Matt was a unique young man, and at the same time he was very typical. He was his parent's son. He was his brother's brother. He was his grandparent's grandson. He was the boy next door, the kid in class sitting next to you. He was the blonde-haired, blue-eyed little boy who used to run down the street with his buddies laughing and playing ball. He laughed, he cried, he felt

106. "Expanding the circumstances under which certain hate crimes may be prosecuted by removing the 'federally protected activity' requirement, and permitting prosecution for bias-motivated crimes of violence that cause bodily injury (or a class of specified attempts) based on the victim's race, color, religion, or national origin, will permit the Federal Government to provide assistance to State law enforcement in a wider range of circumstances . . . The investigation conducted into the death of James Byrd in Jasper County, Texas, is an excellent example of the benefits of an effective Federal/State investigative partnership in a high-profile hate crime case . . . The fact that the crime at issue appeared to violate established Federal criminal civil rights law was critical in the FBI's decision as to its legal authority to lend assistance to the State prosecution...Unfortunately, the 'double-intent' requirement of 18 U.S.C. Section 245(b)(2)—particularly the 'intent to interfere with a federally protected activity' requirement—has precluded the Department of Justice from performing an effective backstop role with regard to a number of heinous hate crimes . . . Currently, Federal authority can turn on such artificial distinctions as whether a racially motivated assault occurs on a public sidewalk as opposed to a private parking lot across the street, or whether a convenience store at which a racially motivated attack occurs has a video game inside that might qualify the stores as a 'place of entertainment.' The Federal Government's authority to participate in State-Federal investigative partnerships, or to step in and play a backstop role when necessary, should not hinge upon such arbitrary distinctions." House Judiciary Committee Report, "Background and Rationale for Legislation," 168–69.

107. "The murder of Matthew Shepard in Laramie, Wyoming, is an instructive example of the limitations in current law. Despite clear evidence that the murder of Mr. Shepard was motivated by animus based on Mr. Shepard's sexual orientation, the Federal Government lacked jurisdiction to act as a full partner with State and local officials in the investigation of this horrifying crime, or to bring Federal hate crime charges." United States Federal Bureau of Investigation, "Hate Crimes Based on Sexual Orientation, Gender, Gender Identity, or Disability," 170.

> deeply, he worried about all people, including those he loved and those he had never met. He followed local and world affairs; he wanted to love, to be loved, and to fit in.[108]

Despite widespread support among legislators for hate crimes legislation, criticisms still remain. Two types of legal criticism have been lodged against hate crimes legislation, even though doing so may have a detrimental effect upon one's status and career.[109] Some have complained that hate crimes legislation violates First Amendment guarantees of freedom of expression and thought. In fact, this tends to be the primary concern of those Christians who oppose such legislation, particularly with respect to attempts by the state to regulate religious speech. Others have, ironically, challenged it on grounds that it violates Fourteenth Amendment guarantees of equal opportunity and due process, as well as Fifth Amendment protection from multiple prosecutions for the same crime.

One approach to arguing that hate crimes laws violate the Constitution is to attack the enhanced-penalty provisions. Nearpass argues that enhanced penalty provisions violate the Fifth Amendment Double-Jeopardy clause, which, in part, protects against one receiving multiple punishments for the same offense.[110] While he also raises questions related to the idea that some murders are worse than others due to the reason for targeting the victim, he is most concerned with how penalty-enhancement is adjudicated; it comes across as a second trial for the same crime, one being the determination of guilt or innocence, and the other being the ascertainment of intent and motive. Additionally and of greater concern, is the assignment of additional punishment under penalty-enhancement, which Nearpass argues is "nothing more than a form of cumulative punishment," which the High Court has "repeatedly declared unconstitutional via the Double Jeopardy Clause."[111]

108. Boulden, "Tribute to Matthew Shepard," 13–14; simultaneously published by Haworth Press as *Journal of Gay & Lesbian Social Services* 13:1/2 (2001).

109. Nearpass argues that the rhetoric surrounding hate crimes legislative discussion makes it almost impossible to criticize or raise objections to its passage, for those who do are often labeled "non-tolerant" or even "bigots," and to do so is "political suicide." Nearpass, "Overlooked Constitutional Objection," 550, 554.

110. He writes, "The term *penalty-enhancement* is itself only a politically correct way to get around double jeopardy." Nearpass, 561.

111. Ibid., 562. Later, Nearpass makes his argument even more explicit: "While there is a separate element of the penalty-enhancement provision that is not contained in the underlying offense, there is not a separate element of the underlying offense that is not contained in the penalty-enhancement. In other words, all of the elements of

The Fourteenth Amendment has been a favorite of civil rights defenders, for its equal protection clause served as the basis upon which the High Court ruled in *Brown v. Board of Education* and desegregated American schools. It rejected the notion of "separate but equal" utilized in *Dredd Scott* as a means of getting around the Fifth Amendment's equal protection clause while upholding racial segregation. The Fourteenth Amendment reads, "All persons born or naturalized in the United States, and subject to the jurisdiction thereof, are citizens of the United States and the State wherein they reside. No state shall make or enforce any law which shall abridge the privileges or immunities of citizens of the United States; nor shall any state deprive any person of life, liberty, or property, without due process of law; nor deny to any person within its jurisdiction the equal protection of laws."

Thus, some criticize hate crimes legislation because it seems to create classes among the citizenry and thereby violate the Equal Protection Clause of the Fourteenth Amendent. Some groups of persons are, on this view, set aside for special protection, and crimes against those persons are deemed more heinous than similar crimes committed against others. At first glance, this argument appears persuasive, for so-called hate crimes are no worse than others, at least concerning the act itself. The murder of someone because of his race, gender, religion, ethnicity, etc., is not worse than the murder of someone else by similar means but for other reasons, at least not from the perspective of the victim or the victim's family, and members of those protected groups are surely no better than other persons, are not more worthy of protection under the law.

Upon further reflection, though, the argument is proven to be in error for several reasons. First, hate crimes laws do not identify specific groups to be singled out for special protection, but rather focus on the intent in the alleged crime being prosecuted. For example, hate crimes protections are not restricted to minority ethnic or racial groups, but may be utilized to prosecute violent crimes perpetrated against those in the majority, provided the criminal activity was directed against the victim because of his/her ethnicity or race.[112] Second, hate crimes laws do not

---

the underlying conviction are also part of the elements needed to invoke the penalty-enhancement provision. Therefore, penalty-enhancement provisions fail to satisfy the *Blockburger* test, as each offense does not contain an element that is not contained in the other." Ibid., 564.

112. *Wisconsin v. Mtichell* is the classic example, where the victim, a white male, was assaulted by a group of black males. At least one of the perpetrators, while

mean to pass judgment upon the relative loss suffered by the individual victims, but rather claim that certain types of crimes have wider effect than crimes of similar outward appearance. Hate crimes have a uniquely broad impact upon the so-called "target communities" (those who share the victim's distinguishing characteristics). As Lawrence puts it, since hate crimes are typically meant to not only harm the immediate victim, but also to intimidate the community of which the victim was a member, target communities experience hate crimes "in a manner that has no equivalent in the public response to a parallel crime."[113] Members of target communities often feel isolated, threatened, hurt and/or scared, and may withdraw from the broader society or feel like they are lower-class citizens as a result. Increased tensions among groups within society can result, and it can thus be argued that hate crimes have a wider cultural and societal impact because they are destructive of community. As President Obama noted when he signed the Matthew Shepard and James Byrd, Jr. Hate Crimes Prevention Act into law, hate crimes legislation is not fundamentally about special rights for some, but about freedom for all people to seek out "their own version of happiness." He likened the occasion to that on which President Lyndon Johnson signed into law the Civil Rights Act of 1964 and proclaimed, "the bells of freedom right out louder."[114] While some may still question whether hate crimes laws create a special class or suspect that they serve a wider agenda, there can be no doubt that they are also meant to reduce fear among certain communities and to protect against racially-, ethnically-, religiously- or other similar motivated violent crimes.

Challenges to hate crimes laws on First Amendment grounds have taken several forms. Some have charged that penalty enhancement effectively punishes wrong thoughts.[115] In the Supreme Court case of *Wisconsin v. Mitchell*, the Wisconsin hate crimes statute was challenged based on its enhanced penalty provisions, which extended Todd Mitchell's aggravated battery conviction from a maximum sentence of two years un-

minority, was convicted under the provisions of the state hate crimes statute because his actions were shown to be racially motivated.

113. Lawrence, *Punishing Hate*, 42.

114. President Obama, "Remarks," October 28, 2009.

115. MacNamara, "New York's Hate Crimes Act of 2000," 519–45. MacNamara notes, "These laws, however, are not entirely without cost. Legislating against subjective thought implicates some of our most important First Amendment protections." Ibid., 545.

der the normal provisions of law, to that of seven years because the jury found the assault to be motivated by his desire to injure the victim due to his race.[116] The Wisconsin Supreme Court sided with Mitchell, holding that the state's law "violates the Frist Amendment directly by punishing what the legislature has deemed to be offensive thought."[117] The United States Supreme Court did not agree, though, making a distinction between one's *abstract thought*, which is protected, and his *specific thoughts directing motivation* for criminal activity, which is not so protected. The Court reasoned that judges have always taken motivation into account in determining sentencing; this is part of why mandatory sentencing is opposed so vigorously by many on the bench—it takes away judicial consideration with regard to the specific details of each case. So the Court may give increased sentences based on the motivation underlying the crime, but cannot punish individuals for their thoughts.[118]

The High Court's ruling in *Wisconsin v. Mitchell* did not put to rest all concerns over the First Amendment and hate crimes statutes. Many have questioned the distinction between motive and intent at the heart of the majority opinion.[119] Others have argued that hate crimes legislation criminalizes improper words. Some have noted that, while legislators have intended to offer enhanced punishment provisions for crimes committed due to, for example, racial animus, often times the law is applied to crimes where other factors were clearly in play, but racial epithets were used. In these cases, then, the guilty is given harsher punishment for his offensive words (because of the racial slurs used during the commission of a crime).[120]

116. Apparently, after watching the movie, "Mississippi Burning," Todd Mitchell and a group of friends were standing outside when Mitchell expressed his desire to "move on some white people." When a young white boy happened to walk by. Mitchell encouraged three of his friends to attack the boy; they beat him unconscious, and left him in a coma four days.

117. *Wisconsin v. Mitchell* 169 Wis. 2d. 153 (1991) at 163; 485 N. W. 2d 807 (1992) at 811. Quill argues that he Supreme Court got it wrong and that evaluation of motivation in hate crimes prosecution is too speculative, especially given the stakes in legal proceedings. Quill, "Motivation, Causation and Hate Crimes Sentence Enhancement," 181–216; See also Brooks, "First Amendment—Penalty Enhancement for Hate Crimes," 703–42.

118. *Wisconsin v. Mitchell* 508 US 476 (1993) at 485. See also *Dawson v. Delaware* 503 US 159 (1992) at 167–68.

119. For example, see Jacobs and Potter, *Hate Crimes,* 129. See also Coker, "Hope-Fulfilling or Effectively Chilling?," 271–99.

120. Ginsberg points out the difficulty of reconciling legislative intent with

Concerns About Free Speech and Free Exercise for Chaplains

Elsewhere, I have discussed at length concerns of chaplains regarding their free speech and free exercise rights, even when their religious convictions run afoul of contemporary American sensibilities or of current Department of Defense (DoD) policies.[121] I argued that military chaplains are particularly vulnerable to what might be called "silencing action," due to their governmental allegiances and responsibilities, coupled with DoD directives and military regulations prohibiting service members from overtly criticizing executive or legislative actions and decisions or engaging in political activism while on duty. However, I also noted that, even though courts typically give wide-breadth to the War Powers Clause of the United States Constitution, and as a result, allow the military to regularly deny service members' rights in order to secure mission effectiveness and readiness, the Court has also recognized the need to preserve the most fundamental rights of service persons when possible. In fact, it is this very need that serves as the justification of a taxpayer-funded military chaplaincy, that is, to preserve service members' First Amendment right to free exercise. The point is that there is almost always tension between Free Exercise and Establishment within the chaplaincy, and the Court has sought to strike a happy medium. It does not take infringement of those rights lightly.

Rigdon v. Perry

One instructive example of the Court's willingness to reject appeals to the War Powers Clause as a means of overriding service members' First Amendment rights is the case of *Rigdon v. Perry*.[122] It is particularly relevant for the present discussion because it involved an attempt by the Armed Services to regulate the speech of military chaplains during worship services on base. In this instance, the speech had clear politi-

prosecutorial application in hate crimes cases. Ginsberg, "Hate is Enough," 1599–1633. See Jacobs, "Should Hate Be A Crime?," 3–14. Jacobs references the case of *State v. Wyant*, where David Wyant was incarcerated for "ethnic intimidation" when he threatened to harm Jerry White, an African American, and hurled racial slurs while doing so, in order to raise First Amendment concerns with hate crimes prosecution.

121. Laing, *In Jesus' Name*.

122. For a more thorough discussion of the case, see Laing, *In Jesus' Name*, 74–81

cal overtones, though it arose out of the chaplains' religious and moral commitments: it had to do with the chaplains' encouragement of parishioners to lobby their congresspersons regarding upcoming legislative talks related to abortion. Despite the fact that DoD directives prohibit partisan political speech and activity when service members are on duty, the court found in favor of the chaplains. In his ruling, Federal District Court Judge Stanley Sporkin concluded that "the compelling interests advanced by the military are outweighed by the military chaplains' right to autonomy in determining the religious content of their sermons."[123]

Since the activities of the chaplains in this case had the potential for more clear and direct violation of DoD directives and military regulations, but the chaplains' religious speech was still protected, it should serve to alleviate concerns about governmental regulation of chaplain speech regarding homosexuality in the context of the worship service, even on military bases and in military chapels. Another case, though, offers even more compelling reasons for confidence that military chaplains will be free to preach about the topic as they deem appropriate, for it was adjudicated by the Supreme Court of the United States and involved speech patently offensive and specific to homosexuality.

Snyder v. Phelps

I was somewhat reluctant to comment on this case, if for no other reason than it could be perceived that I am advocating the policies, positions, or activities of the Westboro Baptist Church, or that my reference may be seen as substantiating the fears and/or suspicions of those in the homosexual community who perceive all conservative Christian opposition to the homosexual lifestyle as equal to that undertaken by the Phelps family and others in the congregation. This is clearly not my intent, and I would argue that most social conservatives find the Westboro speech and activity just as repulsive and just as hateful as any more socially progressive persons do. Still, there are good reasons for seeing the case as applicable to the current question, since it touches upon concerns related to religo-political speech that could easily be considered in violation of hate speech statutes, and thus, may add clarity to the complex issues at stake in the

123. *Rigdon v. Perry*, 962 F. Supp. 150 (D.D.C. 1997).

discussion of hate crimes and First Amendment protections regarding free speech and free exercise.

The case of *Snyder v. Phelps* involves members of the controversial Westboro Baptist Church, most notably pastor Fred Phelps and two of his daughters, and the family of Marine Lance Corporal Matthew Snyder, who was killed in Iraq in the line of duty. The members of Westboro picketed Snyder's funeral with signs such as "Thank God for Dead Soldiers!," "God Hates You!," "God Hats Fags," and "Thank God for IEDs," presumably in an effort to communicate their belief that God's judgment is imminent upon America due to its acceptance of homosexuality, abortion and other sins, and that God is angry with the United States military for protecting, defending and supporting such a sinful nation. Albert Snyder, the father of the deceased, filed suit under state tort law, claiming acute emotional distress. Initially, a jury awarded the Snyder family millions of dollars in damages, but then the District Court ruled the damages excessive and reduced the award. Upon appeal, the Fourth Circuit reversed, finding the Westboro speech to fall under the protections of the First Amendment, and the Supreme Court agreed. Chief Justice John Roberts wrote the majority opinion.

Westboro won the case on First Amendment grounds, largely due to the fact that the speech was determined to be "on matters of public concern, were not provably false, and were expressed solely through hyperbolic rhetoric."[124] Presumably, if the signs were directed specifically at Snyder or specifically referenced Lance Corporal Snyder's death, the judgment could have gone the other way, for then the speech could reasonably be seen as intending to inflict emotional damage upon the Snyder family through *intentional* and *reckless, excessive* and/or *outrageous* conduct or speech, but as it was, the speech was general enough to be deemed "public." Thus, even though the language on the signs could be deemed *hateful* under provisions of hate speech laws, it remains federally protected because of its general nature and due to the fact that it represents the sincerely held beliefs of the speakers. The Court argued that mere location of speech cannot, in itself, transform the nature of the speech. Even though the picketing was hurtful to the Snyder family and was done in conjunction with the Snyder funeral, it was still done in a peaceful manner, in accordance with local ordinance, and on public property. The majority found that these facts mean that the only reason

124. *Snyder v. Phelps*, 563 U.S. (2011).

Westboro was sued and found liable was the content of its speech, and the Court is loathe to put itself in the position of public censor.[125]

The Court rejected the notion that Westboro could be held liable because its speech was "outrageous," since such a moniker is so malleable as to almost defy definition, and because its speech, taken as a whole and due to the reasons already cited, falls under the protections of the First Amendment. Similarly, the Court rejected Snyder's claim that he was a captive audience and thereby, could not have been prevented from being impacted by Westboro's hurtful speech, largely because the church members' activity did not interrupt the funeral or internment ceremony in any way.[126]

Some may question the applicability of this case to the free speech and free exercise rights of military chaplains because they are employees of the state. However, this would not be correct. In this case, the Court referenced earlier cases where it has explicitly addressed the question of whether public employees may engage in protected speech regarding matters of public concern. It has consistently found that they may, so long as the speech does not adversely affect the department for which the employees work.[127] Chaplain speech in chapel services regarding

125. Adding to Westboro's claim that its speech was not directly aimed at Snyder and his family was the history of Westboro's picketing activity and public demonstrations of a similar nature to that engaged in at the Snyder funeral. Justice Roberts writes, "The record confirms that any distress occasioned by Westboro's picketing turned on the content and viewpoint of the message conveyed, rather than any interference with the funeral itself. A group of parishioners standing at the very spot where Westboro stood, holding signs that said 'God Bless America' and 'God Loves You,' would not have been subjected to liability. It was what Westboro said that exposed it to tort damages. Given that Westboro's speech was at a public place on a matter of public concern, that speech is entitled to 'special protection' under the First Amendment. Such speech cannot be restricted simply because it is upsetting or arouses contempt." *Snyder v. Phelps*, 562 U.S. (2011).

126. In fact, Mr. Snyder could not see the wording of the signs while en route to the cemetery, but instead became aware of their contents while watching the local evening news. This may not lessen the impact the signs had on Mr. Snyder's emotional well-being, but it does speak to the Westboro members' proximity to the funeral proceedings. It is this fact that led Justice Breyer to concur with the majority opinion. He agrees with the spirit of Justice Alito's dissent, which notes that even public speech on public matters cannot always be protected, e.g., if it causes severe emotional harm to another. However, Breyer takes the facts here regarding the shielding of Mr. Snyder to be determinative for the legality of Westboro's speech in this case.

127. See *Keyishain v. Board of Regents of University of State of New York*, 385 U.S. 589 (1967) at 605–6; *United States v. Treasury Employees*, 513 U.S. 454 (1995) at 465, 475; *San Diego v. Roe*, 543 U.S. 77 (2004) at 83. There are, however, some situations in

their sincerely held religious and moral convictions can hardly be seen as impeding military effectiveness or combat readiness.

Justice Alito issued a dissenting opinion, which expresses, I suspect, the feelings of many in our country, especially those who have served in the nation's military. His opening statements are worth quoting at length:

> Our profound national commitment to free and open debate is not a license for the vicious verbal assault that occurred in this case.
>
> Petitioner Albert Snyder is not a public figure. He is simply a parent whose son, Marine Lance Corporal Matthew Snyder, was killed in Iraq. Mr. Snyder wanted what is surely the right of any parent who experiences such an incalculable loss: to bury his son in peace. But respondents, members of the Westboro Baptist Church, deprived him of that elementary right. They first issued a press release and thus turned Matthew's funeral into a tumultuous media event. They then appeared at the church, approached as closely as they could without trespassing, and launched a malevolent verbal attack on Matthew and his family at a time of acute emotional vulnerability. As a result, Albert Snyder suffered severe and lasting emotional injury. The Court now holds that the Frist Amendment protected respondents' right to brutalize Mr. Snyder. I cannot agree.[128]

In fact, Justice Alito goes on to point out the missive released by the Westboro Church leadership, which does seem to attack the Snyder family directly, as opposed to the general nature of the signs and placards displayed at the funeral. While I am inclined to agree with Alito's opinion and am disgusted (and not a little embarrassed) by the Westboro Church's words and actions, the fact remains that the Court has seen fit to rule speech such as that presented by the Westboro congregants here, as federally protected.[129] The caustic nature of the

which the government may, even without appeal to the War Powers Clause, regulate speech of its employees, even though it cannot so regulate that of its citizenry. See *Shahar v. Bowers*, 114 F.3d 1097, 1110 (1997); *Pickering v. Board of Education*, 391 U.S. 563 (1968); *Garcetti v. Cebdlos*, 547 U.S. 410 (2006); *Connick v. Myers*, 461 U.S. 138 (1983); *Berg v. Claytor* 436 F.Supp. 76 (D.D.C. 1977).

128. *Snyder v. Phelps* 563 U.S. (2011).

129. In fact, I have wondered if the actions of Westboro should be regulated more closely, especially given the fact that they include young minors in these activities. The animosity they invoke by their actions put themselves and their children at risk. It is irresponsible, and if anything were ever to happen whereby a by-stander were to attack the group and injure or even kill one of the children present—something I take to be a very real possibility, given the high incidence of PTSD among returning

language, specifically with respect to homosexuals and homosexuality, goes far beyond typical religious objections to homosexuality in terms of communicating animus or hatred. This fact alone should lead most chaplains to feel more secure about preaching their convictions about any topic, including homosexuality, without fear of intimidation, prosecution, or incarceration.

Conclusion

Political activity related to homosexuality evokes passionate feelings and elicits high-spirited reactions and dialogue/debate. Whether it is social conservatives expressing concern for the safety of their children or for their parental rights regarding what their children should be taught about human sexuality, or homosexual lobbyists arguing against what they perceive to be an encroachment upon their fundamental human rights, all parties believe the stakes could not be higher. To be sure, both sides have legitimate concerns and can point to specific instances in the not-so-distant past where wrongs were committed and from which pain still remains.

The history of gay rights involves instances where the dignity of homosexual men and women was stripped from them and they were right to resist.[130] Sometimes this was due to the actions of the state, but many times it was the words of Christians which produced the most damage in dehumanizing ways, and it is for this reason that many gays and lesbians are hostile to the Church. Christian ministers (including chaplains) should be sensitive to this history and remember to clearly connect the image of God in humanity to those in the homosexual community—gays and lesbians are bearers of the *imago dei* and should be treated as such.

To say that Christian ministers should treat those in the gay community with respect and dignity is not to say that homosexual sex must be affirmed and may not be condemned as sin. Some gay activists and apologists take issue with this claim, arguing that repudiation of gay sex

service members—the inclusion of children in their picketing activities would border on criminal negligence. I have even wondered if they include children in these activities as a sort of defense mechanism, akin to criminals using human shields to protect them from attack.

130. Some may wish to contest this claim, arguing that no one can take another's dignity, but the point made remains: homosexuals have, on many occasions, been treated in undignified ways.

is itself somehow a dehumanization or a rejection of those in the homosexual community. For example, Childers writes, "So wouldn't it be heresy for a Christian—evangelical or otherwise—to believe homosexuality isn't sinful? Wouldn't it place the believer in direct opposition to God? From my own experience, I have found the opposite to be true. Once I walked away from the church's teachings of rejection and condemnation, my relationship with God transcended to a higher spiritual plateau. I realized an unparalleled sense of spiritual clarity when I opened my heart and mind to a genuine expression of love, compassion, and acceptance of gays."[131] OK Explain

This argument is flawed for several reasons. First, it is largely an emotional appeal with little rational basis. Emotional arguments are not, in themselves, false, but must have facts undergirding their emotional force, and this argument provides none. Second, it confuses the person with his/her sexuality. While sexuality is clearly an aspect of lived experience for most creatures (not just humans), it should not be key or primary for one's identity. It is no wonder that gay persons identify their humanity with their sexuality, since they have been so identified by such terms, as "gay," "fag," "dike," and the like, but they should be helped to see that they are so much more than sexual beings; they are human beings. When Christians proclaim gay sex a sin, then, they mean only to speak against the acts (or perhaps the proclivity), not the being (to use a more philosophical term, *ontos*) of the person.

Chaplains should not fear prosecution, punishment, censure, or liability for proclaiming their sincerely held religious beliefs about homosexuality in the context of their sermons or counseling work. Careful examination of legal cases demonstrates that legislators and the judiciary in the United States have tended to hold in tension the individual rights of homosexual persons, with the moral standards and concerns of the wider community. There have been some significant victories for homosexuals along the way—the mere mention of the topic is not a violation of decency laws and they now enjoy privacy rights with regard to adult consensual sex—but also significant

131. Childers, "An Evangelical Christian Apologizes," 92. Childers rejects the reality/possibility of hating the sin while loving the sinner. Even though this belief is grounded in his own subjective experience/his own previously-held attitudes, it is reflective of the attitudes of many in the Christian community, whose hatred of the sin of homosexuality is expressed as hatred of homosexuals. Childers is correct in his claims that his ought not be, but is incorrect in his assertion that love of homosexuals requires acceptance of their lifestyle and/or expression of sexuality.

victories for those who wish to uphold traditional values and/or speak against the normalization of homosexuality. Both should be affirmed, as homosexual men and women ought to be acknowledged as human beings who may enjoy the basic rights of humanity, while the religious rights of those who disagree with the morality of gay sex are simultaneously upheld. While it would be the height of naiveté to think that open dialogue would remove all disagreement, it seems that some open communication could help move the issue forward toward greater understanding. It is hoped that this chapter has provided some fragments toward that end.

Part Two

Responding to Homosexuality

4

"An Abomination?"

Homosexuality, the Bible, and Christian Theology

—Page Matthew Brooks

Introduction

AT THE CENTER OF the homosexuality debate in the Christian church is how scripture is interpreted. Most Christians will agree that the scriptures should inform our practice of the Christian life, but there are still disagreements over the relative roles of scripture, reason, and contemporary culture in biblical and theological reflection. References to prohibitions against homosexuality encompass the entire corpus of scripture. This essay reflects on the biblical and theological ramifications of those scriptures.

Though most readers of the Bible can agree on what it *states*, they may disagree over what it *means*. Readers may agree on what words are contained in the Bible, but may disagree on how to translate certain words from the original languages and render their meaning into contemporary language. The science of interpretation is called hermeneutics. Thus, arguments over what the Bible teaches about homosexuality may be called a hermeneutical debate.

Hermeneutics plays a significant role in every day life. How we interpret anything involves hermeneutics, whether it be a book, web page, traffic signal, or conversation. A person literally cannot go through any significant part of his or her day without using hermeneutics, but there can be great variance in how persons do hermeneutics, or how persons interpret signs, signals, and words. Our concern here has to do with how hermeneutics inform persons' interpretations of the key Bible passages related to homosexuality.

Every person comes to a given text with a set of presuppositions. No one can escape presuppositions when discerning meaning from any form of communication. Part of the process of hermeneutics is understanding one's own presuppositions, as well as those of others. This is especially true when dealing with biblical passages concerning homosexuality. Conservative, evangelical Christians approach a text commonly using what is called the historical-grammatical approach: the meaning of the text is determined by how the historical, linguistic, and grammatical background of the text determines its meaning. In other words, contemporary generations try to find how the original recipients of the message would have understood it.

Those who use what might be called a "homosexual hermeneutic" approach the text with certain presuppositions as well.[1] Homosexual interpreters typically presuppose that the Bible does not condemn homosexuality itself, and therefore, use a variety of methods to dismiss or reinterpret passages critical of homosexual activity. They conclude that the Bible either supports homosexuality, or does not address it. For example, while proponents of the homosexual hermeneutic typically read Old Testament law in such a way to argue that it either does not address or does not criticize homosexuality, they will also emphasize passages that exhibit close personal relationships between persons of the same sex, such as those between Jonathan and David or Ruth and Naomi.[2] Such presuppositions and hermeneutical methods will be examined with each scripture passage.

This chapter is organized into sections examining key passages and themes/stories from the scriptures that are debated. Each passage is examined in its original context with an explanation of how the scripture bears on an understanding of homosexuality. Then, common explanations are given from advocates of homosexuality. A response is given

1. Throughout this essay, I use the term "homosexual" to denote both homosexual and lesbian behavior, unless otherwise specified. Often times the homosexual community is known more widely with the acronym LGBT, which stands for lesbian, gay, bisexual, and transgender. While the examinations of this essay may be applied to bisexual and transgender issues, the more specific examination will be on homosexual and lesbian behavior and how it is addressed in the biblical text.

2. Horner, *Jonathan Loved David*, see especially chapters 2 and 3.

from an evangelical perspective, taking into consideration the historical and grammatical background of each reference.

Homosexuality and the Hebrew Bible/Old Testament

The *Imago Dei* and Human Sexuality

Genesis 1–3 gives the account of the creation of the world. Chapter 2 specifically gives an account of the creation of humanity. God created the man (*adam*) to work in the garden of Eden. Seeing that man needed a companion, God also created a woman (*ishshah*).[3] Several concepts should be noted here. First, God created Eve to be a helper to Adam. The Hebrew word for helper (*ezer*) means one who supplies what is lacking in the one who is helped.[4] The term can imply either helping someone who is stronger or weaker (Gen 2:18). In the Genesis account, Adam named the animals but could not find an animal that would be a suitable helper to him. So, God created Eve to be that suitable helper. The picture which emerges from the story is that God created both man and woman, each with needs for the other. This is not to say that what God created was not good from the beginning. Just because something or someone compliments something or someone else does not necessarily imply lack or weakness. Rather, the Genesis account shows God's underlying principles for how man and woman fully compliment each other in their roles.

Second, God created Eve by taking Adam's rib from his side. Adam states in Genesis 2:23 that Eve is "bone of my bones" and "flesh of my flesh." Similar wording also appears in Gen 29:14. Such wording not only indicates that woman was created from man, but also communicates that the bonding of man and woman is the closest of all human relationships. Later in Genesis 2:24, the Bible states that a man will leave his father and mother and "hold fast" or "cleave" to his wife. Such language is used in general in the Old Testament for speaking of covenant faithfulness,

3. Greek and Hebrew terms from the biblical text are offered in parentheses using English transliteration.

4. The term *ezer* is used to denote that one supplied what is lacking in another, not necessarily an inferior position. For example, in Psalm 121:1–2, the Lord is called the "helper" of Israel. The overall connotation is that one complements the other by supplying a need that may be lacking in the other. See Dearman, "Marriage in the Old Testament," 65; Myers, *Discovering Women*, 85; and Gowan, *From Eden to Babel*, 85.

and in this immediate context, covenant faithfulness between a man and woman.[5]

Third, one can see from the Genesis 2 account that God instituted the covenant of marriage to be a reflection of His character displayed in creation. The way in which God brought about the creation of the first two humans shows they were meant to be complimentary to one another. No other creature could provide companionship for Adam. By God creating the opposite sex from Adam and instituting the covenant of marriage, it becomes clear that the two together reflect the *imago dei* and how two persons can have the closest of any kind of human relationship in marriage. Only two persons of the opposite sex, coming together in marriage, can fulfill God's commission to multiply and fill the earth, but the emphasis upon the complementary nature of the man and woman in the creation story goes beyond mere procreation, though it is surely there as well. Regardless of the view one holds concerning the historicity of the Creation account, even reading the narrative from a purely literary and theological standpoint produces these themes: only the complementarity of a male and female can fulfill God's vision for physical, interpersonal, spiritual, and procreative mandates given in the Creation account.[6]

Sodom and Gomorrah

A text often used in the debate over homosexuality is the account of Sodom and Gomorrah. In Genesis 13, the story of Abram and Lot unfolds by stating that the Lord abundantly blessed them. In fact, they were so blessed that they had to go separate ways because they were literally running over each other's livestock and possessions. Lot looks toward the Jordan River Valley and notices the grass is greener in that direction.

5. See Deuteronomy 10:20. Also see 1 Corinthians 6:16–17 for how the Apostle Paul brings the idea of covenant faithfulness together. In the Old Testament, cutting an animal in half and laying the halves on either side of a path made a covenant. The participants would walk down the short path, in between the bloody animals, as a symbol of the covenant. The imagery given is that they will fulfill the covenant, even to the point of death. When the Bible states a covenant is "made," the Hebrew word used literally means "to cut" a covenant. When a male and female come together in the covenant of marriage, they are literally "cutting" a covenant together, till death parts them.

6. Often one finds those who hold to a homosexual hermeneutic will also have a low view of biblical inspiration. Even if one holds to such a view and doubts the historicity of the creation story, merely taking the literary and theological themes from the Creation account can show the case for a complementary view of marriage.

Notice, however, in Genesis 13:13, a small comment is inserted concerning his decision: that the men of Sodom were extremely evil and sinners in the eyes of the Lord. Notice that the biblical writer specifically mentions the *men* of the city, whereas in other scripture references groups of people are specifically referred to as evil (Gen 11:6, 14:16).

Abram is then visited by three "men" in Genesis chapters 18 and 19. The biblical writer identifies these men as two angels and the Lord Himself (Gen 18:22, 19:1). After Abram and Sarah show hospitality to the visitors and the Lord informs Abram of a prophecy that Sarah would give birth to a son, the Lord tells Abram that the two angels were being sent to Sodom to see if the outcry against the people of Sodom and Gomorrah regarding their sin was true. Abram interceded on their behalf, and was able to secure an agreement from the Lord to not destroy Sodom (where Lot was living), if at least ten people could be found who loved the Lord. When the two angels arrive at the city center, only Lot shows hospitality to them and invites them to his home (Gen 19:3).

Before the evening was done, the men of the city gathered at Lot's home and stated that they wanted to "know them" (Gen 19:5). Lot went out to the doorway to meet them and shut the door behind himself. He offered his two virgin daughters, but the men were insistent upon "knowing" the other men (the two angels). Since Lot would not step away, the angry men threatened to treat Lot worse than their original intentions toward the visitors (Gen 19:9), but the angels reached out, brought Lot back into the house, and caused a blinding light to fall on the men outside so that they eventually grew tired of trying to find the door and went away. The angelic men then confirmed to Lot that they had been sent to the city to destroy it because of its wickedness. Nevertheless, the angels coax Lot and his family out of the city early in the morning. Lot's wife was turned into a pillar of salt because she looked back. Then, while living in a cave in the hills, Lot's two daughters got him drunk so that they were able to sleep with him for two nights because they wanted to preserve the offspring of their father (Gen 19:30–38). Such was the story of Lot.

At the center of the controversy over this narrative is exactly what is meant by the term "to know" (*yada*). Derrick Bailey, whose seminal work *Homosexuality and the Western Christian Tradition* paved the way for much of today's homosexual hermeneutics, argues that "know" in Genesis 19:5 means to "get acquainted with" and not to "have sexual intercourse with."[7] While it is true that the Hebrew word *yada* can mean simply "to know," the surrounding context can only support a sexual connotation. Why else would Lot offer his daughters, who have not "known" a man, though they were engaged to two men of the city? The same word is used in the parallel story of the Levite and his concubine (Jdg 19:22–25), and leaves little room for doubt regarding the sexual context. Few scholars adopt Bailey's argument, even among those who use a homosexual hermeneutic.[8]

Some scholars, such as Bailey, argue that the real sin of Sodom and Gomorrah was a lack of hospitality towards the visitors. Certainly the reason given by Lot for not handing over the men is because he wants to act as a proper host towards his visitors and provide protection. Such practices were placed in high value in ancient society because the honor of the home would be at stake if protection were not given. Lot's own self-interest becomes apparent when he offers his own daughters instead of himself to the men. Such self-interest could be motivated by the devaluation of women in ancient culture. Nevertheless, given the entire context showing the depth of depravity of Sodom, it is likely that the sin of Sodom is not merely a failure to show hospitality toward visitors, but rather a whole range of sinful activity, with the attempted rape of male guests by the men of the city serving as the culmination of a godless culture, or as final proof of the depths of depravity of the inhabitants and their guilt in the face of divine judgment.

Daniel Helminiak, a Roman Catholic priest, argues from other portions of the Bible that the sin of Sodom was inhospitality, not homosexuality. The prophet Ezekiel states that the "guilt of Sodom" was that its populace had food and enjoyed prosperous living, but did not render aid to the poor and needy. Helminiak states that the sin of the Sodomites in the story of Lot and the angels was that they refused to take in the needy visitors (16:48–49).[9] While Ezekiel does imply that the people were inhospitable (surely rape is inhospitable!), the following verse makes it clear that they were guilty of even graver sin; they committed "abominations" (v. 50).

7. Bailey, *Homosexuality and the Western Christian Tradition*, 3–4.

8. See the refutation of Bailey and others in Haas, "Exegetical Issues in the Use of the Bible," 387–88. See also De Young, "The Contributions of the Septuagint," 158–65; Boughton, "Biblical Texts and Homosexuality," 142–43.

9. See Helminiak, *What the Bible Really Says About Homosexuality*, 39.

Sodom and Gomorrah are mentioned in other parts of the Bible. Some may point out that Jesus mentioned Sodom and Gomorrah but never connected the sin of the city with homosexuality (Mat 10:14–15). While it is apparent that Jesus does not connect the sin with homosexuality, it is also apparent that he does not connect it to inhospitality either. The immediate connection between the situation of the disciples and that of Sodom and Gomorrah is that all the cities refused to hear the Gospel and repent. Jesus is merely stating there will be a more bearable judgment for Sodom and Gomorrah than for the cities of Jesus' day because they experienced the visitation of the Apostles themselves with the clear message of the Gospel.

Sodom is also referenced in Jude and Second Peter. Jude 6–7 mentioned Sodom and Gomorrah as a symbol of God's punishment upon exceeding immorality. Jude makes a theological connection with angels who gave up their proper place in heaven with the men of Sodom, who desired strange flesh. Some may point out that sin of the Sodomite men was that the desired the flesh of the angels, but the Genesis account clearly shows they did not know the men were angels.[10] The sin of the men of Sodom was not inhospitality, but rather the sexual desires and acts that brought God's judgment.

Leviticus and the Old Testament Law

Two central passages from the Old Testament Law are fiercely debated. In fact, perhaps more than any other passages, these two passages lie at the heart of the same-sex debate: Leviticus 18:22 and 20:13. Daniel Helminiak admits that these two passages are fairly clear about prohibiting homosexual acts. After citing the two verses, he states, "This sound pretty straightforward, and it sounds pretty bad."[11] John Boswell clearly admits the Leviticus passages are prohibitions against homosexual behavior as well.[12]

Unlike narratives, commands such as those in Leviticus are not just descriptive but prescriptive. Both commands occur in a larger block of laws that many scholars refer to as the Holiness Code of Leviticus. To borrow a phrase from the real estate industry, it's all about "location,

10. See also 2 Peter 2:4–10.

11. Halminiak, 51.

12. Boswell, *Christianity, Social Tolerance, and Homosexuality*, 100–4.

location, location." In the same way, it is all about "context, context, context." Notice some features of the context in which these commands appear. First, the command that a man shall not lie with a man as with a woman (Lev 18:22) appears in a larger block of laws prohibiting certain sexual relationships, including incest, bestiality, and adultery. Second, the choice of the word "abomination" (*toeva*) for the homosexual act shows the degree of revulsion. The Hebrew word communicates something particularly revolting against the boundaries established by God in His law. After the list of all the prohibited practices, the word "abomination" is used (18:24–30), but note that it is specifically attached to the homosexual act (18:22).[13] Last, this is one of the few prohibitions directly carried over into the New Testament. It will be shown later how Paul was simply carrying over a law from the Old Testament Holiness Code and not invoking something new based upon his own cultural preferences.

Central to the controversy of the Levitical passages is the meaning of the Hebrew word for abomination (*toevah*). According to John Boswell, the word *toevah* does not usually signify something that is evil in and of itself, such as eating pork. He notes specifically that it would *not* include acts like rape or theft. He states, "It is used throughout the Old Testament to designate those Jewish sins which involve ethnic contamination or idolatry . . . the Levitical enactments against homosexual behavior characterize it unequivocally as ceremonially unclean rather than inherently evil."[14]

However, such a dichotomy between the meanings is not supported from the surrounding context. Normally whenever the word *toevah* is used, the sexual act described is characterized as a detestable act before God and one worthy of the death penalty. Homosexual intercourse is specifically singled out in Leviticus 18 and 20 as worthy of the label *toevah*, or abomination.Thurston argues that homosexual sex is specifically singled out because it involves a violation of the distinction between

13. In pointing this out, I also mean to note that the person who engages in homosexual sex is not, himself (or herself), an abomination. This is an important point and distinction, as judgment against homosexuality is not a referendum on the value of the individual. To be sure, he is of immense value to God, so much so that He gave His Son for their redemption.

14. Boswell, 100–2. Some claim that *toevah* is used to denote a socially constructed constraint. Kamionkowski, *Gender Reversal*; Goldstein, "Reading *Toevah*," 48–60. Others have argued that the labeling as *toevah* was a later addition by a redactor(s). Olyan, "And With a Male You Shall Not Lie," 182–83.

male and female and the boundary between the two.[15] Similarly, Boyarin argues that the prohibition of homosexuality was universal because the confusion deals with a boundary established in the natural order at the time of creation.[16] There is difficulty in setting up a distinction of how these acts would simply be "ceremonially unclean." David Greenberg writes, "Leviticus does recognize forms of ritual uncleanness that are not morally condemned . . . purification from these pollutions is accomplished quite simply through bathing and sacrifice . . . That intercourse with a menstruating woman is also classified as an abomination along with homosexuality is an indication not, as Boswell suggests, that the latter offense was considered trivial, but rather that the former was considered extremely grave."[17]

Though one may overcome the argument concerning the meaning of "abomination" in the Levitical passages, the question is constantly raised if Leviticus carries any contemporary authority. Some scholars and theologians argue that the Old Testament prohibitions concerning homosexuality are not longer binding to contemporary society. David Bartlett makes an argument concerning this with an analogy from slavery. Slavery, which is tolerated in many biblical texts, would be vehemently opposed today. Bartlett makes a similar point by stating that Bible never condemns slavery. Yet, because of its innate inequalities and oppressiveness, Christians have come to condemn it. In similar manner, though the Bible condemns homosexuality, recent empirical studies and the experiences of homosexuals requires a reinterpretation of scripture using the larger principles of love and equality.[18]

Further, several New Testament references speak to the abrogation of the Old Testament law. Walter Wink argues that Christians accept some prohibitions in the Old Testament but reject others. For example, Christians still reject rape, incest, adultery, and bestiality; however, Christians today practice intercourse during menstruation, exogamy, and birth control. Given this state of affairs, Wink believes that Christians may reevaluate biblical prohibitions against many sexual practices in light of changing times.[19] Rabbi Jacob Milgrom teaches that the ho-

15. Thurston, "Leviticus 18:22 and the Prohibition of Homosexual Acts," 7–23.

16. Boyarin, "Are There Any Jews," 342.

17. Greenberg, *Construction of Homosexuality*, 195–6.

18. Bartlett, "A Biblical Perspective,"142.

19. Wink, "Homosexuality and the Bible," 33–49.

mosexual prohibitions were only for the Jews living in the Holy Land. He argues that it is wrong to place such prohibitions on persons living outside the Holy Land.[20] Nevertheless, the reason why the Old Testament law code still carries moral teaching for all time is because the God of the Old Testament is still the same God of Jesus Christ. The debate really is an argument over the continuity and/or discontinuity of certain aspects of the Old Testament.[21]

Not sure?

It is true that the Holiness Code of the Old Testament is very much concerned with matters of purity and that many of the requirements from the code no longer carry enforcement today. For example, there is no longer a reason to adhere to the prohibition against rounding off the hair on a person's temple (Lev 19:27). Many of the commands given in the Holiness Code were meant to keep the Israelites separated from the nations around them and maintain clear social and religious boundaries.[22] Some commands were of a practical nature in how to maintain physical health and purity.[23] Others related to the organizing and structuring of the nation as Israel at the time was a theocracy.[24]

Most of Leviticus 18–20 can be seen as an extended commentary on the Ten Commandments, with applications given for each commandment. The Holiness Code includes ritual and moral laws, as well as eternal and contingent laws. Christians must know how to carry over the Holiness Code into contemporary settings.

The same God who gave the law codes to Moses is that same who inspired the New Testament. The Apostle Paul saw considerable continuity between the two testaments, even in the matter of sexual behavior and

20. Milgrom, "Does the Bible Prohibit Homosexuality?," 11. Milgrom's argument cannot be justified based solely upon geography alone. Why would homosexual prohibitions be in effect only for a certain geographic area and not other places? Why would a Jew not be able to practice homosexuality in the Holy Land but would be able to practice it anywhere else? Milgrom does not offer any conclusive arguments.

21. The debate over the continuity of the Old Testament and New Testament carries over into many theological and practical issues in the church, not just the Old Testament law: ecclesiology, dispensational vs. covenant theology, circumcision and baptism, security of the believer, and eschatology.

22. Deuteronomy 12:29–32.

23. Deuteronomy 18:19; 20:18. For an excellent discussion on the Holiness Code and social and religious boundaries, see Gagnon, *The Bible and Homosexual Practice*, 111–20.

24. The issue of how the Old Testament applies in New Testament times will be addressed later in the chapter.

ethics. For example, Paul's commandment against incest follows a similar format as is found in the Levirate Code (Lev 18:6–18). His language in Romans 1:32 about homosexual sex echoes the same "death" language as was used in Lev 20:13. In addition, the Greek word Paul uses in Romans 1:24 (*akatharsia*) is also used in the Septuagint (Greek) translation of the Old Testament in several Levitical passages (Lev 18:19 and 20:21, 25). Paul was well trained in the Hebrew Scriptures and had studied with one of the foremost rabbis of his day, Gamaliel. Paul was using not-so-subtle hints throughout his writings to show the continuity of sexual ethics from the Old Testament to the New Testament.[25]

One may notice that the Holiness Code specifically prohibits male homosexuality. Why would the biblical writer mention primarily males in the Holiness Code? Several reasons may help explain this. First, there may be illusions to all-male cultic homosexual practices by the surrounding Canaanite peoples. To maintain the sacred distinctiveness between the two peoples, God could have commanded against the type of prominent homosexuality known in that time.[26] To be sure, the LORD was concerned with ritual and religious purity of the Israelites, but the entire context of Leviticus chapter 18–20 gives precepts and prohibitions concerning the entire created order: family relationships, incest, bestiality, etc. One may infer that the intention of the law code in these chapters is to preserve the created order as God had ordained. Paul uses similar language and reasoning in Romans 1, as will be explained below.

Second, tradition regarding rules for determining cases of adultery may offer some insight. Daniel Boyarin, a proponent of homosexual hermeneutics, explains why he believes females were not mentioned. He states that only male anal penetration was mentioned in the Babylonian Talmud. Female on female rubbing did not disqualify a woman from marrying a priest. Also, a woman was not guilty of adultery if she had intercrural intercourse, only intercourse that penetrated the vagina or anus.[27] Boyarin's point seems to be that adultery was not committed unless penetration of flesh was made and male semen ejaculated. Of course, one may carry such technical cases to the extreme, especially when comparing the Holiness Code of the Bible to extra-biblical sources.

25. See, for example, Kaiser, *Toward Old Testament Ethics*, esp. chapter 19; Schrage, *Ethics of the New Testament*, 201–7.

26. See Snaith, "Leviticus and Numbers,"126; Scanzoni and Mollenkott, *Is the Homosexual My Neighbor?*, 59–61; and Driver, "Deuteronomy," 264.

27. Boyarin, "Are There Any Jews," 336–47.

For example, a person may go quite far in sexual stimulation of another person without technically committing intercourse. Such activity among unmarried persons (or persons not married to one another) is still sinful, even if it does not technically violate rules against fornication.[28]

Other factors possibly explain why lesbian intercourse is not mentioned. Penetration may be the overriding concern in the Holiness Code. The penetration and transfer of semen enact a real merging of beings in a definitive manner. Take the example of the prohibition of bestiality, where both males and females are mentioned because they both may have penetration. It may have been that lesbianism was something handled by the discipline of fathers and husbands in private and not by public authorities.[29] Nevertheless, the Apostle Paul certainly expanded the prohibition to include women, not just men, in Romans 1.

Ceremonial and Moral Law

One final objection to the prohibitions of Levitical law and the Holiness Code still relates to the issue of the relationship between the Old Testament and the New Testament and to the question of the applicability of the Holiness Code to New Testament believers. The distinction must be made in the Old Testament as to what God meant to be temporary and what He intended to be permanent. The Bible does indicate, via context, what was intended to be applied only to the Israelites, and what was intended to be binding upon all people in all places at all times.

Some laws related specifically to the priesthood, dietary laws, and ritual purity practices of the Israelite cultus. These laws are called the ceremonial law, and are typically viewed as temporary and incidental: they applied to the ancient Israelites at the time of the conquest and settlement of Canaan in an effort to establish a theocracy. Other laws are binding on all people at all times, such as laws relating to murder, adultery, and idolatry. These laws are called the moral law, and are typically viewed as permanent and universal: they apply to all persons of all times and places.

Thus, the ceremonial law referred to those ordinances and regulations that instructed the Israelites in correct worship, based upon the covenant obligations made in the Mosaic Covenant (see Exod 19ff). These temporary statutes pointed forward to the time when the Messiah would

28. Jesus' prohibition of lust may serve to prove the point.

29. Greenberg, 190.

fulfill these ceremonial codes. From a certain perspective, one could argue that the codes are still in effect today, but are fulfilled in the person of Jesus Christ; therefore, individuals do not have to execute them.[30]

Likewise, the moral law referred to those aspects of code that were binding on all people at all places at all times. Murder, idolatry, adultery, covetousness, stealing, and lying still have the same characteristics from several thousand years ago as they do today. While the penalties for violating the moral law were specific to Israel, the principles behind the moral law still remain unchanged. While the ceremonial law was specific to the nation of Israel, the moral law was binding on everyone, including the other nations. For example, the Prophet Obadiah addressed his prophecy to Edom; Jonah was a messenger sent to Nineveh; Ezekiel referenced several nations surrounding Israel (Ezek 25–32), and each pronounced judgment for violations of God's moral law. Context, after careful examination, can clearly show what was binding during the time of the Israelites (ceremonial law) and what was binding for all time (moral law).

David and Jonathan

It is sometimes alleged that David and Jonathan had a homosexual relationship, based upon the account of how close they were (1 Sam 18–23) and the wording of David's eulogy for Jonathan (2 Sam 1).[31] One can possibly now understand more clearly the context and expressions used after the previous examination of Old Testament passages. A review of the story below will explicate some of the allegations concerning this story.

David first encountered Jonathan shortly after he killed Goliath and was brought before King Saul. Their story is told starting in 1 Samuel 18:1–16. A key phrase, however, is found in verse 3 where it states that

30. The book of Hebrews gives a New Testament picture of how the ceremonial law would be fulfilled in the person of Jesus Christ. Christ, as Messiah, provided the sacrifice once and for all that was demanded by God for sin. An example of how such a demand would still be binding today but fulfilled in Christ would be the Old Testament sacrifice. God still demands a sacrifice for sin; this is binding on people still today and, from this perspective, may still be "binding" on New Testament Christians. Nevertheless, Christ has provided the final sacrifice needed for this demand from God; therefore, the Old Testament ceremonial law has been satisfied, or fulfilled, in Christ.

31. For some representative sources concerning such arguments, see Homer, *Jonathan Loved David*; and Schorer and Staubli, "Saul, David, und Jonathan-eine Dreiecksgeschichte?" 15–22.

Jonathan loved David *as his own soul.* Jonathan's love is portrayed as part of a much larger love affair of the Israelites with David, who was a successful military and political leader. Jonathan, instead of acting jealously, completely submitted to David. By making a covenant with David, Jonathan was in essence adopting David into the royal household, despite Saul's spiteful actions toward David.

David and Jonathan had now become family, but not in a romantic sense. Similar phrases speaking of the binding of souls is used elsewhere in the Old Testament, but with no romantic connotation. For example, Judah references his brother Benjamin in this way, and no homosexual relationship is intimated or in view (Gen 44:30–31). The Hebrew word for bound is *qasar*, which refers to the binding of people together for political purposes. In this sense, we see that Jonathan and David's relationship might be a political union of sorts, but that it goes far beyond that into a deep friendship. And, if David becomes king, Jonathan is telling David he will rejoice out of loyalty, and not out of jealousy even though Jonathan is the rightful heir to the throne.

Several pieces of information help to bring the background into focus. Such language of love as is seen in the act of handing over his robe and armor was not only an act of love but also personal and political investiture. This pattern is seen in various parts of scripture. Saul tried to clothe David with his own armor in First Samuel 17:38–39. After David defeated Goliath, he took Goliath's armor and placed it in the tent as a sign of defeat. The giving of the robe to another person could have been a sign of transferring rights and power.[32]

While the story continues to unfold (too much to detail here), we see in First Samuel 20:41–42 where the weight of Saul's pursuit is too much and the two must depart from each other for good. The text states that David bows three times and kisses Jonathan. The three-fold bowing again shows the political undertone of the story. Kissing as a greeting was common in the Ancient Near East, especially for two men in sorrow. These were not erotic kisses. Even David's eulogy in Second Samuel 9 shows the sorrow and grief expressed from the loss of a deep friendship.

None of the texts suggest any type of homosexual relationship. The two terms that are normally used to communicate some type of sexual relationship ("to lie with"-*sakab* and "to know"-*yada*) are never used in the passages examined. Both David and Jonathan went on to have wives

32. McCarter, "1 Samuel," 305.

and children of their own (1 Sam 18 and 1 Sam 20:42), and David took in Jonathan's son and treated him well as a result of his love and respect for Jonathan. While heterosexual relationships do not necessarily preclude homosexual relationships, the biblical writer's attention is particularly drawn to the eroticism between the two men and their wives, not between the two men.[33] Biblical writers were never remiss to point out homosexual behavior before. Instead the biblical writer emphasizes the personal bond of brotherhood that matured between the two men, even with all the political undertones that developed as well.

Before moving to New Testament texts, let us summarize what the Old Testament teaches. The Old Testament texts that speak of the perversion of homosexuality are scattered throughout the Old Testament. From the very beginning, God designed male and female to be complementary toward one another. Usurping that design by way of homosexuality is considered to be a grave sin, worthy of death by stoning. While some may read the stories from the Old Testament and claim they do not teach against homosexuality, or that homosexual undertones can be read into the text, a close reading of the language and context do not support such conclusions.

Homosexuality and the New Testament

Jesus and Homosexuality

In continuing the arguments over scripture, inevitably the question of Jesus arises. Jesus never mentions homosexuality specifically in the Gospels, though He does reference marriage many times. What was Jesus' stance toward homosexuality? Some argue that Jesus showed a more loving and merciful attitude toward sexual ethics and would not want to exclude anyone.[34] Nevertheless, when we read more closely in the Gospels, we see that Jesus continued the same path as was given in the Holiness Code of the Old Testament. Jesus' silence on the issue should

33. David is especially known for his (heterosexual) sexual appetite with his many wives and concubines, including the detailed story of Bathsheba (See 2 Sam 11).

34. For example, see Rogers, *Jesus, The Bible, and Homosexuality*, 56–57. For a helpful response to such arguments, see Grenz,. *Welcoming but Not Affirming*, especially chapter 3.

not be misconstrued as acceptance. Rather the overall context of Jesus' ministry shows just the opposite, for several reasons. His silence on the subject actually might speak louder than His words.

First, it is highly unlikely Jesus would have adopted such a radically different approach toward same-sex relationships from that of his own culture and faith. We must remember that Jesus was first and foremost a Jew, even before there was anything "Christian," and to read him as a modern sexual libertarian is anachronistic. Also, Jesus was seen as a Rabbi during his time. While he did confront contemporary attitudes toward the law in His day, he also showed the right motivations and fulfillment of the Law. Since Jesus challenged many of the conventional beliefs during his day, it is reasonable to suppose that he would have mentioned homosexuality if he held a position contrary to that of the majority of Jews. His silence shows acceptance of, not a challenge to, the Old Testament teaching on the morality of homosexuality.

Strengthening this claim is the fact that Jesus boldly stated that he came not to abolish the law, but to fulfill it (Matt 5:17–18). Following his address, he brought into greater focus six different points of the law and expanded upon their meaning (Matt 5:21–48). While Jesus did not advocate the death penalty for adultery and prostitution, he certainly did not overturn it.[35] While examining each specific reference to the law is outside the scope of this essay, one focus becomes clear. Jesus was emphasizing that rigid conformity and keeping of the law was not the intent of the law. Examining the motivation and attitude behind the keeping of the law was also important.

While Jesus' did not make explicit reference to homosexuality, his teaching on sexual ethics certainly imply his disapproval of it, and his approval of Levitical sexual purity laws. For example, in Mark 7:21–23, Jesus uses the word "sexual immoralities," using the root word *porneo* (from which comes the English word "pornography"). In fact, Jesus uses the plural form, indicating the many sexual immoralities: adultery, licentiousness, etc., should be condemned. A first-century Jew would most likely have understood that Jesus was referring to the forbidden acts listed in Leviticus 18 and 20, thereby having in mind homosexuality as well as those prohibited acts specifically mentioned.[36]

35. One could argue the death penalty was taken away by Jesus fulfilling the ceremonial law.

36. Turner, "Biblical Texts Relevant to Homosexual Orientation and Practice," 441.

Second, Jesus appears to appeal to the Genesis account to understand the sexual relationship. In Mark 10:1–12, Jesus refers to both Genesis 1:27 and 2:24. He then states in Mark 10:6–9 that what God has joined together no human should separate. Jesus appears to understand that marriage was ordained by God from the beginning of creation as that of the union between a man and a woman and show no acceptance of another pattern. While this may be an argument from silence, He certainly does not endorse monogamous homosexual relationships (or any homosexual relationship), even though homosexuality was rampant among the Roman culture at the time. But with Jesus' reference going back to Genesis 1–2, a first-century Jew would have clearly understood the implication from the Torah that marriage should be between a man and woman in lifelong sexual union together.

Many depict Jesus as having a more acceptable stance towards people who practice various sexual ethics. However, a survey of the Gospels shows that Jesus actually had a more restrictive sexual ethic, in continuity with the Old Testament law, because he closed loopholes that had developed in practice among the Jews. His teachings even exceeded what the law required.[37]

We actually see a model of love, justice, and righteousness coming together in Jesus' ministry. One can look at the parables of Jesus, such as the Prodigal Son (Luke 15:11–32) and see an example of the kindness of Jesus. What was unusual about Jesus' ministry was that more often than not, He raised moral standards above those of His fellow Jews. Yet, Jesus also showed an incredibly merciful spirit to those who had been in perversion and disobedience to the law for years. For example, Jesus often stated how he would go after the one lost sheep, leaving the ninety-nine, just to return the sheep to the fold (Luke 15:3–7). Jesus showed mercy and grace to those who were not shown mercy and grace, even moreso than the religious establishment of His time (who were supposed to show such mercy and grace). Jesus' model can serve as a model for churches today to show how to exercise incredible love and grace to those who have a repentant heart while maintaining high moral standards.

37. See Matthew 5:31–32 and Mark 10:11–12.

Paul and Homosexuality

It has been demonstrated that the Old Testament clearly prohibits homosexual behavior in the Levitical Code. It has also been shown that Jesus, though not explicitly addressing homosexuality, builds on what the Old Testament taught by making affirming references to that Holiness Code. Paul, likewise, builds on the tradition of the Old Testament Holiness Code, but also addresses homosexuality even more explicitly.

Why did Paul address homosexuality explicitly while Jesus addressed it more implicitly? Perhaps the difference is due to the audiences. Jesus was primarily addressing the Jewish nation (though He certainly interacted with Gentiles in many accounts), and Paul primarily worked among the Gentiles. Jewish believers would have automatically had an understanding of the Law and its prohibitions against homosexuality. Paul, on the other hand, was ministering among the Gentiles where homosexuality was practiced more explicitly and knowledge of the Law more scant. Therefore, one can possibly understand why the differences of address would have taken place when comparing Jesus and Paul.

The first chapter of Romans stands as a central text in the homosexuality debate because of its explicit address. Not only does it address male homosexuality, but also female lesbianism. The overall context for Paul's first 3 chapters of Romans is his argument that everyone is under the influence of sin (Rom 3:10, 3:20, 3:23). His point is to show that there is no distinction between Jews and Gentiles. All are guilty of sin before God and in need of his merciful salvation. One does not obtain salvation by simply adhering to Torah (Law or Holiness Code), but rather it is only through the Gospel that one can find liberation from sin's power.

Paul's writing in Romans has a strong social and ethical tone. In later chapters (14 and 15) he exhorts the strong Christian not to look down on the weak Christian with regard to food, religious holidays, circumcision, and other issues. While some may say that Paul encourages believers not to judge others, especially those who may practice homosexuality (Rom 14:1–15:13), he only takes this approach with issues of indifference. He does not take the same approach when looking at matters of sexual ethics. One need only compare the language Paul uses in chapter one with that of chapter fourteen to see the difference.

Romans 1:26–27 are the central verses in which Paul addresses homosexuality. Leading up to those verses, Paul gives several important points. First, the character of God and His most basic laws are revealed in nature itself (v. 18–20). It may be argued exactly what these basic laws may be. Would it be the Torah? The Ten Commandments? From Genesis 1–3, we know that God placed in each person the *imago dei*. The *imago dei* gives each person a basic understanding that there is a god and creator, and that he has revealed himself in creation. Similarly, there are certain moral laws that are most basic to every person; there is something in people that tells them that murder is wrong, for example.[38] Paul continues this argumentation later on describing how sexual relations between a man and woman are *evidently* natural, but homosexuality is unnatural (v. 26).

Second, Paul explains that even though persons knew the law of God, they suppressed the truth of God by their foolish thinking and darkened ways (v. 21). Notice that in response to the hardening of their hearts, God gave them over to further sin. Also notice the connection between the dishonoring of God and the dishonoring of self. A failure to honor God and His ways leads to an unfit mind and perverted conduct (v. 23, 25).

Third, Paul uses homosexual and lesbian relationships as particular examples of how dishonoring God leads to perverted action (vv. 26–27). Paul's reference to homosexuality and lesbianism is quite clear: women exchanged natural uses of their organs for unnatural and men committing the same acts with other men, burning in lust for one another. The point Paul makes here is decisively against homosexuality: it is "against nature" (*para physin*).[39] At a minimum, Paul means to refer to the complementary anatomical and procreative functions of male and female. In the most basic of terms, the male organs fit the female organs. Paul goes on to argue that even the Gentiles, who do not have access to the law, do things according to the law and know that homosexuality is contrary to nature. For Paul, it was a simple matter of physical observation and the use of the mind to observe how God created male and female in a complementary fashion.

A number of scholars and theologians attack Paul using various descriptors: homophobic, chauvinist, sexist, intolerant, and bigoted. We

38. C.S. Lewis uses the moral argument to show proof for the existence of God in *Mere Christianity*.

39. Wright, "Homosexuality: The Relevance of the Bible," 291ff. Other essays on this debate include the following: Balch, ed., *Homosexuality, Science and the "Plain Sense" of Scripture*; Brawley, ed., *Biblical Ethics and Homosexuality*; Siker, ed., *Homosexuality in the Church*.

have seen how Paul based his prohibitory arguments concerning homosexuality on the creation account, God's design, nature itself, and the Old Testament Holiness Code. Margaret Davies, however, argues that Paul devalued the procreation mandate, valued a stronger role for women, and devalued war. She suggests that Paul's attachment to the prohibition on homosexuality was merely an "emotional hangover" and should be read as such. In other words, we should read past Paul's emotions and see what we think he was really meaning in the text: that homosexuality should be accepted. Despite the dubious conclusions Davies draws, and despite Paul's lack of attention to procreation and war, it is actually Paul's attention to homoerotic activity that should catch the attention of the reader to show his emphasis.[40]

Paul also makes quick references to homosexual behavior in 1 Corinthians 6:9–11 and 1 Timothy 1:8–10. In both contexts, Paul lists certain behaviors that cannot be a part of fruitful Christian living. In 1 Corinthians 6:9–11, Paul first mentions the sexually immoral, which again comes from the Greek word *porneo*. Paul then uses the more specific word, *malakoi*, often translated as "homosexuals" but literally translated "soft ones," or "effeminate." He also uses *arsenokoitai* (both in 1 Cor 6:9 and 1 Tim 1:10), which literally means a male who takes another male to bed, or is sometimes translated as "sodomites." The two terms taken together may have a broad range of meanings.

Concerning the term, *malakoi*, Paul clearly has in mind more than those who might be said to have a "limp wrist" or more feminine behavior (in a non-sexual way). Some homosexual hermeneutics advocates, such as Dale Martin, propose that the word *malokoi* has too broad of a range of meaning to know precisely what is intended.[41] It might be said those who are *malakoi* are those who are more passive in a homosexual relationship or who engage in a process of intentional feminization which would result in lead towards the tempting of someone else into a sexual relationship.[42] Combining the understanding of both *malakoi* and *arsenokaoita* in the context of Paul's discussion of sexual immorality, leads to the conclusion that Paul is condemning the intentional feminization which leads to homosexuality, along with homosexual sex.

40. Davies, "New Testament Ethics and Ours," 320–27. In the same article, Davies advocates that persons should see themselves as people first, instead of males and females. She argues for the unity of the whole rather than the distinctiveness of the parts.

41. Martin, "Arsenokoites and Malakos," 117–36.

42. Fee, "The First Epistle to the Corinthians," 243–44. See also Collins, *First Corinthians*; and Grenz, *Welcoming But Not Affirming*, 57.

For Paul, homosexuality (and lesbianism) are explicitly prohibited. Paul moves beyond simply stating homosexuality is prohibited merely because the Holiness Code said so. Rather, he shows from natural reasoning why homosexuality is not in accordance with God's creative design. Paul is often attacked because he gives the most explicit prohibition on homosexuality. Nevertheless, Paul flows in the same tradition as the Old Testament and Jesus Himself with regards to this teaching. Paul is often times said to be homophobic and bigoted. Those who make such statements often accept one part of Paul's teaching and dismiss others. Either all of Paul's teachings should be accepted or all should be dismissed. Paul's critics must also share the burden of proof to show how they arrive at their own conclusions based upon the context. Even in explaining the prohibitions, Paul shows the mercy and grace of God in 1 Corinthians 6:11 by stating that though his readers used to be counted among the unrighteous, there is freedom through the justification and sanctification of Jesus Christ.

Conclusion

In conclusion, from start to finish the Bible gives clear prohibitions against homosexual behavior and motivations. God's original intentions from the beginning were that two humans, male and female, would come together to show a reflection of God's glory. Together, male and female are complementary, not competitive. Just because they are complementary does not imply weakness in one or the other, but rather shows the glory of God's design. Homosexuality is prohibited not only because it goes against God's holiness and righteousness, but because it goes against the very design God created for male and female. Jesus' implied teachings on homosexuality show acceptance of the Old Testament teachings concerning homosexuality, despite the lack of explicit mention. Paul, likewise, flows in accord with Old Testament tradition on the prohibition of homosexuality but emphasizes the role of nature and reason to show how homosexuality is corrupt and contrary to God's design. As Gagnon aptly puts it,

> Arguments put forward by advocates of homosexuality to undermine the contemporary relevance of Scripture are weak. Scripture does not reject same-sex intercourse because of some alleged ignorance of non-exploitative forms of homosexual

behavior or genetic causation factors. It does not reject homosexual intercourse because of some misperception that only idolaters in the strict sense could engage in such behavior or because of some superstition about defilement and purity. It does not reject homosexual practice, at least not primarily, out of some need to assert the rule of men over women. Rather, Scripture rejects homosexual behavior because it is a violation of the gendered existence of male and female ordained by God at creation.[43]

43. Gagnon, *Bible and Homosexual Practice*, 487.

5

"Virtue or Obedience?"

Homosexuality, Repeal of DADT, and Chaplains

—John D. Laing

Introduction

In this chapter, I hope to offer a response to the repeal of the Don't Ask, Don't Tell [DADT] policy that conservative chaplains can use to engage the secular political culture, while retaining their prophetic voice and avoiding court-martial or accusation of harassment and/or intimidation. As the public and political debates over the repeal of the Clinton Administration's policy commonly known as "Don't Ask, Don't Tell," continue to rage, military chaplains are increasingly finding themselves in the center of controversy. Many chaplains and their endorsing agencies have expressed particular concern over the effect that the repeal of DADT will have on the free speech and free exercise rights of conservative religious service members, including chaplains.

Repeal of DADT has already taken place; now it is a matter of implementation, which has, at least at this point, been left to the discretion of the Department of Defense [DoD]. Prior to the repeal, and in an effort to measure the effect a repeal might have upon military readiness, the DoD commissioned the RAND Corporation to conduct a study of military member attitudes toward open service of homosexuals by means of survey. News reports which referenced the survey noted that the most fierce opposition to the repeal has come from members of the chaplain corps.

There are several avenues which conservative chaplains can take in response to the repeal. First, they can combat implementation of the repeal on the basis of legal concerns that the issue raises for chaplains and other members of the armed forces whose faith opposes the normalcy of homosexual relations. This has been the most common approach, with chaplains claiming that the repeal will violate their First Amendment right to free speech and free exercise. This argument, while raising legitimate areas of concern for dialog and debate, is somewhat premature and speculative, since the mere presence of homosexuals in the military does not, in itself, constitute a violation of anyone's free speech. The repeal would have to entail some sort of regulation of speech regarding homosexuality, and it does not. Further, legal arguments can only be brought if there is harm, and none exists as yet. As noted in chapter two, these concerns are not completely unfounded, but there are good reasons for thinking chaplains will continue to enjoy their First Amendment rights. Second, they can oppose the repeal on the grounds of the sinful or unbiblical nature of homosexuality. While this is also a legitimate concern of chaplains, this approach will by and large, prove ineffective for the audience in view here (i.e., secular government). Third, they can argue that open homosexual service will be detrimental to unit morale or will lead to increased problems with sexual harassment or even violence among service members. Again, another legitimate concern, but this is not proper to chaplaincy and instead belongs to the military command. Additionally, it is speculative and there are steps that can be taken to address it without a wholesale rejection of the repeal. Each of these approaches has attractive features and will be considered in somewhat more detail to follow. Nevertheless, I will argue that they are ultimately unhelpful and will prove ineffective or even counter-productive. If the points made here are correct, then it may seem that chaplains' only alternative is to support homosexual service. After all, this approach will preserve the important concept of freedom of choice/conscience, so central to the legal justification for military chaplaincy; however, it has the unsavory consequence of the chaplain arguing for something he/she deems ultimately at odds with God's Word. There is, however, another approach available which retains the chaplain's prophetic voice, preserves the principle of freedom of conscience/choice, and also allows for limits on the range of appropriate beliefs/choices: he can appeal to universal morality, natural law, or virtue theory. Thus, the chaplain can uphold the philosophical concept of freedom of choice while refusing to advocate an "anything goes" or relativistic approach to ethics. I will argue that this is the best approach for the thoughtful conservative chaplain to take.

Legal Concerns with Repeal of DADT

First, chaplains may wish to challenge homosexual service on legal grounds, or at least voice legal concerns that arise specifically for chaplains and other peoples of faith. In fact, the primary concerns that have been raised pertain to the Constitutional rights of chaplains and their constituency. In a widely publicized open letter to President Obama and Secretary Gates, 65 retired chaplains from across the services expressed concern that the proposed repeal of DADT "would threaten the religious liberty of chaplains and service members."[1]

The letter first expresses concern that chaplains will feel pressure to water down their teachings, which seems to go against both the free exercise and free speech clauses of the First Amendment. The letter also warns that an official ban on speech deemed "discriminatory" could essentially remove the ability of chaplains to express their beliefs on homosexuality, with the result being to effectively establish liberal religion as the official government faith.[2] It claims that chaplains will be hampered in their ability to preach passages which address homosexual behavior, to condemn homosexual practice in their counseling, and to draw upon the full moral instruction of their faith backgrounds in official classes on moral leadership and ethics. Worse, chaplains could face disciplinary action or adverse litigation for refusing to allow homosexuals to serve in leadership positions in their ministries or homosexual couples to attend chaplain-led "Strong Bonds" marriage enrichment retreats. The letter concludes with a statement of intent to encourage chaplains to love and

Is this True?

1. Letter to President Barack Obama and Dr. Robert M. Gates, September 16, 2010, page 1. Letter is available for download via link at http://www.npr.org in an article entitled, "Chaplains Worry About Careers If 'Don't Ask' is Lifted," Accessed March 1, 2011.

2. The letter states, "If chaplains are limited in teaching and counseling on their beliefs, then the men and women in uniform who share their faith and rely on their instruction will face a reduction in the free exercise of their faith. Likewise, if chaplains with beliefs that contradict the proposed policy are kept from roles that are prone to generate conflict—such as administering the Army's Strong Bonds program—then they, the faith groups they represent, and the Service members whose religious beliefs they serve will all be marginalized. The armed forces would effectively establish preferred religions or religious beliefs." Ibid., page 5.

minister to all people, along with a plea for Congress to include "comprehensive and robust religious liberty protections" in any official policy change on the issue. The concerns raised were not intended to be inflammatory, caustic, or alarmist, but rather to engender discussion and debate regarding the potential fallout from this far-reaching shift in policy.

Unfortunately, when issues as highly charged and emotional as these are aired publicly, a certain measure of sensationalism and misinformation will abound, and this case is no different. Some have charged that DoD documents which outline plans for implementation of the repeal essentially prohibit chaplains from preaching against homosexuality and suggest that those who disagree with the homosexual lifestyle should leave the military. For example, former naval chaplain Gordon Klingenschmitt, famous for claiming to have been brought before a court-martial for praying in Jesus' name (he was, in fact, court-martialed for wearing his uniform at a political rally), has been a vigorous opponent of the repeal. He suggests that President Obama is secretly attempting to force conservative Christian chaplains out of the military, and that the Obama Administration has "quietly begun writing policies that will result in discharge of Christian Chaplains [sic] and troops who cannot 'reconcile' with homosexual sin."[3]

Klingenschmitt points to four "shocking proofs" that the purge has already begun: (1) the existence of DoD documents which state that chaplains who can't "reconcile" with homosexual sin will be separated; (2) those same documents limiting chaplains' religious freedom to Sunday chapel services; (3) Battalion Commander was relieved of duty because he refused to teach respect for (homosexual) sin; and (4) The Left has demanded the punishment of a Christian Colonel who has taken a stand for his right to witness for Christ. The first two claims reference the DoD Working Group's implementation support plan for the repeal of DADT and will be of concern here. According to Kingenschmitt, the wording of the plan requires Christian chaplains to "reconcile" with homosexual sin or face discharge from the service. He quotes the specific wording of the report, which reads, "If a chaplain is unable to reconcile serving with or caring for gay and lesbian Service members with his or her faith, the chaplain may request that the relevant endorsing agency withdraw its

3. Klingenschmitt, e-mail to supporters, dated Wednesday, January 26, 2011.

ecclesiastical endorsement for him or her. This would trigger an administrative separation under DoDI 1304.28."[4]) WOW!

Klingenschmitt interprets the wording of the plan as a concerted effort to force conservative chaplains to compromise their beliefs or to leave the military. As he puts it, the Obama Administration is "officially on record pressuring Chaplains to quit the service if they cannot 'reconcile' with homosexual sin that violates their Christian conscience."[5] He suggests that Congress must pass laws offering "bold protection" for the religious rights of military chaplains.

In support of the second claim, Klingenschmitt argues that the DoD report, which states that chaplain speech is protected in certain contexts, is misleading at best. Drawing from his own experience of alleged religious discrimination for his Christian views, he argues that the free speech rights of Christian chaplains will be greatly diminished, confined to the Sunday morning worship setting. Elsewhere, Klingenschmitt argued that his prayer at a political rally constituted public worship and that his commander's guidance regarding the wear of his naval uniform was unclear. He uses this incident to suggest that chaplains will not be allowed to preach against homosexuality in most situations, even if during a worship service.

Klingenschmitt accurately quotes the report, but his use of the quotation is misleading, for the context within which the statement is made has to do with those service members who, as a result of their religious convictions and opposition to homosexuality, wish to separate from the military. The recommendation from the working group is that service member contracts should remain non-negotiable and in effect. Commanders will retain the ability to review individual requests and make recommendations to their respective Service Secretaries, but the repeal of DADT should not serve as the basis for a DoD-wide renegotiation of service contracts. Generally speaking, service members who still have time to serve on their contracts will be expected to serve out the duration of their obligation, regardless of their personal feelings about the repeal.[6] This, it seems to me, makes good sense, as a military-wide,

4. Johnson and Ham, co-chairs, *Support Plan for Implementation*, 24. See also page 57.

5. Klingenschmitt, e-mail to supporters.

6. "The Department of Defense does not establish a specific policy permitting the early discharge of Service members based upon opposition to repeal or to serving or living with gay and lesbian Service members...Service members may request to be voluntarily discharged under the Military Department Secretary's plenary authority.

across-the-board rewriting of contracts on all service personnel without "indefinite" status would unnecessarily create a burden of paperwork and waste untold resources and time. The report then goes on to point out that chaplains who wish to leave the service due to their objection to the repeal and their inability to serve with homosexual service members can separate by having their endorsing agency drop their endorsement. The loss of endorsement, the report correctly notes, will lead to an administrative separation. It should be noted that this is nothing new; such an option is always available to chaplains who wish to separate from the service. In this case, the working group for implementation of the repeal is just stating the fact that chaplains have an option that most military service members do not. It does not appear to be malicious, but rather a reasoned response to the widely publicized concerns of evangelical leaders. It should further be noted that these words regarding the chaplain's option are given after the report had already addressed the major concern of most within the military chaplaincy: the possible infringement upon the chaplain's first amendment rights to freedom of religion and free speech.

The implementation report notes and affirms the constitutional rights of chaplains (and all service members who object to homosexuality on religious grounds). It states:

> Policies regarding Service members' individual expression and free exercise of religion already exist and are adequate...Service members, to include chaplains, will neither be encouraged nor required to change their personal views and religious beliefs; they must, however, continue to respect and serve with others who hold different views and beliefs. Specifically for chaplains, the existing guidance developed by and for our chaplains, should be reiterated as part of any education and training concerning repeal. These regulations strike an appropriate balance between protecting a chaplain's First Amendment freedoms and a chaplain's duty to care for all.[7]

The point here seems to be that any given service member's religious objections to homosexuality should be treated in much the same way

---

As under currently policy, such discretionary discharge may only be granted when the Military Department Secretary has determined the early separation would be in the best interest of the Service." Johnson and Ham, co-chairs, *Support Plan for Implementation,* 24 and 57.

7. Ibid., 16.

as religious objections to competing religions. Evangelical chaplains are allowed to proclaim the exclusivity of salvation in Christ in the context of their ministry work, but are not allowed to proselytize. Similarly, chaplains can proclaim the sinfulness of homosexuality in the context of their ministry work, but are not allowed to engage in protracted or heated discussions in times and places where those who may not wish to be part of the debate will be exposed nonetheless. If a member of another faith group comes for counseling, the chaplain has an obligation to make every effort to get a chaplain or qualified religious leader of the service member's faith group to talk to the individual. Similarly, if a gay man or lesbian comes for counseling, the chaplain should try to find a counselor who finds his/her lifestyle acceptable (assuming the issues is one in which his/her homosexuality is a factor). Thus, the implementation report specifies some protection for chaplains: "Chaplains, in the context of their religious ministry, are not required to take actions that are inconsistent with their religious beliefs. Existing policy regarding chapalins' free exercise of religion and duty to care for all continues to apply."[8]

Thus, at least from the standpoint of the authors of the report, the concerns of many within the chaplaincy are unfounded. However, the minimalist approach to addressing these very complex issues suffers from a severe lack of clarity. For example, the previous statement assumes that there is an agreed-upon definition of "context of their religious ministry." More specific guidance regarding what are and what are not acceptable ways to express religious concerns about homosexuality is needed. Similarly, more direct guidance on when a chaplain is considered to be working in the context of his religious ministry and when he is not is called for. This position that the existing regulations are adequate to address all these issues, while seemingly reasonable, is terribly naive.

Retired Army Chaplain (COL) Dennis Camp claims that the concerns of evangelicals are unfounded, referring to them as a "smoke screen." He argues that a distinction should be made between the legal and moral issues: "They have made it an issue because they want to fight this thing on moral grounds . . . That's not the kind of fight it is. It's a civil rights issue."[9] Camp's claim is based on the questionable (though popular in American culture) assumption that a clear distinction exists between legal and moral issues. This assumption is vigorously debated

8. Ibid., 50.

9. Quoted in Hagerty, "Chaplains Worry About Careers," http://www.npr.org.

in philosophical and legal circles and will be addressed later, but even if it is granted, it seems that Camp has missed the point. The concerns of chaplains are legal as well as moral; both are in play and legitimate. The First Amendment rights of Christians to hold, and act upon, their religious conviction that homosexual behavior (at a minimum) is immoral, is what is at stake. Additionally, it should be noted that the sharp division between legal, religious, and moral concerns, especially with reference to civil rights, cannot be sustained. Civil rights have traditionally been understood as "God-given," though the meaning of this has morphed into a less religious conviction as American society has become more secular. But while the religious basis for civil rights may be questioned today, there can be no doubt that there is a moral basis. Even the proponents of homosexual rights use morality-based language to make their case: to violate one's civil rights is not merely a legal faux-pas; it is a moral outrage! Thus, what is at stake are two competing moral positions, both with claims to protections under the First and Fourteenth Amendments. Homosexuals argue for the right to privacy under the Free Speech clause of the First Amendment (the same legal justification for so-called, "reproductive rights"), while chaplains argue for the right to practice their faith without fear of repercussions under the protection of the Free Exercise clause of the First Amendment.

While the legal issues surely need to be addressed, it seems that it is somewhat premature, as no adverse legal action has been taken against chaplains speaking out against homosexual practice. A court challenge seems doomed to failure, as it is doubtful that standing or damages can be proved. Additionally, it seems that these concerns can more appropriately be addressed by those in the legal profession and the courts rather than the chaplaincy. Attorneys for the DoD and for chaplains, if wrongly disciplined or dismissed from service for speaking from conviction, should battle these issues in the courts.

Unbiblical Nature of Homosexuality

Second, chaplains may appeal to biblical arguments against homosexuality in an effort to combat the wisdom of repeal and to argue against open homosexual service. A strong biblical case surely can, and must be made against homosexual practice and its acceptance within society, and as ministers of biblical truth, it is wholly appropriate for the chaplain to make it. Many gay lobbyists and proponents of the mainstreaming of gay lifestyles have recognized the ongoing powerful force of biblical morality in American culture, and have sought to mount arguments against claims that the Bible condemns homosexuality. These arguments take many forms, from critical dismissal of difficult passages, to limiting biblical condemnation to homosexual practice within paganism and idolatry, to claims that homosexual couples are held up as exemplars within the biblical narratives (e.g., David & Jonathan). All of these efforts are designed to argue that the Bible does not declare homosexuality an abomination worthy of condemnation. For example, Helminiak can boldly proclaim, "The Bible does NOT condemn homosexuality as such but is, rather, neutral on the matter."[10] So an answer ought to be given.[11]

The problem with using biblical arguments against homosexuality to challenge the repeal of DADT is that, while biblical morality is still a political force to be reckoned with, it cannot serve as a basis for legislation that will stand the test of judicial scrutiny (at least not at this point in our nation's history). That is, because of the power that biblical morality wields within the political arena, one may persuade legislators to, as it were, repeal the repeal, but in a country where any suggestion that religion and law are linked is met with great consternation, it is doubtful that such a move would go unchallenged. Further, it is beyond doubt that the Supreme Court would rule against a continuing ban on homosexual service which is grounded in biblical faith and reasons.

the challenge

Pragmatic Issues/Unit Cohesion and Effectiveness

A third strategy some chaplains have adopted to questioning the repeal has been to note the various pragmatic problems which will invariably attend open homosexual service. As already noted, some chaplains have expressed concern over the Strong Bonds program, that homosexual couples may seek permission to attend and when denied, could file charges of harassment against the chaplain in charge. This, it seems to me, should be the cause of little concern at this time, even with the Obama Administration's stance on same-sex marriage and its refusal to enforce the Defense of Marriage Act [DOMA]. If the federal government were to officially recognize same-sex marriages, then there could be a problem, but it does not do so at this time. Just as the federal

10. Helminiak, "The Ethics of Sex," 261.

11. See chapter 4 of this book, "'An Abomination?': Homosexuality, the Bible and Christian Theology."

government does not recognize "common law" marriages (which some states recognize) and does not give benefits to common law spouses, so also it seems doubtful it will give benefits to homosexual spouses even though some states recognize the marriages. Thus, just as chaplains can exclude co-habitating couples (even those with supposed common law marriages), so also they will be able to exclude homosexual couples, at least until the Supreme Court rules on the Constitutionality of DOMA. If it is deemed Constitutional, then same-sex marriages will not be recognized by the federal government, no matter what the Executive Branch wants, and that should be the end of it.

Other pragmatic issues have been raised as well, many having to do with various logistical problems associated with homosexual integration and the looming threat of a spate of sexual harassment charges. For example, it has been suggested that separate shower facilities and quarters should be provided for gay and lesbian service members, in order to guard against their being accused (either wrongly or rightly) of sexual harassment.[12] The DoD has sought to address this issue by denying the request and ordering service members to conduct themselves with professionalism and respect toward others.

The most common pragmatic argument has to do with the negative effect homosexual service will have upon military readiness and effectiveness due to a breakdown in unit cohesion. The issue of unit cohesion and effectiveness is one of considerable interest to all military personnel, chaplains included. After all, the lives of all service members depend in large part (at least in combat situations) upon the members of the unit working well together under particularly stressful conditions. Historically, the military has argued against homosexual service based on pragmatic concerns,

12. Those who have complained that homosexuals should not be allowed to share shower facilities with their heterosexual counterparts have a legitimate concern. If "professionalism" were an adequate response to such concerns, then it would seem that separate facilities for male and female members would not be needed. This fact notwithstanding, it seems to me that the greater danger here is to the "outed" homosexual service members, for several reasons. First, they could be falsely charged with harassment by those who wrongly perceive their natural glances at their surroundings as leering. Second, they could face physical attack by those who wrongly conclude that they are having lustful thoughts about them while in the open shower facility. Third, they could be falsely accused by those who are opposed to homosexual service and see this as a way of cleansing the force (or at least the unit). There are virtually innumerable ways in which open service could lead to false charges of inappropriate relationships, fraternization, or sexual harassment. The DoD has not adequately addressed this myriad of concerns.

the most common having to do with the detrimental effects it would have on military culture, unit cohesion, and the warrior ethos.

Retired General H. Norman Schwarzkopf testified before the Senate Armed Services Committee that open homosexuality in the military would destroy "the very bonding that is so important for the unit's survival in war," predicting that, ultimately, it will result in the U.S. having a "second-class armed force" and service members being "forced to execute orders they don't believe in." A. J. Bacevich, executive director of The Foreign Policy Institute of The Paul H. Nitze School of Advanced International Studies, and no friend to the continued exclusion of homosexual service, summarizes the argument: "No amount of money can buy cohesion, morale, esprit, discipline; these qualities arise out of the very essence of what it means to be a soldier, something which military leaders alone understand and for which they alone should retain proprietary responsibility. For the ignorant to tamper with the fabric of military life—its distinctive culture—simply to satisfy the dubious demands of some political constituency is to place the nation's security at risk."[13] While some may find Bacevich's summary a bit condescending and paternalistic, it gets at the essential components of the argument, which can be summarized in three propositions: (1) The military has a unique and separate culture which helps foster esprit de corps, (2) such esprit de corps is a necessary component of a successful fighting force, and (3) homosexual service undermines that cohesion.

Bacevich questions the first two assertions and therefore believes homosexual service is compatible with modern military service. First, he argues that the concept of military culture is largely a thing of the past, noting that, for a variety of reasons, in the post-Vietnam era, "the integrity of American military culture has given way to pressures tending to make the job of being a soldier more and more like any other job in post-industrial society."[14] Second, he points to the success of the air campaign during Operation Desert Storm to question the necessity of unit cohesion for military success: precision-guided missiles and other technologies are what win wars in the modern age and therefore, technology and the skills needed to exploit its potential is most critical, not

13. Bacevich, "Military Culture and Effectiveness," 44.

14. Ibid., 46. As evidence of this claim, Bacevich cites the growing number of military spouses who follow careers of their own, increased use of business terminology within military units, and the trend among military members, especially leadership, to choose off-post/base housing rather than BOQ.

small-unit ground force operations.[15] It is worth noting that the major studies that have historically been cited regarding the tie of unit cohesion to military performance (the Shils-Janowitz study of de-integration of the Wehrmacht, Marshall's study, *Men Against Fire*, and Stouffer's *American Soldier*) have been questioned by some.[16] David Segal, professor of sociology, government, and public affairs at the University of Maryland, claims that though they are interesting, they "have absolutely no value as scientific research."[17] But this does not mean that the conclusions to the studies were false; it only means that their methods were either flawed or inconclusive, and while Bacevich's arguments may have worked well at the time of writing, the wars in Iraq and Afghanistan have proven them wrong. Ground forces are still needed to win wars, and small-unit operations are most effective. Such operations do seem to function better when there is a high state of morale and strong unit cohesion.

But what of the third proposition—that open service by homosexuals is destructive of unit cohesion? At first glance, some may be inclined to accept it, while others may be dismissive. There are some good reasons to question it. First, there are documented cases of homosexuals who have served admirably in the armed forces—even openly—and received recognition and honors from their commanders and peers alike. In some cases, when steps were taken to remove them from service, their commanders and senior leadership came to their defense. Surely such concrete examples, even though admittedly anecdotal, carry some weight!

Robert MacCoun, a social psychologist who served on a committee working under the auspices of the RAND Corporation when it was commissioned by the Clinton Administration to study the effects of lifting the ban on gay military service, notes that most studies of group dynamics make a distinction between social and task cohesion. Social cohesion

15. Ibid. There is some truth to his point that competence is most important for success. When my life is at stake, I want those upon whom it depends to work well together, but more importantly, to be skilled/competent, and to act with a high degree of professionalism. This is not only possible, but to be expected whether homosexuals serve or not. For example, consider a situation in which a unit comes under attack and some members are injured. Just as under DADT, I would expect homosexuals who have to hide their sexuality to act professional, and render proper aid, comfort, etc. to those who oppose homosexuality, so also I would expect heterosexual opponents of the repeal to treat injured homosexual unit members if the ban were lifted.

16. See Shils and Janowitz, "Cohesion and Disintegration in the Wehrmacht," 280–315; Marshall, *Men Against Fire;* Samuel Stouffer, et. al. *The American Soldier.*

17. Belkin and Bateman, eds., *Don't Ask, Don't Tell: Debating the Gay Ban,* 91.

refers to the interpersonal relations in the group, or how well the members like one another, while task cohesion has to do with the shared commitment of group members toward the group goal(s). MacCoun points out that many studies which fail to account for this difference actually get the relationship between cohesion and performance backwards. While there is a correlation, sometimes a lack of cohesion results from poor group performance rather than poor performance flowing from a lack of cohesion. Still, even taking this into account, the question of a breakdown in cohesion as a reaction to the repeal of DADT is still a valid concern. But MacCoun argues that in many cases, poor social cohesion does not always lead to poor task cohesion or performance. In fact, he notes that performance can be negatively tied to strong social cohesion: "...task cohesion is linked to performance. Having a shared sense of mission improves performance. But social cohesion—liking each other—is not correlated with performance. And in fact, for a variety of reasons, high social cohesion is actually detrimental to performance."[18]

Some argue that the timing of the repeal implementation—wartime versus peacetime—should be determinative, but not the way one may initially think. Desch argues that, while task cohesion tends to matter most in times of war and that homosexual service affects task cohesion only minimally, it is really social cohesion that rules the day in a military environment during peacetime, and that open homosexual service could lead to a breakdown in this area. So, for example, Desch notes, "...we ought to think about making this change in wartime or in a period of fairly intense international security threats, rather than doing it in this period [2000] of relatively diffuse and amorphous threats."[19] According to Desch, the analogy to race and gender integration works well here. Racial integration was more easily accepted because it took place in the context of the Korean War.

Most experts agree that leadership and regulation are vital factors in successful implementation of any integration of gays in the military, but even here, there are mixed analyses. For example, Laura Miller argues that the key is not just leadership, generally construed, but specific leaders on the ground supporting implementation of integration: "We need to get away from the idea that if we just have the right policy or the right regulation, then we could make service members behave the way we want them to. . . .The evidence shows that when the leadership fail to support

18. Ibid., 78–79.

19. Ibid., 88.

an issue, any change will not be effective."[20] So, unit cohesion is a military issue that falls in the purview of the command, and for this reason, it is not an avenue that the chaplain should pursue in responding to the repeal of DADT.

Ultimately, the problem with all of the pragmatic objections to homosexual service is not their veracity or plausibility. In fact, it seems that the DoD has not taken them as seriously as it ought, and the armed services could be overburdened with logistical and personnel issues as a result of its failure to take greater precautions in preventing these difficulties before integration. The problem with these objections is that they are not the purview of the chaplain(s), but are properly the concern of the commander(s). Thus, while there are legitimate concerns, many in which the chaplain himself has a personal interest and stake, they are not appropriate for the chaplain to raise, at least not publicly. He should let the commanders and non-commissioned officers take care of the troops and remember his role as advisor.

The "Sanctity" of Freedom of Conscience

As noted in the introduction, then, it may seem that if the repeal of DADT should not be opposed on legal, biblical, or pragmatic grounds, it should be supported. Some chaplains may conclude that, all options being exhausted, the only response one can have is to support open homosexual service. To be sure, at least in some ways, it appears to involve a civil rights issue and civil rights concerns. It does seem to touch upon one of the most sacred rights in American culture, the right to personal freedom.[21] Persons should, generally, not be discriminated against for hiring; all persons have a right to expect to be given the opportunity to earn a living. In fact, this could be seen (and has been by the Courts) as a by-product or direct implication of the God-given rights articulated in the Constitution. It is somewhat puzzling that those who are against homosexual lifestyles should be opposed to homosexual military service; after all, if a homosexual wants to put his/her life on the line in defense of the country, why should anyone

20. Ibid., 90.

21. I have written elsewhere of the danger, particularly among military chaplains, of making an idol of personal freedom. While part of the justification for military chaplaincy, and every chaplain must uphold individual autonomy with respect to religious devotion, care must be taken to avoid making freedom so sacred, that autonomy or personal choice/preference overshadows religious conviction and for the Christian, biblical fidelity.

else care? I must admit that I always feel a bit of indignation at those who offer up sage advice on the topic when they have not served in the military themselves; it seems that they have not earned the right to comment on the topic and certainly not to criticize brave homosexual men or women who have served. They should thank them!

However, we should note that this general principle does have some exceptions which are also associated with those same rights. Thus, certain kinds of employment entail a measure of discrimination in hiring policies; certain employers or organizations, by their very nature, require or prohibit certain beliefs, lifestyles, etc., of their employees, but this should not be seen as violating civil rights, but rather should be seen as a proper application of what is typically referred to as "common sense." For example, consider the organization, the National Association for the Advancement of Colored People (NAACP); no one would fault executives of the organization for failing to consider a candidate for a position who is a member of the Ku Klux Klan or who has expressed (and never retracted) racist beliefs. It is assumed that employment by the NAACP entails a commitment to the ideals, values, and goals of the organization, and that certain views on race simply disqualify one from consideration, but this hiring policy should not be seen as discriminatory, or at least a sort of discrimination that violates the liberties of the individual in question.

Pro-homosexual lobbyists have constantly attempted to couch the discussion in terms of civil rights, likening their struggle to those of suffrage (for women) and racial equality (for African Americans). This has led some to characterize the opponents of homosexuality as a legitimate lifestyle as "bigoted" or "homophobic." But as may be guessed, this oversimplifies the issue. In a relatively recent article in the Washington Post, Sandhya Somashekhar points out the difference in attitudes from chaplains on this move toward integration. She writes, "Officials say they did not encounter objections from chaplains during past efforts to integrate African Americans and women into the military. But homosexuality presents a particular difficulty because many religions object to it on moral grounds."[22] This is an important point, one lost of many of the supporters of homosexual rights. Religions are not inherently discriminatory or prone to discriminatory attitudes. In fact, they have often [and unfortunately, not always] led the ranks in the fight for social justice. Problems arise when a secular morality and its notion of justice are at

22. Somashekhar, "Pentagon 'don't ask, don't tell' report," http://www.washingtonpost.com.

odds with religious morality (as in the cases of abortion and homosexuality for many).[23])

Natural Law and Virtue Ethics

Natural Law, Homosexuality, and Procreation

The most common natural law arguments against homosexual acts and marriage have come in the form of appeals to the natural or proper use of sex and its role in human bonding. The reproductive nature of male-female sex acts is normally appealed to as constitutive of proper sexual relationships. For example, George argues that marriage is a one-flesh communion of persons that can only take place in the context of reproductive-type acts (because a biological connection takes place in actual reproduction).[24] Thus, proper sexual relations in marriage do not treat the bodies as instruments or means to an end—for pleasure, as expressions of love, or even to reproduce—but rather serve the union of marriage itself. He writes, "The central and justifying point of sex is not pleasure (or even the sharing of pleasure) per se, however much sexual pleasure is sought—as an aspect of the perfection of marital union; the point of sex, rather, is marriage itself, considered as a bodily ('one-flesh') union of persons consummated and actualized by acts that are reproductive in type."[25] He contends that marriage is not only constituted in love, but also in a "one-flesh communion of persons," which proponents of same-sex marriage deny. According to George, the union effected in reproductive-type acts distinguishes them at a fundamental level from the only types of sexual acts available to same-sex partners. Opponents of this view typically characterize it as an instrumentality of a different sort; rather

23. For many evangelicals, the pro-life movement is to be seen as women-friendly, not the opposite.

24. John Finnis, responding to Stephen Macedo's complaint that people, or in his words, "penises and vaginas" do not biologically unite, but rather only sperms and eggs do, writes, "...one might declare that sperm and egg unite only physically and only their pronuclei are biologically united. But it would be more realistic to acknowledge that the whole process of copulation, involving as it does the brains of the man and woman, their nerves, blood, vaginal and other secretions, and coordinated activity is biological through and through. Finnis, "Law, Morality, and 'Sexual Orientation,'" sec. 5.

25. George, *Clash of Orthodoxies*, 78–79.

than seeing sex as a means to pleasure or as an expression of love, this view sees sex as a means to procreation, and on the basis of this sort of argument, they charge proponents of traditional marriage with creating a double standard. So, for example, Stephen Macedo asks what the point of sex in an infertile marriage is, and avers that it could not be procreation; it would have to be something like mutual pleasure or communication of love.[26] George denies this argument because it presupposes that the value of sex in marriage is, and can only be, instrumental, but the traditional view is that the value of sex is the intrinsic good of marriage itself, which "is actualized in sexual acts which unite spouses biologically and, thus, interpersonally."[27]

George's argument here seems to beg the question, suffers from circularity, or is contrived [I must admit that I have been unable to put my finger on which, as yet]. He claims that true marriage requires "reproductive-type acts" because marriage is not mere contract or loving relationship, but is a biological union of two persons into one being insofar as in reproduction, the male and female components unite to form a new being, and the union of sperm and egg cannot be separated from the entirety of the reproductive act. But he does not want to say that only sex within marriage which has reproduction as its goal is good or allowable, for that would, in his view, reduce marital sex to the same kind of instrumentality that his opponents adopt. Thus, he claims that infertile couples can marry and engage in sex because it is "reproductive" in form, which is the basis of the [biological] union of man and woman. He writes, ". . . the intrinsic, and not merely instrumental, good of marital communion gives spouses reason to fulfill the behavioral conditions of procreation even in circumstances in which they know the non behavioral conditions do not obtain. This is true just in case the fulfillment of the behavioral conditions of reproduction is, in truth, unitive."[28]

While there may be good reason to question the logic of this assertion—the biological union is constituted in the actual event of reproduction and therefore, unions which cannot reproduce appear to preclude such a union, even if similar forms are present—what seems most problematic with George's argument are the prospects for sexual expression

26. Macedo, "Homosexuality and the Conservative Mind," 278.

27. George, *Clash of Orthodoxies*, 82.

28. Ibid., 83.

(within marriage) which are not reproductive in form. That is, either George (and Finnis, etc.) has to claim that non-reproductive-type acts (e.g., oral sex) are out of bounds for all persons, even married couples, which seems to be the most logical conclusion, or they are only allowable within marriage (or heterosexual relationships?) because the marriage relationship has already been justified by the biological union through reproductive-type acts and therefore, anything goes. But this seems specious and contrived, at best.[29]

Suppose, though, that one does not want to rule out non-reproductive sex acts within heterosexual marriage, but finds the appeal to reproductive-type acts as justifying all else to be a questionable move. Is there any other argument he can mount against homosexual acts or homosexuality in the military, without the appeal to procreation as constitutive of proper human sexuality? It seems that one can construct an argument which involves the use of natural law philosophy and virtue ethics to argue that homosexual service is detrimental to military community, core values, and good order and discipline. It should be noted that this argument, while quite possibly applicable to American society and culture at large, will be limited to an examination of the effects of open homosexual service in the military at this time. George makes the point well that, while morality can and should be legislated, it is always context-dependent, even if a timeless or universal morality is accepted:

> There are often compelling reasons for legally tolerating moral wrongdoing; these reasons are, however, prudential. As such, sound legislative judgment in the matter of prohibition or toleration will necessarily take into account circumstances that are local and contingent. To say whether a certain form of what one reasonably judges to be immoral ought to be prohibited or tolerated by law, then, requires an understanding of the invariably complex circumstances of particular communities at particular times.[30]

29.. There is another problem which arises with arguments such as George's; it seems to reduce marriage to the biological union which takes place in heterosexual sex. But this suggests that all heterosexual sex—within and without marriage—is thereby sanctioned, since it always involves "reproductive-type acts." While George does make arguments for monogamy and exclusivism within marriage as important for stability and the like, his argument seems unable to escape the conclusion. Time and space constraints do not permit an extended discussion of this issue here.

30. George, *Making Men Moral*, viii.

The argument I wish to make draws upon an analogy between acceptance of homosexuality and acceptance of pornography, such that, the philosophical basis allowing or excluding the one, may also serve as the philosophical basis for allowing or excluding the other. As it stands, anti-pornography and decency laws still remain on the books in many states and local communities, and the Supreme Court has consistently ruled in favor of their Constitutionality, though admittedly by a narrow margin. Conversely, since *Lawrence v. Texas*, the Court has essentially ruled Unconstitutional all state and community anti-sodomy laws.[31] These rulings, it seems to me, are at odds, but it is not my purpose here to question the wisdom or logic of the High Court. Rather, I only seek to determine if the ethical rationale for censorship of pornography may be used to question the morality of the repeal of DADT. In order to do this, we must first examine the general argument for censorship, and then its application to the question of pornography and obscenity.

Natural Law, Virtue, and Censorship

The philosophical basis for laws upholding censorship begins with basic assumptions about the nature of Society and the nature of Law. It also makes assumptions regarding the necessary components for a liberal democratic society. Each will be considered in turn.

Nature of Society/Community

Proponents of censorship see society as a definable group of persons with shared goals, values, desires, etc. It is not merely a composite of individuals, but is itself an entity by the union of persons. By definition, then, there is a core set of unifying values that are typically manifested in shared goals and aspirations. Inherent in this view of society is the claim that it entails more than a raw utilitarian arrangement of the Hobbesian sort. Societies are not formed merely to protect personal interests, but rather have deeper, more important—more uniquely human—purposes in mind. Humans are, by nature, social creatures and have psychological, emotional, and (dare I say) spiritual needs that can only be satisfied

31. *Lawrence v. Texas*, 539 US 558 (2003). For discussion of this case, see chapter 3, "'Rainbow Rights?': Homosexuality, Political Activity and the Law,'" in this volume.

and/or met when living in community.[32] It should be clear that on this view of society, its preservation is dependent upon the maintenance and inculcation (within the people) of those goals, values, desires, and the like, or at least of virtues which point persons toward the realization and attainment of those goals, desires, etc. This leads to the second basic idea in the argument that has to do with the purpose of law.

Purpose of Law

Proponents of censorship reject the majoritarian view of the function of law, derived from John Stuart Mill, which holds that law is meant only to maintain the public peace by punishing particular acts which injure specific persons or disturb the peace, and that law is, for all intents and purposes, morally neutral.[33] The claim that morality cannot be legislated is explicitly rejected. In fact, they claim that it should be obvious that the very nature of law and the concepts upon which it rests is dependent on some notion of morality; justice, ideals, and the concept of right and wrong are all axiological concepts. While George has correctly noted that laws cannot make men moral in a direct or immediate way, he still claims that law has a legitimate positive role in promoting morality. He writes, "Nevertheless, it is an evident fact that laws regularly, and often profoundly, affect notions abroad in society about what is morally acceptable, forbidden, and required. People shape their own lives (and often treat others differently) in light of these notions."[34]

Thus, law can play an important part in character formation and virtue development, and it does so in at least four ways: 1) prevents some levels of self-corruption by criminalizing certain immoral behaviors; 2) prevents bad examples that others might emulate; 3) creates a moral climate in society which is conducive to morals formation and development; and 4) educates people about right and wrong.[35] There is no need

32. Aristotle developed these ideas in his examination of the *polis* in his *Politics*.

33. Clor argues that those who follow Mill, if consistent, would render the law morally neutral: "No act could be prohibited because of its unethical or vicious character. The law would tend to become little more than a body of convenient utilitarian rules for the protection of life and property and the prevention of violence, physical or psychological." Clor, *Obscenity and Public Morality*, 179.

34. George, *Making Men Moral*, 2–3.

35. It is readily acknowledged that inner (or what may be termed, "spiritual") corruption cannot directly be affected by law; an individual may entertain all sorts of

to address here all the concerns one might have with such a conception of the function of law: paternalism, forced or coerced homogeneity, lack of equality among the citizenry, "tyranny" of the majority, etc., but rather to note that this is the view of law adopted here. George has already convincingly answered the strongest of them.[36] Thus, it is argued that the rule of law contributes to moral formation, but it should also be noted that the way it does so is dependent upon the nature of the particular society and its politic. This leads to the third major component of the argument for censorship in the United States: the nature of democracy.

Nature of Democracy

In a democratic society, the law must be used to both preserve individual freedom and rights, but also to promote those virtues which unite its members and which are deemed necessary for its survival. It may be thought that in a liberal democratic society, *freedom* would serve this unifying function, and in fact some libertarians have argued that a sense of community can be formed around the ideal of personal freedom; that the concept of individual liberty and the value of tolerance bind persons together in fraternal relationship. As Macedo writes, "Liberalism stands, above all, for the positive value of freedom, freedom to devise, criticize, revise and pursue a plan of life, and it calls upon people to respect the rights of others whether or not they share the same goals and ideals."[37]

However, there is good reason to doubt this conception, as the individuality which Macedo envisions seems to work against fraternity. As Harry Clor puts it, "Isn't it rather counterintuitive that people can be truly bound together in anything approaching a fraternal association on the basis of a principle of personal autonomism—the sovereign right of each individual to choose independently his own goals or ideals and go his own way? A celebration of individuality above all else, and a policy of maximizing it, might have some valuable results, but it's hard to see how communal

evils within his own mind. However, the law can prevent the further corruption of the individual by preventing, or at least giving incentive for refraining from, that activity, and thereby incurring the corruption that comes from actually engaging in immoral behavior. Similarly, it is assumed that the law can be given enough force to actually convince some persons to refrain from immoral activity in which they would have otherwise engaged.

36. See George, *Making Men Moral.*

37. Macedo, *Liberal Virtues*, 258.

consensus or identity could be one of them."[38] Thus, it does *not* appear to be the case that a shared commitment to individual freedom can serve as the basis for democracy, but to say this is to in no way minimize or make light of the importance of freedom in a society so constituted. In fact, republican forms of government are designed to mitigate against the problems of pure democracy; just because shared values are constitutive of society does not mean that the majority's concerns or desires can always take precedence over the individual's. Thus, as Clor maintains, a liberal society must seek to strike a balance between honoring the beliefs and desires of the majority while protecting the rights of the minority. He notes, "Of course, we value our multiplicity, but that isn't all that we value and all that we are. Insofar as a kind of *liberal community* is what is wanted, our respect for diversity and need for unity have to be accommodated in some sort of balance. Consequently, the expectations and demands of both radical purists and radical communitarians will be frustrated, and appropriately so, in favor of the search for a middle ground."[39]

So, for democracy to be tenable, some values in the citizenry are necessary beyond a love and celebration of freedom. That is, there are certain virtues, the inculcation of which, help make the people capable of self-rule and of being ruled. Various lists have been proposed for which virtues that might entail, but they typically include something like self-control and temperance, respect, selflessness, neighborliness, honesty, loyalty, and the like. Clor argues that democracies are particularly needful of a virtuous populace; it is in the government's own self-interests to ensure that the people have a sense of selflessness: "The argument that citizen responsibilities cannot be performed in the absence of certain virtues of self-discipline is most suitably addressed to politics in which the citizens participate in governing and in the making of public policy."[40]

At times, though, the two roles of the law—preservation of freedom and development of virtue—can be at odds. When one's personal choices and/or preferences lead him to engage in activity which is destructive of these core virtues, it is up to the legislature (and often times later, the judiciary) to determine which should prevail. At the heart of the controversies over censorship is the question of whether it is more injurious for society to limit freedom or to permit vulgarity, obscenity, debauchery,

38. Clor, *Public Morality and Liberal Society*, 55.

39. Ibid., 59.

40. Clor, *Obscenity and Public Morality*, 188.

and the like. Proponents of censorship argue that there are some cases where a limitation of freedom is, at a minimum, the lesser of two evils.[41]

Argument Against Pornography

Philosophical arguments for censoring pornography have tended to follow the foregoing argument for censorship in general, and have claimed that it has deleterious effects on society at large. Specifically, claims are typically made against its tendency to corrupt virtues such as respect, self-control, and temperance, which are necessary for the survival of the society.

It destroys mutuality and respect in a variety of ways in both the participants ("actors" seems an inadequate descriptor here) and the consumers. Perhaps the major complaint against pornography is that it debases humanity by objectifying the participants—by viewing them as objects to be used in order to perform a given function—and debases human sexuality by viewing it instrumentally, or as a means to an end. This treatment of sexuality and of the human body can lead to self-hatred in the participants, but it can also lead the consumer to adopt an essentially instrumental view of humanity, including himself. Respect of others, as well as self-respect is in dire straits when humanity is so diminished.

The instrumental view of sexuality which pornography promotes also leads to a deep-seated selfishness in the consumer, for, building upon the lack of respect for and objectification of the other, it arouses and encourages unbridled passion and lust with self-gratification as its ultimate goal. Such a selfishness which has little or no regard for the humanity of the other and places personal fulfillment above all else is not conducive to community or to the rule of law (not to mention the notion of public service as a good in itself!). In this way, some have argued that pornography threatens the very foundation of liberal democratic society by creating a citizenry which is, for all intents and purposes, uncontrollable and ungovernable.

Berns harkens back to the arguments of 18th and 19th century thinkers (Tocqueville & Rousseau to name two), who noted that a healthy sense of shame is both natural to humanity and necessary for democracy, and ultimately, the rule of law. If humans are naturally inclined to community, and such requires restraint for proper rule and social order,

41. Of course, in some cases, the limitation on freedom can itself be a good, insofar as it can teach temperance, humility, or other core values.

then the unnatural disposition of shamelessness can make governance virtually impossible. Anarchy or tyranny seems to follow. Berns writes, "There is, therefore, a political danger in promoting shamelessness and the fullest self-expression or indulgence. To live together requires rules and a governing of the passions, and those who are without shame will be unruly and unrulable; having lost the ability to restrain themselves, they will have to be ruled by others. Tyranny is the natural and inevitable mode of government for the shameless and self-indulgent who have carried liberty beyond any restraint, natural and conventional."[42]

However, one need not be quite so apocalyptic in order to argue that pornography is destructive of society. George has convincingly shown that society is dissolved when a breakdown of social cohesion occurs, even if social order remains; people may continue to live in relative peace and security while being detached from one another. In his attempt to defend Lord Devlin's claim that the acceptance of gross immorality—even if performed in the privacy of one's own house—leads to social disintegration, against Hart's empirical counterargument that history does not bear this out, George argues that societal breakdown does not necessitate a situation in which anarchy reigns. He summarizes what he takes to be the strongest version of Devlin's argument: "His claim was not the trivial one according to which changes in a society's morality by definition entail the 'destruction' of that society and its replacement by a new one. Rather, it was the substantial, partly axiological and partly 'empirical', claim that, in consequence of the erosion of a dominant morality, social cohesion, that is, integration understood as something worthwhile in itself (independently of its utility in supporting social order), would be lost."[43] Thus, selfishness may not necessarily lead to widespread crime and violence, but it can nevertheless harm social cohesion and the interrelatedness of persons within the community, and in *this* way, it can be destructive of society.

Pornography also violates the virtue of temperance because it puts on display what most people believe to be properly private, namely human sexuality. The naked body and sex acts, are properly intimate, private matters, and they are degraded when made public. Some have argued that shame and embarrassment are natural to humans, and that pornography detracts from these virtues. For example, Kristol argues

42. Berns, "Pornography versus Democracy," 20.

43. George, *Making Men Moral*, 66.

that anthropological and sociological studies of human sexuality point to the uniquely human sense of privacy regarding sexuality. As he puts it, "Our 'private parts' are indeed private, and not merely because convention prescribes it. This particular convention is indigenous to the human race. In practically all primitive tribes, men and women cover their private parts; and in practically all primitive tribes, men and women do not copulate in public."[44]

Thus, Clor summarizes what he refers to as the *traditional ethic* (of sexuality), which is characterized by a decidedly "anti-hedonistic" attitude; it is an ethic of *self-control*, which aspires to human goods beyond mere physical impulses and sensuality, and of *civility*, which views others as individuals worthy of respect and/or honor.[45] He then moves to note the particular aspects of sexuality which give rise to these concerns. Drawing upon the Supreme Court's rationale for its ruling in *Paris Adult Theater v. Slaton*, Clor points to the two key issues: sexuality is particularly vulnerable or prone to distortion and debasement, and it is something of fundamental importance to the well-being of the community. Clor sees the fragility of sexuality to be a function of its unique combination of our most elevated and base sensibilities. It can serve as the utmost expression of deep and abiding love, and it can also be used to meet some of our most basic instinctual urges. He writes, "Eros is the arena for a unique interaction of compelling animal impulses and delicate, distinctively human sensibilities. Frequently it is an arena in which primitive or powerfully self-centered urges and elevated aspirations are in competition for predominance."[46] The point Clor hopes to make is that a kind of self-restraint is necessary with regard to one's life. Individuals must subdue the passions—though not quench them—in order to put any potential means of gratification to the test of propriety by means of rational scrutiny and evaluation. The State has an interest in the development of restraint, and this takes place in the context of communal relationships with some input from the rule of law.

As an interesting (and relevant) aside, morals laws jurisprudence has tended to uphold the local community's right to decide what to allow and what to outlaw with respect to pornographic and/or obscene material. In the landmark *Miller* case, the Supreme Court ruled that obscene material does not enjoy protection under the First Amendment's Free

44. Kristol, "Case for Liberal Censorship," 48.

45. Clor, *Public Morality and Liberal Society*, 63.

46. Ibid., 64.

Speech Clause. While it acknowledged that a strict definition of obscenity cannot be given, it nevertheless allowed for certain criteria to serve as a means for evaluation of any work: 1) Whether the average person, applying contemporary community standards, would find that the work as a whole appeals to the prurient interest; 2) Whether the work depicts or describes sexual conduct in a patently offensive way, and 3) Whether the work as a whole lacks serious literary, artistic, political or scientific value. What is of interest here is that the decision regarding standards is left to the community itself. As Justice Brennan, writing for the majority noted, "It is neither realistic, nor constitutionally sound to read the First Amendment as requiring that the people of Maine or Mississippi accept public depiction of conduct found tolerable in Las Vegas, or New York City."[47] The lack of a national standard has led some to call for a complete abandonment of morals legislation.[48] But the Supreme Court has been reluctant to do so, even in the face of potentially upholding conflicting standards (in different states and communities).[49] This is due in part to the deference given to the rights of the community and its citizens.

The argument for censorship of pornographic and obscene material and depictions, then, has to do with the way that they detract from those virtues deemed valuable to democratic society. They violate the virtues of respect, selflessness, and temperance, and instead promote vices of objectification, self-centeredness/selfishness and intemperance, which could potentially lead to lawlessness and anarchy, and which do diminish a communal sense of mutuality and interconnectedness. Thus, they lead to a breakdown of society, and therefore, the law properly restricts their use/existence.

47. *Miller v. California*, 413 U.S. 15 (1973), 32.

48. See, for example, Cenite, "Federalizing or Eliminating Online Obscenity Law," 25–71. Cenite argues that local laws governing obscenity are too diverse and virtually impossible to enforce, given the global online community, but a national law would encounter pragmatic and constitutional problems. Thus, he suggests, obscenity laws should be eliminated.

49. Wallace argues that obscenity laws cannot use minors as the standard, as doing so would violate the First Amendment. While it is acknowledged that the desire to protect minors from the harmful effects of pornography is a laudable goal, Wallace argues that using criminal statutes to do so is neither the most effective nor the least intrusive method. Wallace, "Congressional Efforts to Protect Minors," 189–98.

Analogy to Homosexuality

Can we say the same thing of homosexuality? Does homosexuality suffer from a lack of restraint, or a lack of self-control? Does it foster the sort of self-centered sexuality whereby those who practice it, like the consumers of pornography, become *infected* with a form of anti-social attitude or focus? It is doubtful that such a case could be made against homosexuality *per se*, in the abstract. However, this is not to say that such a claim could not legitimately be made against the homosexual lobby and agenda in its current manifestation and with specific reference to the repeal of DADT. In fact, it does seem to be the case that the homosexual lobby violates many of these standards and virtues, if not in the same ways, then in sufficiently analogous ways.

It is clear that some homosexuals violate the virtue of respect and objectify others and human sexuality. When one-night-stands are a regular feature of one's life and has become part of that community's culture, there can be no doubt that an instrumental view of sex and the bodies of those involved is in play. Of course, this only speaks against the worst of persons in the homosexual community and can be charged against many a heterosexual. These considerations could be used to justify the legal restriction of casual sex in general, but such an argument is not the goal or aim of this paper. An argument could be made which claims that homosexual sex, because it *cannot* function in a way that is proper to the body's construction, must take an instrumentalist view of sex. That is, one could appeal to teleology in order to charge homosexual sex with objectification of the sex act. This move, though, reverts to something of a procreative natural law position and suffers from the same problems already noted.

There does, though, seem to be a form of objectification that is common among homosexuals and is a constituent part of the homosexual lobby. When one identifies himself/herself primarily in terms of his/her sexual orientation, then an objectification of sorts takes place because much of what makes him/her human is ignored or put in a position of secondary importance. Love, for example, is secondary to the object, or more properly, the nature/gender of the object, of that love. Such a self-identity is dangerous to both the individual and to society. Some may wish to respond that this kind of self-identity was somehow thrust upon homosexuals by an often hostile and even violent society, but this claim cannot be sustained, for self-perception comes not from without, but from within. External factors can have an influencing effect, but can never be determinative. A legal concession to the homosexual lobby feeds and justifies this sort of self-abasement and objectification.

Objectification (which is a derivative of this sort of self-identification), like with pornography, works against the virtue of selflessness and instead cultivates selfishness. An inordinate focus on sexuality, such as that promoted by the homosexual lobby, is at crossed purposes with the ideals of a self-governed people. As Clor puts it, "A people devoted exclusively to the satisfaction of sensual appetites is not, strictly speaking, a citizen body at all. It is a collection of private individuals, each concerned with his private gratifications."[50]

Short argues that the gay rights movement violates the virtue of temperance (he uses the term, "discretion") because, like pornography, it puts sexuality on public display. He writes, "But in essence the 'gay-rights' movement is an attack on privacy and on the very idea of sexual morality. It seeks public approval for every variant of sexual activity, at least among consenting adults, and it makes public display of one's sexuality the norm. It studiously avoids any thought that social cohesion and stability might be adversely affected by total sexual freedom; hence, it denies the virtue of discretion."[51]

Thus far, the argument (if accepted) has only spoken against the radical homosexual lobby and it may appear that it has offered nothing which calls into question the repeal of DADT, but such a conclusion would be wrong. First, it should be obvious that the repeal of DADT, not to mention its original construction and passage, was itself a bow of the government to the homosexual lobby; in fact, repeal of DADT could be seen as the greatest victory of homosexual lobbying efforts since *Lawrence v. Texas*. Second, the argument put forth extolling the value of preserving community and how selfishness is destructive of it speak against the repeal. When integration is forced upon an unwilling society *and* there is a legitimate question or discussion to be had regarding the propriety of the activity or the morality of the issue at hand, that integration is destructive of society and should be seen in negative terms.[52] In this case, the repeal

50. Clor, *Obscenity and Public Morality*, 200.

51. Short, "Gay Rights or Closet Virtues?" 44.

52. The caveat regarding the legitimacy of ongoing discussion/debate regarding the morality of that which is to be integrated (i.e., homosexuality) is what distinguishes the integration of homosexuals into the military from the integration of racial minorities and women into the military. There was no legitimate discussion to

of DADT is detrimental to military culture partly because many within that culture oppose it. While most of the news reports claimed that the DoD-commissioned survey of military members showed that repeal of DADT had widespread support among service persons, the report itself paints a very different picture. It notes that "many" respondents were happy with DADT because they were "more comfortable suspecting someone was gay, rather than knowing for sure."[53] Similarly, "many" respondents expressed concern that a repeal of DADT would undermine what the military stands for because homosexuality is at odds with core military values.[54] In addition, the report notes that "most" of the focus group participants had grave concerns about the way the United States military would be perceived by other countries' militaries and more importantly, by the enemy.[55] It is also detrimental to the military culture because, in forcing itself upon an unwilling society (and here, we are claiming that the military is, in some ways, a distinct society), it shows itself to fail to incarnate core military values such as duty, respect, honor, and selflessness. The fact that the implementation plan has to address the potential tidal wave of requests for early discharge speaks volumes about the negative effect the repeal is expected to have upon military cohesion.

It was noted earlier that a breakdown in social cohesion, even if it is not followed by a concomitant breakdown of social order, can lead to the destruction of a society. Presumably, people can live in proximity to one another in relative peace, even when they are not integrated with one another in close and cohesive relationship, just as married persons can stay together even though they no longer feel any love for one another. But they will no longer constitute a community because the integration which comes from shared values, beliefs, and goals will be lost. This is the argument that military leaders have made against the repeal, but they mistakenly tied the argument to military effectiveness, which may or may

---

be had regarding the equality (in their humanity) of minorities and women. Even the DoD recognizes a difference here, as charges of discrimination due to sexual orientation will not be handled under the Equal Opportunity Program, which handles civil rights complaints and issues. This policy is, perhaps surprisingly, consistent with the Supreme Court jurisprudence, which has typically refused to consider homosexuality cases based on the due process clause of the Fourteenth Amendment (which would lead to the equation of sexual orientation as a protected class, alongside race, creed, religion, and gender).

53. *Support to the DoD Comprehensive Review Working Group*, 32.

54. Ibid., 31–32.

55. Ibid., 31.

not be provable or even true, as noted previously; just as social cohesion does not necessarily lead to a breakdown of social order, so also a loss of unit cohesion does not necessarily lead to a loss of military effectiveness. But nevertheless, something is lost in the unit, and ultimately, in the military itself. As George notes, this loss can be terribly detrimental:

> From the individual citizen's [or military service member's] point of view, what is lost is not necessarily security in one's person and property. One might very well retain *these* goods. The good that is lost, rather, is the good of interpersonal integration. While this good is, in one sense, irreducibly social, it is nevertheless fundamentally the good of individuals who together participate in and realize it. Its loss is their loss. They may continue to live in proximity to one another, perhaps even in a state of peace and mutual accommodation, but they will no longer constitute a society.[56]

Perhaps we could say that, after repeal of DADT, we may have to mourn the loss of the military society. Some may think this to be a good thing; that *that* particular military society—the one which discriminates against homosexuals and women, and which instills a sense of outdated bravado—ought to be destroyed. But the Federal government, in the form of the legislature and the judiciary has recognized the separateness and value of military culture and society. The rules for the military are different from those of American civilian life precisely because, in order to accomplish its mission of prosecuting war, the military must constitute a separate society.

Possible Objections

I am not unaware of the fact that many may wish to dispute the argument I have presented for a variety of reasons. The most immediate complaint that I suspect objectors will raise is that I have constructed a straw man. It may be argued that my characterization of homosexuality with the vices named is simply unfair and false: surely not *all* homosexuals are selfish (at least not in an inordinate way), and not *every* homosexual relationship is characterized by selfishness, intemperance, and the like! Further, the objector may claim, the *fact* that some homosexuals have served admirably

56. George, *Making Men Moral*, 69–70.

and with distinction undermines both the premises and conclusions of the argument.

In response, I should point out that these are highly charged and emotional issues, and therefore, judgments are particularly prone to being clouded, and that is what seems to be in play here, for I nowhere suggested that every homosexual (or even most homosexuals, for that matter!) displays or exhibits an unusual level of selfishness. Similarly, I did not claim that homosexual relationships are inherently flawed because of their grounding in vices such as selfishness, intemperance, and disrespect. While some may wish to make such arguments, I did not do so here and, in fact, expressed doubts about the prospects for success of such an endeavor. Instead, I only meant to call into question the motives, tactics, and actions of the homosexual lobby with specific reference to the repeal of DADT at this time, and therefore, the first two aspects of the objection have no bearing on the issue.

The third aspect—the appeal to honorable service by homosexuals in the past—deserves separate comment because it should properly be seen not only as an objection to opposition of the repeal, but also as a positive argument for open service of homosexuals. In basic form, it claims that some homosexuals have served honorably and contributed to the betterment of the military itself and the war effort in the past, that there is no reason to think present and future homosexuals cannot/will not make similarly beneficial contributions if allowed to serve, and that therefore, the armed forces do themselves a disservice when/if they bar homosexuals from military service.

Much could be said by way of response to this approach. At its heart, it includes an assumption that some homosexuals have, indeed, served admirably, and an assumption that there are truths about how things would in fact be if things were different. Leaving aside the complicated debates over the possibility of true future contingents and counterfactuals, we ought to at least comment on the first assumption. Some opponents of repeal may wish to question the claim that homosexuals served honorably by noting that in most cases, the individual either lied on his/her initial enlistment papers, or did so in his/her ongoing service.

Such an approach would be wrongheaded, not only because it would be a public relations nightmare for the individual, and not only because it would be hypocritical, holding homosexual service members to a standard that is rarely met among any persons (i.e., complete honest and transparency in all areas of life), but most importantly because it would be both false and slanderous. The fact of the matter is that there have been some individuals who, by all accounts, have served honorably and even did so while admitting their homosexuality![57]

Nevertheless, this argument still does not speak against the view presented here, for it considers the whole of the military and the effects of open service on the armed forces as a whole. It does not question the competence or sincerity of individual service members. In fact, the basic point of this pro-homosexual service argument could be sustained while open-service itself is rejected for the reasons given in this chapter. That is, one could agree that barring homosexuals from military service does cost the military quality persons by excluding some competent individuals from the personnel pool, but still reject homosexual service because, on the whole, its current manifestation is destructive of military culture and inculcates values contrary to core military values.

Another objection has to do with other forms of government-mandated integration: racial and gender integration were *forced* on an unwilling military and the culture was not destroyed and mission effectiveness was not detrimentally affected on the long term, and therefore, there is good reason to conclude that homosexual integration will not have a negative effect as well. However, as already noted, there is an important distinction between the two integrations mentioned and the integration of homosexuals into the military. There is a *legitimate* ethical discussion to be had regarding the activity of homosexuals, while there is no legitimate ethical discussion regarding the nature or activity of racial minorities and women. This distinction of a values-based difference in the oppositions to these integrations makes the analogy tenuous; there is good reason that open service of homosexuals at this time will adversely affect morale, culture, and possibly effectiveness.

Some may wish to question the validity of the analogy between the homosexual lobby and pornography. It must be admitted that there are good reasons for such disputation. After all, the similarities appear superficial at best: both deals with sexual issues of an ethical nature, both present a challenge to traditional mores with regard to sexuality, and both have made appeals to human freedom and rights for their justification, but beyond these, they appear quite different. One has to do with appropriate entertainment, while the other involves personal sexual behavior; one is directly related to the public square, while the other is

57. For example, the protracted battle of SSG Perry Watkins with the United States Army. See Mezey, *Queers in Court*, 144–47.

really a private matter (pornography is in the marketplace, which by its very nature, is public, while homosexuality deals with actions in one's personal residence).

However, even if all of these differences are acknowledged (and I am not inclined to do so for the homosexual lobby even if they pertain to the individual homosexual lifestyle and sexuality), they do nothing to speak against the analogy as it has been drawn here, for the argument simply rests on the applicability of the vices to the homosexual lobby, not on the degree of similarity between pornography and the homosexual lobby. In fact, the philosophical argument made here could have been constructed against the homosexual lobby and specifically against the repeal of DADT without any reference to pornography at all! I simply noted the analogy for purposes of demonstrating precedent (in American legislation and jurisprudence) and as a thought experiment. But if the analogy is rejected as too loose, or deemed inappropriate or offensive, the argument itself still stands (or falls) on its own merit (or lack thereof). The question that really needs to be asked is, "Do the vices described properly apply to the homosexual lobby specifically in its efforts at securing the repeal of DADT at this time?"

Some who are sympathetic to the concerns outlined here may nevertheless criticize the argument because it seemingly opens the door for revision in the future. The argument, as presented, is limited in scope, and thus, appears to suggest that, if at a later time, homosexuality is widely accepted by those in the military, then open service of homosexuals would be allowable or even advisable. This objection has a lot of merit, at least insofar as it expresses a concern with the limited nature of the argument offered here. However, just because this particular argument is (I believe) the strongest objection against the repeal of DADT that can be offered now, it in no way follows that other arguments cannot be given. So while it is true that this argument will not work if there comes a time when military members exhibit widespread acceptance of homosexuality, it does not follow that repeal of DADT would be advisable or wise. All that follows is that repeal of DADT would then need to be discussed in light of the situation which prevails at that time. It could very well be the case that other reasons for its retention will, or should succeed on different grounds.

Conclusion

The argument, at least so construed, will have limited application. It will not work against, for instance, Sullivan's proposal for a non-liberationist gay rights movement characterized by "virtuous homosexuals" who reserve sex for monogamous, stable, loving relationships (e.g., same-sex unions).[58] But why should that matter? A wholesale assault on homosexuality is not my aim here. While I believe other, more broad, and quite possibly equally compelling arguments can be given for questioning the morality of homosexual acts from a natural law perspective, the goal of this paper has been simply to offer a critique of the repeal of DADT at this time.

Some may note that it is impossible to go back, that once the proverbial Pandora's box has been opened with regard to sexual orientation and military service, it can never be closed. Berns certainly seems to think so.[59] This may very well be the case, but I find solace in the fact that others (who are far more intelligent and skilled than I) have faced similar critiques, and yet have made the argument anyway. After all, if the argument is true, then it is a worthy one, whether or not governments or society at large wish to accept it. As Clor wrote in the epilogue to his *Obscenity and Public Morality*:

> Friendly critics have observed that, since the trend of recent developments seems to be so contrary to the thesis of this book, its author should face the fact that the thesis may be unrealistic or impractical. I have not thought it likely that the policies suggested in the concluding chapter, or any similar policies, would be adopted in the near future, and I did not write with any such expectation in view. It was my hope and intention to contribute to serious thinking about this subject and particularly to thinking

58. Sullivan, *Virtually Normal*. While Sullivan still argues for what many would take to be liberal positions on gay rights, he is opposed to an activist form of it which seeks to subvert traditional institutions and force homosexuality on an unwilling populace. For example, he opposed affirmative action for homosexuals, but supports gay marriage; he rejects the use of legal proscriptions to deny private discrimination based on sexual orientation, but supports homosexual rights to serve in the military. At the heart of his proposal, then, he seeks to make room for homosexuals in the public realm while preserving individual freedom (of those opposed to homosexuality) in the private sector.

59. Berns, "Taking Virtue Seriously," 126. Berns points to Jean-Jacques Rousseau's comment that "Censorship can be useful for preserving morals, but never for reestablishing them."

of those who might be dissatisfied with some of the prevailing trends. These developments need not be regarded, in the long run, as wholly irresistible, unmodifiable, and irreversible. When moderate men—both liberal and conservative—become aware of their basic agreement on certain principles and values, they can have an effect on events.[60]

60. Clor, *Obscenity and Public Morality*, 279.

6

"Hate the Sin, Love the Sinner?"

Chaplain Ministry to Homosexual Service Members and their Families

—Scott N. Callaham

Introduction

Military chaplaincy is a unique profession. A chaplain may preach, lead worship, baptize, marry, bury, or counsel at one moment, then engage in any number of other, non-religious military activities the next. Though serving in a thoroughly secular setting, evangelical Christian chaplains practice and share their faith with a degree of freedom that those who serve in other mission fields rarely experience.

Serving the military and the church simultaneously, the chaplain lives and works at the intersection—and collision point—of worldviews. The worldviews that meet at the secular-religious interface and diverge most sharply are the prevailing postmodern worldview of Western culture on one hand and a biblically-based Christian worldview on the other, and perhaps no issue raises this opposition into sharper relief than that of sexual ethics. Due to the fact that sexuality is a central component of human identity, sexual problems frequently arise at the forefront of service members' concerns. The passions of youth and the immanent pressures of contemporary military life only amplify the intensity of these issues.

Past policies such as "Don't Ask, Don't Tell" drove the expression of homosexuality underground in the military to some degree, but even so, the complete confidentiality of chaplain counseling facilitated ministry to those service members who disclosed their homosexuality to chaplains. Now, especially following the repeal of "Don't Ask, Don't Tell," chaplains should be prepared for expanded opportunities to minister to homosexual service members and their families. Accordingly, the following essay offers reflection upon preparation of Christian ministers for chaplaincy, and the public and private ministry of military chaplains.

Preparation for Chaplain Ministry

Theological Preparation

Interpreting Biblical Teaching on Homosexuality

Christian chaplains academically prepare for military ministry through graduate-level training, in most cases with a Master of Divinity degree. The requirements of these degrees vary from institution to institution, and may or may not include specific training on sexual problems. Such courses can foster chaplains' preparedness for dealing with homosexual issues in ministry, and the findings of social science research can shed light on the vexed questions of human sexuality. However, far more crucial to the work of the Christian chaplain than any other resource is the Bible, for knowledge of the Bible's timeless message and submission to its authority constitute essential foundations for a biblical worldview.

Acquaintance with biblical texts addressing homosexuality must extend beyond surface-level familiarity due to the contemporary challenge of progressive, deconstructionist, reader-centric hermeneutics. According to the assumptions of this postmodern reading strategy, no written text carries meaning uninformed by the issue advocacy of its reader. Furthermore, since truly setting aside one's vested interests is actually impossible, the reader need not attempt to disentangle personal, subjective impulses from the act of reading.

Acceptance, and indeed promotion, of issue advocacy in reader-centric hermeneutics shapes the reader's attitude toward the authority of the biblical message. Most significantly, the true "authority" in the act of reading the Bible becomes the reader rather than the text, for the reader appropriates the text in order to serve his or her own ends. Therefore, in practice, homosexual activists counter-contextually reinterpret biblical passages that do not cohere with their agenda or adopt reading strategies that, in effect, justify ignoring these selections of Scripture altogether.[1]

In contrast, a biblically-based worldview requires submission to the message of the biblical text through text-centric exegesis. This interpretive strategy focuses upon a text as an effective vehicle for communication of an author's ideas, not primarily as a stimulus for a reader's open-ended imagination.[2] Since the source of the text's meaning is independent of the reader, the message of the text likewise stands apart from the agenda of the reader. A person can read a text whose message runs against the grain of cultural predispositions and can even choose to employ the text as a critical dialogue partner rather than an echo chamber for reinforcing his or her own ideas. Studying the results of detailed, text-centric exegesis of the key biblical passages concerning homosexuality is therefore one necessary component of the chaplain's theological preparation for ministering to homosexuals.[3] Ministering with biblical integrity also requires properly locating homosexuality within the broad themes of biblical theology. Specifically, one must recover the biblical conceptualization of homosexuality as sin.

Sin

Sin is an uncomfortably personal subject. While some may experience little or no temptation toward homosexual sin in particular, sin itself

1. For example, the slogan "Jesus never said anything about homosexuality" supplies a common rhetorical flourish for side-stepping or short-circuiting discussion of biblical teaching on homosexuality. A significant, necessary philosophical assumption of the sloganeer remains unstated: Authoritative biblical teaching for Christians derives solely from the words of Jesus. This theological reductionism not only repeats the Marcionite heresy of rejecting the scriptural authority of the first three-quarters of the Christian canon known as the Hebrew Bible or Old Testament, but also radically pares down the breadth of accepted revelation within the New Testament. Even more problematically, "Jesus-only" Christianity then drains the lifeblood from the teachings of Jesus through de-contextualization, setting the teachings of Jesus in opposition to the rest of the Bible. Thus the postmodern imagination molds a pliable, context-free Jesus into an advocate of homosexuality—tellingly, through an argument from silence.

2. Stimulating flights of imagination can, of course, be an author's actual objective. Even so, in this case the reader would still receive signals prompting such an outcome from within the text.

3. Treatment of these passages appears in Chapter 4 of the present volume, "'An Abomination?': Homosexuality, the Bible, and Christian Theology."

crouches at everyone's door and follows all people through life (Gen 4:7). Sin corrupts and stains all human endeavors, including both the writing and the reading of this book. Any reflection upon the topic of sin runs the risk of a dismissive attitude toward some sins—namely one's own—and selective criticism of the sins that bedevil other people (Matt 7:3–5, Luke 6:41–42).

Discomfort with discussion of sin can result in evasion of the responsibility for critical thinking by seeking refuge in thoroughly shopworn expressions such as "hate the sin, love the sinner." Though this saying presents itself as a pithy distillation of truth, it remains problematic for several reasons. First, "hate the sin, love the sinner" carries overwhelmingly negative connotations; its most prominent and emotionally-charged word is "hate." While the saying literally promotes "hate" only toward an impersonal sin, no sin is a mere abstraction in human experience. People who struggle with homosexuality receive supposedly impersonal "hate" of homosexuality as hatred expressed very personally toward them. Whatever the one who utters "hate the sin, love the sinner" attempts to communicate, "love" for the sinner falls in a distant second place in the saying. Furthermore, an overriding perception of "hate" renders any such theoretical "love" impotent and irrelevant.

Similarly unhelpful is the expression "all sins are equal." According to the Bible, sins of all kinds separate humans from God in his holiness. Sin consigns unrepentant, unredeemed sinners to a Godless eternity in hell. While all sin prompts God's judgment and in this respect yields an identical effect, the temporal consequences of individual sins are vastly different. Thus even the mention of minor peccadilloes like jaywalking in the same breath as repulsive evils like child abuse is patently offensive. Yet the standard for grading the theological consequences of sins is not civil law, as would be the case with state-administered punishment of poor pedestrian conduct or assault of a child. Neither can the measure of sins be personally-favored ethical codes or subjective opinion. Instead, one gains proper theological perspective only through the interpretive lens of the word of God.

According to Scripture, the act of sin constitutes a declaration that the authority of the human self eclipses that of God. Sin is an explicit rejection of God's dominion. Hence sin is a platform for self-idolatry, a brazen usurpation of God's supreme place of worship, honor, obedience, service, and love in human life. In common with the pagan logic of idol worship, sin taps into the primal craving of humans for the power to manipulate circumstances and environment in order to grant free reign to self-serving desires. The "self-idol" worshiper seeks significance, security, and blessing in life from him- or herself rather than God, and as is the case with all sin, homosexuality feeds an ever-increasing, addictive appetite for more sin. In the absence of divine constraint, the result is tragic enslavement to a depraved and insatiable master who hates God and wrenches its slaves away from him.

Embrace of homosexuality entails advocacy of sin as a way of life. Deliberate promotion of sin constitutes a radical departure from Christian orthodoxy, for it is an explicit denial of the biblical requirement that people turn from sin in repentance. Unless one indeed turns from sin in repentance, Jesus is neither Savior nor Lord. Advocacy of homosexuality is thus incompatible with biblical Christianity. The problem with homosexuality—the central problem that generates and exacerbates all other problems—is that homosexuality is sin.[4]

Ministerial Preparation

Spiritual Life

Dealing with homosexuality as sin in the course of chaplain ministry requires both theological acumen and sharpened spiritual senses, for all people are sinners, including the chaplain (1 Kgs 8:46, Prov 20:9, Eccl 7:20, Rom 3:23). Yet as a follower of Jesus, the Christian chaplain is also a bearer of the message that faith in Christ sets a person free from captivity to sin (Rom 6:6–7; 8:2). Therefore chaplains must model submission to God in imitation of Christ through holiness and freedom from sin. In order to align their lives with the message they bring, chaplains must stay closely connected with God.

In pursuit of vital connection with God, a regular devotional and worship life is absolutely essential.[5] Prayerful reading and reflection

4. For a moving biblical, theological, and ethical discussion of homosexuality in light of human fallenness, see Hays, *Moral Vision of the New Testament*, 379–406.

5. Here it is important to emphasize that an active devotional and worship life is not solely the domain of the individual; these are also communal activities. In the Bible, God engages in relationship with individual people in the context of his interactions with the covenant community, wherever such a community exists. Since military chaplains work as a missional extension of the covenant community (the church), they

upon Scripture highlights God's anger and grief over human sin, as well as God's merciful love for people in spite of their sin. Whatever personal disciplines a chaplain must enact in order to experience daily fellowship with God, including arising from sleep early if necessary, these sacrifices fade in significance in light of the sustaining peace one experiences in intimate communion with the Holy Spirit. This peace only comes from God, and it directly affects the chaplain's heart and mind (Phil 4:7). In contrast, attempting to function as a communicator of the Gospel without the continual, reforming work of God upon one's inner being is an empty and spiritually fruitless exercise. A vibrant spiritual life is essential for chaplain ministry.

Professional Accountability[6]

Professional military ministers require endorsement from denominations or other similar cooperative religious groups. These "endorsing agencies" expect their chaplains to perform their duties in accordance with certain doctrinal commitments. Therefore, at the very least, chaplains from churches that profess accountability to the scriptural prohibition of homosexuality should hold likeminded convictions. These chaplains should also communicate their beliefs to fellow service members in culturally-appropriate situations and ways as a matter of personal and professional integrity. In order to support chaplains adequately in this task, endorsing agencies should clearly state their expectations of chaplain ministerial conduct. Explicit guidance is all the more crucial in the post-"Don't Ask, Don't Tell" era. In turn, chaplains should proactively inform their military chain of command and endorsing agency of potential or developing situations that could draw attention from outside the military community, such as in the press.

---

must plant and nourish their spiritual roots in a local church to the degree that their work circumstances allow.

6. This section and the section on religious military ceremonies benefitted greatly from conversation with B. Keith Travis and David E. Mullis.

Elements of the Chaplain's Ministry

Public Ministry

Worship Services

Facilitating and preserving the free exercise of religion for military service members is the central task of their chaplains, and it is the Constitutional principle upon which the legal rationale for American military chaplaincy rests. The most visible means of upholding free exercise of religion is the leadership of public worship services. According to United States law, chaplain leadership of public worship services takes place in accord with denominational norms.[7] Thus when only one chaplain leads worship, that chaplain is completely free to shape the content of the worship service. However, when multiple chaplains partner to lead worship, careful negotiation and observance of theological boundaries is necessary to preclude compromise of individual chaplains' integrity in ministry.

The principle of respecting boundaries in matters of religious ministry shapes customs of leading worship in the military. To draw out only a few examples for the purpose of illustration, evangelical Christian chaplains do not lead worship alongside non-Christian chaplains. Only in very generalized settings like a prayer breakfast, which in the military setting can more closely resemble a ceremony of civil religion rather than of Christianity, would Protestant and Catholic chaplains take visible leading roles together. If service members are adherents of a different religious faith than that of their unit chaplains, a chaplain-screened and command-appointed lay leader takes the leading role for worship services instead of a chaplain. Each of these practices is commonplace, and all carry both a lengthy history of precedent and the support of regulations that protect a chaplain from pressure to conform to the beliefs and practices of others when performing the duties of religious ministry.

However, the military problematically classifies a broad swath of chaplains as "Protestant," a category that implies shared faith and practice but in reality denotes a wide spectrum of churches from multi-ethnic to mono-ethnic, "free church" to liturgical, conservative to liberal, and even orthodox to heterodox. Fault lines that divide these groups can run deep, yet commanding officers and lead chaplains frequently expect

7. See "Chaplains: divine services," U.S. Code 10 (2011) §6031(a).

their "Protestant" chaplains to lead worship together, at least in a "general Protestant" service.

On one hand, partnership in trans-denominational worship opens unique opportunities for strong Christian witness, such as when conservative and orthodox chaplains, who happen to differ in their liturgy or ethnic backgrounds, successfully unite their worship leadership under the guidance of the Spirit for the glory of God in Christian unity. On the other hand, the potential for theological compromise among Protestant chaplains under pressure to lead worship together is all too apparent. In the wake of the "Don't Ask, Don't Tell" repeal, evangelical Protestant chaplains must now reevaluate the extent to which they can faithfully cooperate with some fellow Protestants in leading worship services. Despite bearing a "Protestant" label, chaplains who promote or openly practice homosexuality advocate a version of Christianity not anchored to biblical teaching, ruling out extensive partnership in leading worship with evangelicals.

As with difficulties stemming from any cause, communicating concerns openly, courteously, and professionally within a team of chaplains can contribute to resolution of problems with co-leadership of worship before such issues arise. Discussion with fellow chaplains should also address the subject of layperson assistance in worship services, such as the appropriateness of appointing an openly homosexual service member to lead music or other aspects of ministry.[8]

Ordinances

Most evangelical Protestants view baptism and the Lord's Supper (Communion) as church ordinances (or sacraments) that carry deep theological significance. Regarding Communion, some Protestant chaplains may particularly emphasize the idea that this act of remembrance communicates God's grace. Since God grants his common grace liberally to all people (Matt 5:45), they may hold that Christian and non-Christian alike should partake in Communion. This practice is incompatible with a view of Communion as an ordinance *of* the church and *for* the church, for which the only authentic participants are those who are part of the community of faith.

8. Issues raised in this section appear alongside other possible impediments to ministry in "Letter to President Barack Obama."

Denominational disagreement on the theology of the Lord's Supper certainly pre-dates the repeal of the "Don't Ask, Don't Tell" policy. However, evangelical Christian chaplains should evaluate the degree to which a radically-open Communion policy can lead to the regular participation of unrepentant homosexual service members. Of course, the regular participation of unrepentant sinners in Communion is a perennial theological problem in Christian ministry that extends far beyond the issue of homosexuality. However, the probability of perception of homosexual advocacy is greater in the case of homosexuality as a "public" sin than for sins that service members actually acknowledge *as sin* and thus choose to keep private. Since the perception of homosexual advocacy can cast doubt upon an evangelical chaplain's faithfulness to the message of the Bible, the practice of open Communion in a general Protestant worship service entails a degree of theological compromise that most likely excludes the participation of evangelical Christian chaplains.

Regarding baptism, many service members seek this important ordinance without having first come to faith in Christ, and even some Christians are confused about the meaning of baptism. Therefore a chaplain should treat the occasion of any service member requesting baptism as an opportunity for presenting the transformative message of the Gospel and initiating follow-on discipleship. Evangelical chaplains should only baptize those who renounce all sin—including homosexual sin—in favor of the Lordship of Christ.[9]

Religious Military Ceremonies[10]

Homosexual marriage is a matter of contemporary political discourse and dispute, therefore much popular discussion of homosexual marriage employs the heavily-politicized language and logic of "rights." However, the premise of "rights" is utterly incompatible with the biblical worldview

9. This discussion of baptism presupposes the biblical model of baptism for believers, which disallows baptism of infants. Incidentally, just as infants are incapable of repenting from sin and turning to Christ in faith, they are also incapable of expressing an orientation toward homosexuality. Therefore chaplains whose system of belief includes infant baptism would need to consider the appropriateness of baptizing a child from a household that endorses or practices homosexuality, one illustration among many of the great theological gulf that separates the baptism of believers only and the baptism of infants.

10. Discussion of military funerals appears in the section on chaplain ministry to families.

in which followers of Jesus are God's slaves, and true freedom only comes to those who become "slaves to righteousness," submitting their own wills completely to that of God in Christ (Rom 6:15–23). In light of biblical teaching, no one possesses the "right" to marry anyone, and the only people who should marry are those whom God draws together: one man and one woman in lifelong devotion to God and each other. Therefore evangelical Christian chaplains cannot perform homosexual wedding ceremonies.

Even if they do not conduct homosexual wedding ceremonies as a matter of policy, evangelical Christian chaplains should view opportunities to attend such ceremonies cautiously and circumspectly. A wedding service is a special event for which voluntary adult attendance carries the cultural supposition of support.[11] Even if an attender happens not to condone the religious framework of a given wedding ceremony with its accompanying truth claims, the act of attending normally communicates support of the participants *as a couple*. An individual may even privately harbor an entirely dissenting belief system, yet at the very minimum, the act of attending a homosexual wedding ceremony tends to impart one's tacit approval to the outcome: the attempted sanctification of sin.

Such perceived approval casts a pall of ambiguity over an attending chaplain's convictions and fidelity to biblical teaching on human sexuality, which could portend conflict with the chaplain's endorsing agency and even loss of endorsement.[12] Requesting endorsement from another agency in such a situation is possible, but the attendant change in theological commitments entails breaking faith with the churches that had previously endorsed the chaplain and carries implications for one's present military chaplaincy as well as post-military ministry later in life.

Keeping in mind the weighty issues broached above, one should also take into account that beliefs and truth claims that vary from those

11. A "voluntary" attender certainly can display publicly contrarian behavior, as in the case of a visibly distraught relative who plainly does not support the union of a certain couple, yet attends their wedding anyway out of social obligation. However, the present discussion focuses upon an entirely different matter: whether an evangelical Christian chaplain should attend a homosexual wedding ceremony voluntarily.

12. See Brumley, "'Wounded' Chaplain," http://www.abpnews.com. The article quotes the Cooperative Baptist Fellowship (CBF) endorsing agent as stating that former Southern Baptist Air Force Chaplain Timothy Wagoner "thought he had done the appropriate thing" when he attended a same-sex civil union ceremony. However, "fallout" from the chaplain's actions apparently prompted his departure from the Southern Baptist Convention (SBC) and new denominational endorsement from the CBF.

of Christianity do not typically prevent military chaplains from attending services of other religious faiths as an observer. Indeed, under the authority of commanding officers, lead chaplains bear supervisory responsibility for all religious activities within a unit and must maintain first-hand knowledge of them. Thus while performing homosexual wedding ceremonies and participating in them as congregants is clearly inappropriate for evangelical Christian chaplains, the federal government's endorsement of religious same-sex marriage ceremonies in the military mandates some degree of personal chaplain presence for the purpose of supervision.[13]

Non-Religious Military Ceremonies

Outside of the context of worship services and religious ceremonies, the military frequently calls upon chaplains to offer prayers for various public, non-religious events such as the Navy's traditional evening prayer on ships, the noon meal prayer at the United States Naval Academy, and rites of passage such as enlistment, commissioning, promotion, change-of-command, and retirement. Chaplains offer public prayer both on weighty occasions such as the eve of battle and at more light-hearted events like unit formation runs. To the chagrin of anti-religionists, chaplain-led prayer is a widely-accepted and pervasive practice in the United States military. However, the ease with which the military drifts into prayer can transform what may resemble a pious tradition into a mere, thoroughly-secularized formality. Generally speaking, evangelical Christian chaplains must always guard against the neutering encroachment of civil religion in their public prayers in order to preserve the integrity of their witness.

A concern that is more specific to the subject at hand is the possibility that the agenda of some non-religious military ceremonies may include advocacy of homosexuality. Despite any contrary laws or policies that may currently be in place, both the trajectory and momentum of contemporary political discourse mandate eventual inclusion of sexual orientation under the rubrics of civil rights and diversity: topics whose various celebrations and observances fill the Department of Defense

13. Normally a chaplain can maintain a low profile while observing a religious ceremony as a supervisor by choosing a location that is one degree removed, such as the back of an auditorium or a balcony.

calendar. As postmodern culture sloughs off the remaining vestiges of Christian morality that impede the wholesale embrace of sin in the public square, more and more public ceremonies will include homosexual advocacy as a premise or subtext. Evangelical Christian chaplains must not subvert the language of prayer by inserting it into the context of the celebration of sin.

Interface with Civilian Religious Personnel

From time to time chaplains relate to civilians who are fellow religious ministry professionals. Most situations that can involve partnering with civilian clergy, such as community service projects and some weddings and funerals, allow ample time for resolving whatever areas of theological disagreement may impinge upon the task at hand. A special type of interaction with civilian clergy concerns referrals. For example, chaplains may direct service members to appropriate civilian clergy as special faith-specific needs arise. Indeed, upon request the chaplain must refer service members who seek religious affirmation of homosexuality to clergy members who match the service member's belief system, whatever reservations an evangelical Christian chaplain may hold toward that faith stance.[14] The chaplain's Constitutional role as facilitator of free exercise of religion in the military requires such actions, though they are relatively infrequent in the context of irreligious contemporary culture.

Private Ministry

Focus for Counseling

A chance conversation in a passageway or in the field transitions into an impromptu counseling session, or a service member sits down with a chaplain in an office space during a period reserved for counseling. A chaplain meets a commanding officer for coffee, and chatting transitions

14. Furthermore, in the case of a service member seeking a religious community that advocates homosexuality, the chaplain must not interfere with that service member's free exercise of religion through deception by diverting the service member to an evangelical Christian outreach to homosexuals instead. An analogous breach of professional ethics would take place if a chaplain were to refer an adherent of Judaism to a Messianic Jewish rabbi, for example.

to deeper matters as the officer reflects on the weight of command or some family crisis. Though some chaplain ministry takes place in public view, it is these kinds of private, person-to-person encounters that uniquely characterize the chaplain's ministry.

The absolute confidentiality of chaplain counseling opens a safe space for discussion of a service member's most troubling issues. Therefore struggles with homosexuality naturally surface in times of counseling with a chaplain. However, identification of homosexuality as a thorny issue in a service member's life is only a prelude in the counseling process. When meeting with a service member, a chaplain must always remember that the central issue is not sexuality *per se*, as if encouraging heterosexual expression would cure all ills. Instead, the root problem is sin, which becomes more and more apparent as homosexual sin wreaks its havoc upon the service member's life. The chaplain must keep the Gospel message of repentance from sin through faith in Christ as the motivating center of chaplain counseling.

Conduct of Counseling

Perhaps following a few minutes of introductory, surface-level chatting at the start of a counseling session, conversation can begin moving toward the service member's motivation for speaking with the chaplain. Especially for chaplains who may have received advanced training in social work, counseling, psychology, or related fields, at this point it is essential to remember that while the chaplain can draw benefit from sources of practical knowledge and experience such as these, the chaplain is neither a social worker, nor a counselor, nor a psychologist.[15] The military employs both military and civilian personnel for these other roles.

Precisely because the chaplain is not a purely secular professional, the chaplain should regard counseling sessions as divine appointments and pray before, during, and afterwards. Counseling sessions retain this

15. In the course of their ministries, chaplains may frequently find themselves carrying out tasks that resemble the work of these professionals. Indeed, at times a military chaplain may feel somewhat like a "jack of all trades" due to the broad scope of chaplain ministry. However, if a chaplain becomes fully redundant—merely a practitioner of secular arts in the garb of a Christian minister—the chaplain ceases functioning as a chaplain. When a service member asks, "Chaplain, what are you doing here?", such a person can no longer answer with integrity, "I am here because God sent me." For an extended meditation on the necessity of retaining the chaplain's primary role as minister of the Gospel, see Milton, "So What are You Doing Here?," 449–63.

sacred air even if, in the chaplain's judgment, the most direct line toward resolving a service member's problem actually runs through someone else's office. God is sovereign over whatever impulses drive a service member to seek a chaplain's counsel, no matter what the faith background or life situation of the service member may be. Christian chaplains should forthrightly identify themselves as followers of Jesus and secure the service member's acceptance of spiritually-informed counseling.[16]

Establishing and maintaining a spiritual basis for counseling requires extraordinary sensitivity to the service member's spiritual state, which the outpourings of mind and heart often reflect. When counseling with a chaplain, a service member may indeed expect to find a listener, but the counselee may have never before shared personal crises with an attentive, spiritually-responsive listener. Prayerful listening can help ease the intensity of high-strung emotions and allow the service member's interpersonal defenses to lower enough to facilitate genuine two-way conversation.

As the counseling session continues and the service member broaches the subject of homosexuality for the first time, sympathetic gentleness should remain a defining characteristic of the chaplain's response (Heb 5:2). A counselee who warily anticipates angry, rejectionist judgmentalism from the chaplain due to past experience with parents, other authority figures, or self-identified religious people may be so taken aback at this point that the emotional tenor of the counseling session may shift radically, allowing greater openness in sharing. In any case, the chaplain should bear in mind that the service member is a hurting person seeking relief. Furthermore, the chaplain must point to God as the source of the relief the service member seeks.

Cross-Cultural Communication in Counseling

A redemptive spiritual response to homosexual sin is an act of cross-cultural communication of the Gospel. Generally speaking, there is an under-appreciated sense in which every act of communicating the Gospel

16. Exceedingly rare are service members who would seek out a chaplain but refuse to receive a word from God in time of need. Even so, respect for service members' freedom of conscience mandates clear identification of God as the true source of help in the midst of trouble (Ps 46:1). Indeed, affirmation of God as source of help is necessary due to the prevalence of theories of pastoral care that assign the primary healing role elsewhere.

is cross-cultural, as well as counter-cultural in many cases. On one hand, every known human culture contains elements, however many or few, that cohere with a culturally-transcendent, biblical point of view. On the other hand, every human culture also incorporates tendencies that the message of the Bible critiques, curbs, or even flatly rejects.

In the specific case of a chaplain counseling a homosexual service member, the cultural gulf may in fact be much wider than for many other acts of communicating the Gospel in contemporary society. In these early years of the twenty-first century it is likely that the chaplain natively thinks in modernist terms and has accumulated significant experience relating the message of the Bible to people who think in modernist categories of right and wrong, innocence and guilt. However, the homosexual service member is most likely a child of postmodernity and does not readily identify with traditional modernist emphases in relating the Gospel story. The surging cultural tide of postmodernism largely dismisses discussion of right and wrong, so from the modernist perspective, postmodernists experience double separation from God; the postmodernist worldview stands apart from the modernist worldview, which itself is distinct from the worldview of the Bible.

Thus the chaplain faces a communicative challenge: effectively calling postmodernists to faith in Christ across a broad worldview gap. One response is to address the postmodern worldview as directly as possible with the corrective influence of the Bible without first requiring the Bible's message to pass through a modernist filter. This is not to suggest that the categories of right and wrong, innocence and guilt detract from the rest of the Bible's message and thus require censoring, as if contemporary theories of cross-cultural communication should somehow stand above the Bible in authority. In contrast, the metaphor of a modernist "filter" suggests that all elements of the Bible's message should remain intact in its presentation, not just those parts that resonate with a modernist worldview.

If any aspect of biblical theology is in danger of excessive "filtering" in the contemporary era, it is the theology of sin. As mentioned previously, sin is the central theological problem with homosexuality, and for modernists, sin immediately calls to mind uncomfortable notions of right and wrong, guilt and innocence. In a misguided attempt to avoid making people feel guilty, a modernist might tend to deemphasize the gravity of transgression involved in sin. Otherwise laudable gentleness might motivate this act of deemphasizing guilt in the case of communicating with a fellow modernist. However, the postmodern conversation partner, who already is not inclined to think primarily in categories of right and wrong, could more readily fail to grasp the stark "wrongness" of sin due to this lack of emphasis. Remaining situationally sensitive in the act of communication, a modernist cross-cultural communicator should not soft-pedal the biblical truth that sin imparts guilt before a holy and righteous God. Homosexuality is sin, therefore homosexuality imparts guilt.

Yet more biblical truth about the effects of sin remains, all of which should pass unfiltered in the presentation of the Gospel message. In addition to guilt, sin also imparts shame and fear.[17] Fear results from breaking God's trust, generating anxiety about sin's consequences. Shame comes from broken relationship with God, resulting in a sense of alienation, embarrassment, and unworthiness to aspire to restored relationship. Salvation from sin through faith in Christ redeems people from God's judgment (removing guilt), rebuilds trust between God and his people (removing fear), and restores relationship with God (removing shame).[18]

For at least three powerful reasons, a special sensitivity to sin as generator of shame should infuse the chaplain's counseling with homosexual service members. First, despite growing cultural awareness and acceptance of homosexuality, many homosexual service members have suffered broken relationships and endured significant shaming from friends and family. Naturally this leads them to associate with friends and surrogate "families" for whom homosexuality neither constitutes a basis for severing relationships nor is a source of shame. Instead, these likeminded circles ascribe some degree of compensatory approval (or "coolness," a postmodern means of ascribing honor) to homosexuality that restores a lost sense of belonging and community standing.[19] Thus homosexual postmodernists deeply identify with the idea of honor and its opposite, shame.

Second, Christian counseling should bring to light how Jesus takes the repentant sinner's shame as his own in his death and leaves it in the grave upon his resurrection. Jesus exchanges the shame of sin for the honor of redemption, loving the repentant sinner on the basis of faith in

17. Genesis 2:25 relates that Adam and Eve are not *ashamed*, despite their nakedness, before they sin for the first time. Then after they directly transgress God's one stated prohibition and eat fruit from the tree of the knowledge of good and evil, God calls out to the man, who responds in Genesis 3:10 that he was *afraid*, so he hid.

18. Müller, *Messenger, Message, and Community*, 198–209.

19. Ibid., 152.

him rather than on the ground of which sins a given community considers "cool" or not.

Third, the chaplain should communicate that committing one's life to Christ includes accepting his welcome into the church. Though composed of sinners, the church rightly lives out its calling as the redeemed people of God when it celebrates restored relationship with God in obedient holiness. Then the church reverses the alienation, embarrassment, and feelings of unworthiness that come from broken human relationships as its members find belonging in the serving and worshiping family of God.

Effective cross-cultural communication of the Gospel invites response. When a service member repents and Jesus takes sin's former place as Lord, the chaplain should be prepared to complete the act of Gospel communication by facilitating discipleship leading to baptism and entry into the local church. In military exigencies such as lengthy deployments, the chaplain should personally take up that critical discipleship task rather than leave it for others at some hoped-for point in the future. For willing service members, this discipleship should teach the foundations of Christian faith through interaction with the Bible. The gauge of discipleship progress should be visible, verifiable obedience to biblical teaching, which includes rejection of all sin, including the specific sin of homosexuality.

Consciousness-Raising through Counseling

Chaplains should pray for service members' acceptance of the Gospel message, which in many cases requires a spiritual pilgrimage through multiple applications of the salve of biblical truth upon the wounds of sin. When chaplains care enough for those whom they serve to tell them hard truths, Christian counseling sessions can provide occasions for discrete acts of consciousness-raising that the Holy Spirit uses in a process of drawing someone to faith in Christ. Discussion of some important consciousness-raising topics appears below.

One key act of consciousness-raising concerns homosexual service members who claim to be Christians already. Perhaps they want the chaplain to help them reconcile homosexual practice with Christianity, and they search for some means of mediating a truce between the obedience God requires and the demands of sin. In truth, neither of these combatants would actually agree to a truce. Yet the service member may begin to grasp the grievousness of his or her actual alienation from God during response to open-ended prompts like, "Tell me about yourself," "What do you like to do?", and "What do you want out of life?" If the chaplain has already set the service member sufficiently at ease to respond forthrightly, answers would likely flow quite naturally in conversation for several minutes. Listening carefully and attentively, the chaplain could then ask the service member who professes to be both homosexual and Christian to answer the same kinds of questions about God: "Tell me about who God is," "What kinds of things does God like to do in the world?" "What does God want from you in your life?" These matters are close to the heart of God as seen in Scripture but far from the heart of unrepentant sinners, so the range of briefer and more hesitant responses will likely include non-scripturally-based clichés about Jesus and emotional generalities like "God wants me to be happy." In truth, the spirit of the life and mission of Jesus does not traffic in clichés, and God's plan for humans centers upon his glorification in Christ rather than individually-customized scenarios for stoking self-esteem or positive emotions. The chaplain should gently draw out the contrast between the fulfillment that comes from living in concord with God on one hand and the spiritual impoverishment of self-focused living on the other. Lack of intimacy with God should trouble a Christian, and the chaplain can offer to help lead the service member back to his or her spiritual home of peace with God through Christ.

Another important act of consciousness-raising applies to service members who are heterosexually married but struggling with the emergence of homosexuality in their lives. In contemporary Western culture a now-familiar narrative demonstrates that homosexual sin especially targets heterosexual marriage for destruction. First a husband or wife experiences a kind of sexual "awakening" upon some exploratory foray into homosexual activity. Then the postmodern value of self-expression demands unleashing this newfound passion in service of self-discovery. Since heterosexual marriage stands in the way of maximal self-realization in this line of thinking, the marriage must finally dissolve in divorce, regardless of biblical teaching on divorce and divorce's bitter consequences. Divorce for the sake of homosexuality constitutes flagrant contempt for one's personal integrity in covenant-keeping, and though the marriage may not endure, the pernicious pain divorce inflicts upon spouses, children, and other family members abates little over time. Often the self-idolatry of sin shrouds these consequences from view until the cruel scythe of divorce has sliced through and dismembered deep family relationships. Chaplains should gently remind homosexual service members of their commitments to people who love them, recognizing the poignancy of discussing divorce with members of a generation whose own parents divorced in record numbers.

In keeping with its basically materialist and atheistic philosophical principles, contemporary culture views human sexuality purely as a biological imperative outside the spheres of influence of ethics or theology. Accordingly, homosexual service members may feel that they must divorce or commit other major life-altering acts because they have no real choice in the matter; the mere existence of homosexual urges mandates fulfilling them. In this situation the chaplain can point out that the service member actually chooses to believe that he or she has no choice. To abandon the power of moral choice in favor of chasing the vacillations of one's primal urges is to dehumanize oneself, to deny the moral agency that is a central element of God's image invested in humans.[20] In contrast, chaplains should affirm that the homosexual service member is fully human, uniquely made in God's image, and a beneficiary of God's self-sacrificial love in Christ.[21] Chaplains should pull back the curtain on postmodernity's restless quest for greater and greater self-knowledge in order to expose how following the path of limitless indulgence of instincts actually causes one to turn his or her back upon the person God created him or her to be.

Especially in the midst of inflamed emotions likely to prompt rash acts, the chaplain can urge that a service member simply *slow down*.[22] Enacting major life course changes within brief periods is unwise, and decelerating a rapidly unfolding chain of events to allow more time for thought is an act of reasonable caution in almost any circumstance. If a

20. Humans exercise moral agency rightly when they act under God's authority and in accordance with his will. See van Imschoot, *Théologie de l'Ancien Testament*, 2:9–10; Eichrodt, *Theology of the Old Testament*, 2:128–9; Waltke, *Old Testament Theology*, 217.

21. Such affirmation can foster the healing of wounds inflicted at the hands (or through the words) of well-meaning Christians. Unbalanced emphasis upon the biblical language of homosexuality as an "abomination" without concomitant reference to full participation in God's image with all of humanity can effectively dehumanize homosexuals.

22. Reflection on advising slowness to act derives from conversation with Mark T. Whitworth.

service member agrees to delay "coming out," filing for divorce, moving in with a same-sex partner, or any other major milestone of asserting homosexual identity, the service member is expressing a willingness to consider alternatives. It is crucial that the chaplain then offer the best alternative: following Jesus as Savior from sin and Lord of life.

This discussion on consciousness-raising through counseling obviously cannot offer a step-by-step guide to chaplain counseling of service members struggling with homosexuality, nor can it aspire to completeness. However, by far the most important act of consciousness-raising often takes place after discussion has ended and the counseling session is drawing to a close. Chaplains should offer to pray with the service member, committing him or her to the care of a loving God who wants everyone to experience his salvation and come to knowledge of his truth (1 Tim 2:4).

Ministry to the Family

Though military chaplains spend most of their careers working among fellow service members, they play a special role in ministry to family members that extends beyond the work of the local church, in that parents, spouses, and children of homosexual service members may also receive confidential counseling with a military chaplain. Throughout all aspects of military family ministry, however, the chaplain must also maintain the strict confidentiality of chaplain communications with the service member. In order to guard against breaking anyone's confidence inadvertently, chaplains should weigh the appropriateness of referring family member counseling to another chaplain, a local church, or a civilian counseling service.

For situations in which the chaplain judges counseling family members to be appropriate, much of the previous discussion translates to the context of civilian life as well. If the family members are followers of Jesus who are wondering how they should respond to a loved one's homosexuality, chaplains should encourage them to take the initiative in repentance and praying for God's intervention in their family relationships. This is the course of action that the Bible commends to believers who face heart-wrenching challenges in the face of seeming divine inaction (2 Chr 7:13–14). Focusing first upon one's own need to turn from sin reminds Christians that the Gospel message is for them as well. Furthermore, personal spiritual renewal through repentance and faith helps Christians to trust God and discern him at work even in the midst of the heartbreaking tragedy of homosexual sin.

Apart from counseling, weddings and funerals are the major life events for which military personnel and their families regularly seek the services of a chaplain. Though military chaplains are free to choose which couples they will agree to unite in marriage, typically the only factor that determines which chaplain will lead a funeral service is the claimed religious faith of the deceased or the surviving family. Therefore Protestant chaplains regularly perform funeral services for "Protestant" fallen service members whose actual religious faith in life may have diverged radically from that of the chaplain. In general, funerals for service members whose lives did not reflect the Gospel of Christ are occasions for honoring their service, extending Christian love to their families, and pointing to the hope of the resurrection for those who will follow Jesus.

Since evangelical Christian chaplains already often performed funerals for non-Christian "Protestant" service members, repeal of the "Don't Ask, Don't Tell" policy introduces few new considerations into chaplain performance of military funeral services. Yet the inevitable normalization of homosexual spousal relationships in the military will entail the formal acknowledgement of same-sex spouses of the deceased at military funerals, so funerals will present a more and more common opportunity to minister to homosexuals and their family members. Christ-like compassion for them should undergird and motivate communication of truth, during both the funeral or committal ceremonies and personal interactions before and after the burial.[23]

Conclusion

As has been the case with other major moral and ethical matters in American military history, chaplains are involved in the tectonic societal shift that has brought about repeal of the "Don't Ask, Don't Tell" policy because the people they serve are encountering moral crisis and are looking to their chaplains for help. Serving men and women in uniform well entails remaining a faithful witness to the transformative power of the Gospel in all areas of life, including sexuality. Chaplains should

23. See John 4:4–26 for a biblical model of compassionate, cross-cultural communication of truth that is worthy of emulation.

prepare themselves for ministry to homosexual service members and their families through familiarity with scriptural teaching and active personal fidelity to its message. They should carry out the public and private aspects of their ministry as acts of cross-cultural and countercultural communication of the Gospel. They should care enough to tell people the truth with opportunities that God grants and, in ways that fit their Constitutional role as providers and facilitators of free exercise of religion in the military, invite people to faith in Christ. Perhaps most importantly, chaplains should remember that God loves homosexual service members and wants them to be among the disciples he is drawing from among all nations. Participating in the fulfillment of Jesus' Great Commission, chaplains should teach everything Jesus commands to anyone who will listen, knowing that Jesus is with them always (Matt 28:18–20).

7

Afterword: The Questions Surrounding Homosexuality and Military Service

Concluding Thoughts

—John D. Laing

IN THE PREFACE, IT was argued that too much of the discourse surrounding the issue of homosexual military service is oppositional and combative in nature, and that this fact lends itself to exceptionally negative overtones. It was also argued that all parties involved in the discussion could learn something of humility and the military value of selflessness, both of which accord well with the Apostle Paul's exhortation to "consider others more important than yourselves" (Phil 2:3).[1] These truths are especially pertinent to those serving in chaplaincy ministry, as humble service born out of a love for others is at the heart of what we do. Nevertheless, due to the content of the book, some may offer criticism that the contributors have not expressed love of homosexuals, but have instead pronounced judgment and condemnation upon them. It is true that much of the book has consisted of arguments against the normative nature of homosexuality, whether from a biological/medical standpoint, a biblical standpoint, or a legal/politico-philosophical standpoint, but these were arguments for public concern, not attacks on individuals or a community. The appearance of being hateful or judgmental is a very real

1. This exhortation is, of course, given in the context of the Christological hymn, wherein Paul encourages reflection on the incarnation as a basis for one's own humility. Emulation of Christ, whose infinite humility and humiliation in the incarnation and crucifixion, is the standard.

concern for all of the contributors, for if chaplains appear this way, they may forfeit their credibility and thereby lose their ministries.

So by way of conclusion, I wish to offer some thoughts on three principles that can serve to answer these concerns and to guide military chaplains and others involved in ministering to the gay military community: judgmentalism, love, and wisdom. These thoughts will be followed by a brief question-answer format prepared by my colleague, which is meant to offer practical answers and suggestions for issues related to these themes. The book has been organized around a number of slogans and catch-phrases used in reference to various aspects of the questions that arise with regard to homosexuality and American culture. We hope that solid Biblical answers, those that are truly loving and gracious, redemptive and reconciliatory, have been presented.

Prohibition on Judging Others

It is arguably one of the most oft-quoted and well-known verses in the Bible, at least with regard to its wording. Jesus teaches his followers to avoid judging others and warns that to do so could be disastrous: "Do not judge, and you will not be judged. Do not condemn, and you will not be condemned . . . For with the measure you use, it will be measured back to you" (Luke 6:37–38). At the base of this teaching is the concept of reciprocity, akin to the *eye for an eye* concept of the Levirate law (Lev 24:20; see also Exod 21:26; Deut 19:21) and the suggestion implied in the Golden Rule: "Therefore, whatever you want others to do to you, do also the same for them—this is the Law and the Prophets" (Matt 7:12; cf. Luke 6:31).

It is appropriate to discuss judgmentalism and love of others together because in the biblical text, the two are intertwined. For example, in Luke's gospel, the prohibition on judging others (Luke 6:37–38) is placed in the context of Jesus' broader teaching regarding interpersonal relations, and immediately follows his commands to love neighbor and enemy alike (Luke 6:27–36). This context lends insight into the meaning of the prohibition, and illumines the concept of loving others, which will be examined in some detail below.

First, when Jesus commands his followers to love their enemies, he does not change words for "love," but rather uses the same term for both neighbor and enemy. *Agape* is one of several Greek words used to render the English word "love," and it is sometimes thought that *agape* is a specially reserved term for divine love.[2] This claim is sometimes disputed, on the grounds that *eros* appears in much ancient literature in reference to love of God/gods and is not restricted to erotic or sensual love, and that *philia* is sometimes used to refer to love that is greater or deeper than mere friendship, even being used interchangeably with *agape*.[3]

These disputes notwithstanding, when Jesus commands his followers to love their enemies, he tells them to do so by using the term *agape*. Thus, even if *agape* is reserved for love associated with God, or is a kind of love that is selfless and pure, Christians are called to exhibit it toward all persons, not just their family, friends, acquaintances, or others who are nice to them. Chastising a self-serving approach to love, Jesus notes that sinners "*agape*" their friends and neighbors too! Clearly, the point has less to do with distinguishing one form of love (i.e., *agape*) from other forms of love (i.e., *eros, philia*, etc.), and more to do with the objects of love. Christians should be unique in loving even those with whom they disagree or strive. How this ought to play out will be discussed in the next section.

A somewhat surprising feature of Jesus' teaching on judgmentalism is tied to the concept of reciprocity. Jesus' claim that the measure used will be applied back to the individual measuring refers to something positive in Luke's rendition. That is, while it is commonly thought to refer to negative judgment and a resulting condemnation (that is, if you judge and condemn others, you will be judged and condemned by God), the context makes clear that it does not. Rather, his comment that it is a "good measure," exceeding the boundaries of the container, point to its positive nature. The imagery is of food, whereby one desires an overflowing container of something good (e.g., an order of French fries

2. While admitting that *agape* and its cognates have a wide range of meanings generally, Brown contends that in the New Testament usage, they "have taken on a particular significance in that they are used to speak of the love of God or the way of life based on it." Brown, *NIDNTT*, 2:538.

3. Stauffer suggests that in pre-biblical Greek, there were some differences in emphases. He suggests that *eros* can best be seen as an intoxicating love,, and that *philia* may be seen as personal love toward others, while *agape* is characterized as weak and variable. Still, he goes on to compare/contrast *eros* and *agape*, noting that *eros* "is a general love of the world seeking satisfaction wherever it can" and "seeks in others the fulfillment of its own life's hunger," while *agape* "makes distinctions, choosing and keeping to its object" and "is a giving, active love on the other's behalf." Stauffer, *agapao*, 1:37.

where some fall out of the cardboard holder and into the bag . . . it's like a bonus). Specifically, it refers back to the previous sentence, wherein Jesus commanded that his followers grant forgiveness liberally (v. 37). Thus, the measure used/measure poured back concept has to do with forgiveness and not judgmentalism: if one forgives, he will be forgiven; if one grants much forgiveness, he will be granted much forgiveness; if one does not grant forgiveness, he will not be granted forgiveness. It is clear that Jesus assumes his followers will not only forgive others, but will do so with abundant grace, a good measure that is overflowing and more than one needs (v. 38).

Such a message is sometimes lacking in churches, or is given lip service but not emulated in the actions of the body. In the biblical material, then, to love others is to extend forgiveness analogous to the forgiveness God offers through Christ to us; to fail to extend forgiveness analogously to that which we have received from the Lord is to fail to love others. The extent of grace we have received is the standard for the extent of grace we are to offer. In his discussion of the atonement, Anselm argued that humans have received infinite grace and forgiveness because they have committed an infinite offense against God's honor. He reasoned that any sin against an infinitely holy God is a sin of infinite proportions; this is why satisfaction could only be made by God Himself.[4] The point here is that the grace we have received is much greater than we can ever return or show toward others, and so our interactions with others ought to be characterized by graciousness. We ought to be known as forgiving and patient, and characterized by grace. For Christian chaplains serving alongside homosexuals, love ought to be clearly expressed, and the possibility for forgiveness, grace, and redemption ought to be the key to our message. We sometimes just tack this on to the last thirty seconds of a message characterized more by judgment, condemnation, and abandonment. We ought to be careful to ensure balance in our preaching, demeanor, and interactions with others.

The imagery of judgmentalism used by Jesus here is quite jarring and graphic: the one judged is depicted as having a speck of sawdust in his eye, while the one judging him because of the speck has a log in his own eye (Luke 6:41–42)! The hypocrisy is clear and the irony rich. One

4. Anselm, *Cur Deus Homo*. It could be claimed that Anselm was trying less to offer a new theory of atonement (i.e., the so-called *Satisfaction* theory) and instead was offering a rational argument for the necessity of an incarnation and subsequent sacrifice. That is, the work is more Christological than soteriological in nature and content.

cannot help but develop a mental picture, as it is simultaneously humorous and disturbing. Jesus' didactic purpose moves beyond the practical application, to give insight into the nature of the prohibited actions and their underlying attitude. The prohibition on judging others here does not mean that one cannot make a moral appraisal of the actions of others. To be sure, Jesus criticizes those who judge others, calling them "hypocrite[s]" (v. 42), but his call to remove the plank from one's own eye *before correcting others* undercuts the popular understanding of the prohibition. Implicit in that call is a moral judgment about the actions of both parties. The plank represents sin in the individual's life and the speck similarly represents personal moral failings. The attack on judgmentalism by Jesus, therefore, is not a general prohibition on moral assessment. Rather, it is a call to an acute awareness of sin and a particular sensitivity to our own sin, as well as sin in general. In addition, the fact that Jesus does not offer an absolute prohibition on moral assessment of others (he seems to approve the removal of the speck) also speaks against that understanding.

In other words, the example Jesus gives does not condemn our assessing sinful actions as sin, and does not prohibit our proclamation of warnings that sinful activity is wrong in God's eyes, separates one from God, and can eventuate in condemnation, but instead, it requires that we make such as assessment, and it assumes we will also offer such a proclamation if we truly love others. However, it requires that we do so out of love, in a loving spirit, with a humble recognition that we, too, struggle with sin and stand in need of redemption. This reading of Jesus' words accords well with the Bible's message about sin and its adjudication by humanity. The story of Israel includes numerous incidents where sin was judged not only by God, but also by human leaders. In fact, the entire concept of Law, with its detailed descriptions of how to handle a host of violations, depends on persons having both the ability and responsibility for evaluating actions as sinful or not. While some may wish to dispute this argument by pointing out the disparity between the two testaments, or the theocratic nature of ancient Israel, such an objection cannot be sustained. Jesus' teaching was wholly consistent with a proper understanding of Torah, and his Sermon on the Mount may rightly be seen as his commentary on it (Matt 5:17–20).

This discussion raises important questions regarding the meaning of Jesus' prohibition and its application by Christians. Did Jesus (and by extension, Paul) overturn requirements for sin's punishment and do away with consequences for sinful activity? What does Jesus mean when he prohibits one from judging others? These questions are interrelated, and thus, both will be examined together, if only briefly.

One narrative often pointed to as proof that Jesus meant to undercut punishment for and/or moral assessment of sin is the story of the woman caught in adultery found in the eighth chapter of John's Gospel. It is well known that the narrative is not found in the oldest and most reliable manuscripts and therefore, some would be inclined to simply dismiss appeals to it for proof of an argument.[5] Such a dismissal, though, is not without its problems, and so an answer is warranted.[6]

It is commonly thought that the story effectively denies consequences for sin, and that it serves as a paradigmatic case which demonstrates the complete forgiveness of sins in Christ. Just as the blood of Christ cleanses sin and grants rebirth for his followers, so also the woman found healing for her sin and was spiritually reborn as a result of her encounter with Jesus. She was allowed to go free because those who sought to condemn (and kill) her were at least honest enough to acknowledge their own sin and were unable to condemn her because of it. The conclusion that any of us with sin cannot condemn others for their sins (and since we have all sinned, none of us can do so) is both correct and incorrect. It is correct in its assertion that we cannot, as individuals, condemn others for their sin, and that we, as sinners, are no better off than they insofar as we require forgiveness from God and stand condemned apart from God's grace poured out to us through Christ. However, it is incorrect in its underlying assumption that the story means that sin itself is inconsequential.

5. For example, Haenchen offers no comment on the pericope, but after quoting the passage, merely includes the following note: "The author did not consider the pericope of the woman taken in adultery to be an original part of the Fourth Gospel. It has been inserted after John 7:52 by D and other old Latin manuscripts. But it is missing in the best Greek manuscripts," and then he lists them. Haenchen, *John 2*, 22.

6. Some commentators have chosen to put it at the end of their discussion of the Gospel, separated out, due to difficulties in assigning it location, authorship, wording, authenticity, etc. For example, Bernard chose to do so, as did (more recently) Borchert. Bernard, *Gospel According to St. John*, 2:715–21; Borchert, *John 1–11*, 369–76. However, this is not to say they dismiss it out of hand, for many still view it as authentically representing the early tradition about Jesus' ministerial demeanor. As Bernard puts it, "All we can assert with confidence is that the passage is very like the Synoptic stories about Jesus; while its tenderness and gravity commend it as faithfully representing what Jesus said and did when a woman who had sinned unchastely was brought before him." Bernard, 2:716.

It may appear, at first glance, that Jesus' actions in the story were meant to call into question all consequences for sin, but his actions here are unique to the situation and should not be seen as normative for all situations. First, the Pharisees and synagogue leaders clearly hoped to catch Jesus in a no-win situation (John 8:6). Jesus saw through their actions and so refused to directly answer their question about the woman's fate.

Second, Jesus called into question the authority of the crowd to prosecute and punish the woman. Other biblical passages, as well as secular sources indicate that capital punishment could only be enacted under certain conditions, which this situation did not meet.[7] Jesus' question regarding their relative sinfulness was not meant to suggest that capital punishment is never appropriate unless the would-be executioner were sinlessly perfect; this would stand in direct opposition to Levitical capital-crimes legislation. Rather, it directly challenged the members of the unruly mob. Only governmental authorities are authorized to carry out corporal punishment; vigilantism is not allowed, and Jesus challenged it here.

Third, there is good reason to question the sincerity of those who brought the woman to Jesus for judgment, even beyond their sinister motives regarding him. The claim was made that the woman was caught in the act of adultery, so there was no question about her guilt. However, the Torah required punishment for both parties in cases of adultery (Lev 20:10; Deut 22:22). There is no mention of the man caught with her; presumably he was not to be condemned. Thus, it appears that the woman was innocent (or at least the conditions for condemnation found in Torah were not truly met). In this case, then, justice required that she be freed.

Fourth, Jesus did not condemn her or allow her to be executed, but he still called her to repent: "Neither do I condemn you...Go, and from now on do not sin any more." (v. 11). Jesus' words include both a denial of condemnation and a call to repentance! The juxtaposition of the two clearly indicates that judgmentalism does not involve the mere call to

7. A number of scholars have argued that the Jews, during the Roman occupation of Palestine, did not have authority to execute criminals. This seems to be the reason given why the Pharisees brought Jesus to Pilate first, then Herod after, for trial and execution. See, for example, Barrett, *Gospel According to John*, 591–92; Morris, *Gospel According to John*, 782; Witacre, *John*, 206; and Keener, *Gospel of John*, 1:737. However, Michaels rightly points out that the text is not clear, as Pilate seemed to accord them such authority when they brought Jesus to him (18:31 and 19:6). Michaels, *Gospel of John*, 496.

repentance or the moral stand against sin. Rather, it involves something more sinister. In fact, it seems that it has to do with the attitude Jesus saw in some of the Pharisees when they would pray and thank God that they were not like the sinners and tax collectors (Luke 18:11–12). The judgmentalism that Jesus so sternly condemned sprang from a hateful and proud spirit, which saw others as inferior and less deserving of God's love. It is true that religious persons can fall into such attitudes, but far from clear that they are inherent in righteous indignation expressed against sin and its inroads into the culture. It seems the key to having a righteous and appropriate anger against sin, as opposed to an unrighteous and inappropriate hatred of sinners has more to do with the inner life of the individual than with the clear manifestation in action. Christians are right to stand against sin and to stand against the normalization of what God's Word deems aberrant or ungodly. Nevertheless, such opposition must be born out of love in all humility; otherwise, it is sinful itself.

Requirement to Love Others

The command to love one's neighbor is one of the most basic in the Bible, yet it often appears to be one of the most difficult to follow. Clearly, it is foundational to Christianity, as on more than one occasion, it is referenced, along with love for God, as the key to the faith and the fulfillment of the biblical requirements (Mark 12:30–33; Matt 22:37–40; Luke 10:27–28; Rom 13:9–10; Gal 5:14; cf., Jas 2:8; Lev 19:18). To love one's neighbor involves great responsibility and intentionality, and touches upon both outward action and inward attitude.

In the book of Leviticus, where the command to love neighbor as oneself first appears, a whole litany of specific examples of loving neighbor is presented (Lev 19:9–18). The section begins with a practical example of how a heartfelt love for others should manifest itself with intentional efforts at charity and hospitality. The requirement to harvest only once and leave gleanings of the crops behind was meant to allow the poor and travellers to have something to eat (vv. 9–10). The Promised Land was not to have any hungry or starving persons, and Ruth benefited from the rule (Ruth 2:15–16). Dishonesty is born out of a lack of love—just as we do not want others to steal from us or to be dishonest with us, so also ought we to respect the property of others and tell them the truth (vv. 11–12). Our loving actions toward others are tied to our respect and love for God (v. 12). Loving others also involves a sensitivity to their physical needs, a concern for their financial stability, and an aversion to even the appearance of taking advantage. Employers are to pay their hirelings at the end of the day so that they may purchase any necessities they lack (v. 13). Loving others also manifests as compassion, and never demeans or ridicules, even when the other is unaware or would never find out (v. 14). Instead, love is shown as justice and truth (v. 15–16), and is more than outward action. The love of neighbor is a heart attitude that leads to honest dealings, forgiveness, and reconciliation (vv. 17–18).

There are two passages from the New Testament that speak loudly to the idea, though with seemingly conflicting results. On the one hand, the story of the rich young man suggests that no one can live up to the ideal, and on the other hand, the story of the good Samaritan provides a concrete example of how to do so. What is clear is that each breaks down common conceptions about loving neighbor which were prevalent in Jesus' own day and seem to persist even today.

The story of Jesus' interaction with the rich young man and subsequent teaching to his disciples, is found in all three synoptic gospels (Matt 19:16–30; Mark 10:17–31; Luke 18:18–30). The point of the story is not to denigrate property ownership; even though Jesus did not own a home, his ministry certainly benefited from the contributions of those who did. The point of the story is also not to teach that money should not be the primary love of the faithful, true though that may be; instead, it serves as a related sub-point in a larger theological proclamation of Christological and soteriological significance. The point of the story, then, is to note that humans cannot, in and of themselves, follow the commandments and earn salvation because love of neighbor (and the other commandments) is not humanly possible, and therefore, salvation can only be found through faith in Christ.

There are two somewhat embarrassing and perplexing statements made by Jesus in the story. The first occurs when the young man initially approaches Jesus and the second immediately follows. In Mark's account, the young man addresses Jesus as "Good Teacher," and Jesus seemingly repudiates the designation, questioning why he referred to him as "good," and noting, "No one is good but One—God" (Mark 10:18). At first glance, this may seem like a denial of the essential goodness of Christ or a rejection of the doctrine of the incarnation, but it is not. Rather, it functions to get the young man (and the reader) to think about who Christ is and what it means to be good. The so-called *messianic secret* looms large here, and plays an important role in the pericope, as at the end of the interaction, Jesus invites the young man to follow *him* (Mark 10:21). Jesus' answer to the young man in Matthew's account makes the problem clear. Included in the list of commandments the young man is enjoined to keep are those which deal with relations with others, culminating in the summary statement, "love your neighbor as yourself" (Matt 19:19). Since the young man claims to have kept all of the listed commandments, Jesus challenges him to demonstrate that he truly loves others as he loves himself: he calls him to give all his possessions away to the poor (Matt 19:21). The fact that the man leaves and does not follow Jesus demonstrates two crucial factors regarding his claim. First, he does not really love others with the same kind of love that he loves himself. Later, it is revealed that such love is only possible with God's help (Matt 19:26). Second, he does not really believe Jesus is the Christ (or good, like God), and thus, Jesus' initial challenge to the young man's sincerity in his address is vindicated.

The story of the good Samaritan is one of the most beloved and straightforward in the New Testament (Luke 10:25–37). As the story goes, an expert in Torah confronted Jesus in order to test him, and asked him the same question as the young man: "What must I do to inherit eternal life?" (v. 25). After Jesus and the man agreed that the proper response includes loving God and neighbor and Jesus admonished him to do so, the man asked Jesus to clarify who his neighbor is, apparently hoping to be justified (v. 29). Jesus then goes on to tell the story of the unfortunate man who was robbed, beaten, left for dead, and ignored by passers-by, including a priest and a Levite, until a Samaritan stopped to help him. The conclusion of the story has the expert agreeing that the one who showed mercy was a true neighbor, and Jesus admonishing him once again to "go and do the same" (v. 37).

While it is true that the story could be read as a critique of the Jewish religious leadership or as a challenge to the prevailing social norms regarding relations between Jews and Samaritans (it certainly includes both elements), the primary focus of the story is on the meaning of neighbor and of loving one's neighbor as oneself. Much can be said regarding the loving actions of the Samaritan, from his disregard for his own schedule in favor of helping another in need, to his taking on the considerable expense and responsibility of ensuring the injured man was cared for and sheltered, to his willingness to put himself at risk of physical injury or exhaustion by allowing the stranger to ride his donkey while he walked in the desert heat, to his throwing off of social constraints (e.g., racism, nationalism, etc.) and the attendant fears that could prevent his stopping to help another in need, to his resourcefulness in rendering first aid, but what is of greatest concern is not the particulars of the example given, but the drive behind his action and the admonishment of Jesus to the questioner.

The context of the story makes it clear that the basis for the Samaritan's actions was love of God and neighbor (Luke 10:27), and as Nolland has rightly observed, the story that follows—that of Martha and Mary, which culminates in Jesus' admonition to Martha to also be devoted to him and his teaching, just as her sister was (Luke 10:41–42)—serves to answer the question of inheriting eternal life. It is found in Christ.[8] Jesus' admonishment to the expert is interesting because it turns the original question on its head. The man's question about who counts as his neighbor can be summarized as asking who he is obliged to love, but Jesus' answer inverted the focus to suggest that the man ought to be asking to whom he could be a neighbor.[9] Jesus tells him to be a neighbor to all people, including those he would typically hate, find unclean, or distasteful, in this case, foreigners, Gentiles and Samaritans. More importantly, though, the way Jesus answered called into question his very attitude, which seemed to desire a minimalist definition. Such a minimalist focus on salvation was what Jesus most criticized among the Pharisees and other religious leadership. Love of God and the ensuing love of neighbor desires to do all it can for the sake of the other, and those who seek to do the least do not really love.

These considerations demonstrate that both stories refer to the requirement to love neighbor, and both make it clear that it order to do so, one must give himself wholly to Christ. Love of others in the required sense involves a work of God's spirit within the individual, enabling him to overcome his own selfishness/love of self. Thus, love of neighbor and love of God are both tied to surrender to Christ's lordship and to the salvation which God graciously bestows when one does so in faith.

Christian community was to be characterized by love for one another so unlike anything in the world that it would distinguish it from

8. Nolland writes, "Luke wants us to see that Jesus pushes the scope of necessary neighborliness beyond every traditionally accepted limit (vv 29–37), and he would have us link the love of God with attachment to Jesus' own person and teaching (vv 38–42)." Nolland, *Luke 9:21–18:34*, 578.

9. Barrett Duke brought this point out quite nicely in his chapel address on our campus earlier this year, in which he referenced this text.

all other religious communities: "By this, they will know you are my disciples . . ."(John 13:35). The Apostle John records this important teaching in the context of Jesus' farewell discourse on the night of the last supper after he has predicted his impending death (John 14:2–3; 16:17) and warned his disciples of a coming persecution because of their faith in him (John 15:18–25). Jesus also reminded them of the incarnation and referenced his person and authority in order to encourage them to obedience, faithfulness, and steadfastness (John 14:12–14; 15:10, 14; 16:19–28). Although he calls the command to love one another "new" (John 13:34; 15:12, 17), it should be clear to all that a mere love for one another was not new at all, and so the unique aspect of this love must be understood in light of the context in which the command was given. In addition to the doctrinal didactic already noted, it is in his farewell discourse as recorded in John's Gospel that Jesus gave his most poignant teachings regarding the person and ministry of the Holy Spirit (John 14:15ff.; 15:26—16:16), and John records Jesus' high priestly prayer, in which he prayed for the unity and empowerment of the disciples and any who would come after them (John 17:20–21).

The love spoken of here and which is supposed to be unique to the Christian community is a love that is generated by the Holy Spirit. It is a love grounded in the new birth given by God due to faith in Christ, effected by the union of God's Spirit with those of believers. It is a supernatural love that only those who have been reconstituted by God, who have been given a new nature and born again, can exhibit. This occurs when the believer yields himself to God's control and allows the Holy Spirit to live through him.

Exhortation to Wisdom & Gentleness

The third broad principle that deserves mention comes from a message Jesus gave to the Apostles just before he sent them forth on a preaching mission throughout Israel. They were to proclaim the imminence of the Kingdom of God, heal the sick, cleanse lepers, cast out demons, and even raise the dead! He told them to trust God working through the inhabitants of the towns to provide for their needs, but also warned them that some (many?) would not be prepared to receive them or their message. In the context of these instructions, Jesus told his most trusted followers and co-workers to "be as shrewd as serpents and as harmless as doves" (Matt 10:16).

Jesus noted that, even though the mission of the disciples (at that time) was to be to the people of Israel—God's special people—and not to godless Gentiles or Samaritans, they should still expect to encounter hostility and persecution. Some of the towns were more sinful than the epitome of Old Testament godlessness, Sodom and Gomorrah (v. 15). Jesus warned of the hostility from both individuals (v. 14) and local authorities (v. 17). In fact, the very culture was fraught with sin and ungodliness, and was hostile to the things of God. Governmental authorities at echelons above the local level would participate in their persecution and punishment because of their zeal for and fidelity to the Gospel (v. 18).

These facts suggest that the exhortation to be both shrewd and harmless is meant to guide the disciples' conduct of faithful ministry in a context that purports to be tolerant and/or friendly to things of God, but is in fact hostile to the Gospel. The relevance of Jesus' advice and warning to the current context should be obvious, though the meaning of the exhortation and its application requires further clarification.

The word used in reference to doves here (*akeraoi*) only occurs three times in the New Testament, and is variously translated as harmless, gentleness, innocence, purity, and incorruptibility. In classical Greek, it referred to the pristine condition of a post-conflict countryside or city wall, untouched by the ravages of war. Thus, in a figurative sense, it connotes an individual who is unscathed by his interactions with an ungodly society. It brings to mind Paul's exhortation to be in the world but not of the world, to refrain from being conformed to the world and instead, to be transformed by the renewing of the mind (Rom 12:2). In fact, Paul uses the same term in his concluding exhortation to the Romans, though he positions it alongside a different term for wisdom than which Jesus uses here (cf. Rom 16:19).[10] In telling the disciples to be shrewd, Jesus used a term (*phronesis*) that is more suggestive of thoughtfulness than wisdom (*sophia*). It is the same word he used in reference to the man who built his house on a firm foundation (Mat 7:24–27). While *sophia*

10. The fact that both Jesus and Paul advise Christians to be harmless as well as shrewd or wise has led some scholars to conclude that there was most likely an idiomatic expression to that effect. Since Jesus juxtaposes *akeraoi* with *phronesis*, while Paul does so with *sophia*, it must be concluded that no such expression was known in Greek. However, the difference in terminology could be explained by appeal to translation; there may be a Hebraism or Aramaic expression to which both Jesus and Paul refer.

normally refers to a deeper insight into the nature of things, *phronesis* suggests a more practical and pragmatic approach to the workings of the mind. The thinking man considers potential outcomes and makes provision for any contingencies that may arise; he uses his brain.

These considerations suggest that what Jesus had in mind for his disciples was that they would go into a hostile environs to preach the gospel, but would do so without being corrupted by that context; it would not sully their reputations, it would not lead them into ungodliness, it would not steal their joy or zeal for God's Word or Kingdom. They would remain resolute in their convictions and mission, unswayed by the pulls of this world. The military context includes many factors that can have an adverse effect upon religious leaders and service members. Pressures to conform or compromise the faith, temptations to sin, and the potential for guilt by association abound. Jesus' words are as applicable today to members of the armed forces as they were then to his disciples.

At the same time, Jesus also exhorted his disciples to be smart as they went out. They were to act not only on their feelings, but were called to use their heads. They would go forth to minister with their eyes wide open to the possibilities of persecution and deceit, and were to act accordingly if the need should arise. Ultimately, he warned them against naiveté, which characterizes many religious persons. The current military context does appear at times to be hostile to conservative religious concerns and beliefs. A healthy sense of wariness and vigilance is called for, lest fundamental religious rights be widdled away as we sit back unawares. Similarly, we must choose our battles wisely and carefully and act in ways that reflect both our trust in God and our use of the brains with which He endowed us.

Conclusion

All religions recognize the frailty of humanity in its current state. Many refer to sinfulness as the primary shortcoming of all persons and call us to repent and turn to God in faith and deed. This book has addressed this fundamental problem and sought to point to its solution. This final chapter can best be seen as an appeal to two parties. First, it seeks to answer the concerns of homosexual service members and others in the homosexual community pertaining to the moral appraisal it offers of their actions and desires. Such moral appraisals are not inherently judgmental in the sense prohibited by God. Second, it hopes to call Christians and other religious persons to evaluate their own attitudes undergirding their moral pronouncements and political/social activism against homosexuality. Those activities must be driven by a God-ordained, Spirit-empowered love. There is no room for hypocrisy in the Christian life. Similarly, chaplains ought not only act out of love, but they must also act out of a correct and valid appraisal of the situations. Wisdom, not naiveté, must drive decision-making and action. In this way, chaplains may effectively engage homosexual service members and the gay community in a loving and redemptive manner.

Commonly Asked Questions about the Bible and Homosexuality

—Page Matthew Brooks

Now that the biblical text has been examined and surveyed on the topic of homosexuality, common questions will be offered and answered. The answers will draw from the biblical and theological reflection and applied to each question. Practical experience will also be offered in the answers, especially when considering how to minister to homosexuals.

Is homosexuality an abomination? Is it a greater sin when compared to other sins?

The Bible never gives a clear list of what sins should be considered "worse" than others. We find no clear categorization of sins anywhere in the Bible. We do find various descriptors given to sins, as has just been surveyed in this essay. But nowhere does God give a clear list or degrees of sin.

Homosexuality, along with other sexual sins, is clearly labeled as perverse, though, homosexuality is singularly labeled as an "abomination." We must be careful when trying to categorize sin, especially when we do not understand everything about the ways of God. I believe homosexuality is listed as an abomination specifically because it reverses the natural order and design God has established, not necessarily because it ranks any higher in a gradation of sins. Paul states in 1 Corinthians 6:18–20 that other sins a person commits outside the body, but sexual sin is done against the person's body. The issue becomes even graver for believers because Christ lives in each believer. When persons prostitutes their body, they are bringing dishonor not only to themselves but also to Christ.

All sexual sin may be categorized as perverse, but homosexuality is uniquely considered an abomination to God because it reverses the natural order and design God has created. Nevertheless, often times people use the "abomination" references to single out homosexuals as worse sinners, or perhaps even imply that a homosexual cannot be saved because of homosexuality. I wish to point back to my earlier comments on First Corinthians 6:9–11 where Paul lists sexual sins, but then in verse 11 specifically states to his readers that some of them "were" those things, but now they have been justified and sanctified by Jesus Christ. There is no sin that cannot be forgiven and washed away by the reconciliation of Christ.

Can one be a celibate homosexual? Can one have homosexual feelings and drives but not act on them? If a person does not act on homosexual feelings, can he or she be a "good" Christian?

These questions really relate to one central question: What is the relationship between the homosexual motivation and the homosexual act. In our Western way of thinking, we have a tendency to dichotomize issues: church and state, science and religion, religion and politics, etc. I believe that this type of thinking has infiltrated into the way we see sin as a part of the person as well. We have separated out the sin and the sinner.

In another question, I answer the issue of if we can love the sin but not the sinner. For the present question, however, the focus is upon the motivation for the behavior and the behavior itself. Often people will use the excuse that they might have the motivation in their mind to perform a sin, but so long as they do not act on it, then it is not a sin.

What does the Bible say about the relationship between the motivation, thought, or drive behind a sin and the sinful behavior itself? Jesus mentioned the issue of adultery in Matthew 5:28–30. In fact, Jesus is quoting from the Holiness Code in Exodus 20:14. The phrase in verse 28 concerning "lustful intent" may be translated literally as "for the purpose of lusting for her." Jesus is teaching that such lust and the motivation for lusting is just as sinful as the act because in the same verse he states that the person has already committed adultery in the heart.

Jesus is not adding any new commandment or any new perspective on the law. If we refer back to the holiness code, we see that just a few verses later in Leviticus 20:17, God gave Moses commandments that specifically prohibited sinful motivations, thoughts and passions (covetousness regarding spouses, houses, animals, etc.).

One time some soldiers in my unit were joking about looking at women lustfully. They used the standard, metaphorical excuse about being able to look at a woman but not commit adultery by saying, "I can shop around, but so long as I don't buy anything, my wife is fine with it!" Actually Jesus is stating not only should you not buy anything, you should not even be shopping in this area!

Applying this to homosexuality, I believe that Jesus is teaching that even the thought or drive for homosexuality can be sinful. Heterosexuals may have the corresponding problem with lust of the opposite sex as well. Even the drive, passion, and thought to have a sexual relationship with a person other than your spouse is sinful. Both the motivation, passion, and act itself for homosexual behavior is considered sinful by the criteria Jesus established. A person who is celibate but still has homosexual lusts and passions would still be considered sinful. A person may be a Christian, and have homosexual desires and lusts in the same way a person may be a Christian and still have a tendency to lie, cheat, or fornicate. One is not considered saved by how much or how little sin is left in his or her life. Rather, the focus should be on if a person has professed Christ as Savior. Nevertheless, if indeed a person has professed Christ as Savior, then the person should be open to the Spirit working in his or her life to gain control and get rid of all sin, be it homosexuality or whatever.

A clear distinction needs to be made between the underlying causes of a motivation or proclivity toward homosexuality and the motivation itself. For example, a person may have homosexual tendencies because of attachment issues, abuse, or traumatic event from childhood. Psychologists call this "imprinting." Based upon our experiences in childhood, things we did or things done to us, we are imprinted with images, emotions, and attachments that could make a person vulnerable to homosexuality as well as other unhealthy attachments. While investigating the causes of homosexuality is outside the scope of this essay, a person need not feel guilty for having some evil done to them. The person who performed the abuse and trauma is responsible for the sin, not the victim. Nevertheless, every person is responsible for how they handle their own thoughts, desires, and behaviors as he or she continues to grow in Christ. By the power of the Spirit of Christ living in a believer, all these things may be brought under the control of the Holy Spirit in the process of sanctification of the believer.

Why do some elevate homosexuality as a litmus test?

Often the question is asked why some people elevate the issue of homosexuality to be a litmus test for fellowship in the Christian church. They may say: Are not other issues more important? Why make such a big deal about homosexuality when other issues are just as sinful? Can't we still get along and be part of the church fellowship? Let's just love others and let God worry about judging people!

At one of the military branch's chaplain schools, a senior ranking chaplain officer said, "We make such a big deal about homosexuality as a sin, why don't we also make other issues just as big, like adultery and pornography?" It is indeed an indictment that conservative evangelicals have made such a large issue about homosexuality that it appears as though all effort and energy is spent on that one topic. Other sins deserve attention just as much. The outcry against all sexual sins should be a part of the prophetic ministry of the church.

The issue for the question of the litmus test is not so much homosexuality itself as what the issue of homosexuality in the church represents. As has been shown at the beginning of this essay, hermeneutics and biblical interpretation are very important. Certain hermeneutical assumptions have already taken place if one accepts homosexuality as allowable in a biblical worldview. Quite literally, biblical authority, inspiration, and inerrancy may be called into question. If a person believes that certain portions of scripture are not normative for all times, then other sections of scripture may be viewed in the same manner. For example, the same hermeneutical assumptions that undergird a homosexual hermeneutic *may* allow someone to accept polygamy. I emphasize *may* because other philosophical assumptions are involved in the process of interpretation.

Nevertheless, it is important to give the correct emphasis where it is needed. Granted, if we are going to call homosexuality a sin, then we also need to give just as much emphasis to other sexual sins to show how they are not part of God's original plan for human sexuality. But, undergirding homosexual hermeneutics are interpretational assumptions that may lead to other biblical issues as well. So, the issues for many conservative Evangelicals is not just homosexuality, but what interpretational principles can lead to acceptance of homosexuality.

Can a person love the homosexual and not homosexuality?

At the root of the question of loving the homosexual but not the homosexuality is the question if one can love a sinner but not the sin. In other words, can believers show love to any person but not endorse the sins they commit?

Several points need to be made to answer this question. In an earlier question, I noted the dangers of separating the actor from the action, or the sinner from the sin. In our Western worldview, we have a tendency to dichotomize issues and fail to see corresponding connections. In other words, we need to recognize that a person sins because he is a sinner. The core of every person has been influenced by the effects of sin since the day he was born.

In the same way, sexuality also reflects the core of who we are. Sexuality is one of the prime identifiers of self-concept and is formed early in childhood. Both homosexuals and heterosexuals have a deep abiding sexual identity that goes beyond merely how that sexuality is expressed in action.

These points are made to bring up a larger and more important question. One really cannot separate the sin from the sinner for the reasons explained above. To do so disconnects the responsibility of the actor from the action. So a person has to either love the sin and the sinner or hate the sin and the sinner. The larger and more important question is, How should believers relate to non-believers or those committing a certain sin?

Again, Jesus provides an example to us. The Gospel accounts are filled with Jesus interacting with tax collectors (Luke 19:1–10), prostitutes (Luke 7:36–50), adulterers (John 4:3–42), and many others considered outcasts of society and the religious establishment. Did Jesus show love to them? Yes, most certainly He did. But, I believe Jesus also loved them enough to point out their sin to them and their need for a Savior. We cannot use the establishment of a dichotomy between sin and sinner as an excuse to overlook sin or to act in hateful ways. When ministering to a person, we need to have a comprehensive view of the entire person, actor and action, sin and sinner.

How can the church and chaplains respond to homosexuals in a practical way?

From a biblical perspective, how can churches and chaplains best minister to homosexuals? While this question is considered throughout this entire book, to answer this question I would like to share some biblical and theological reflections but also some reflections from practical experience. Various resources are offered in both print and electronic publication, and I would encourage churches and chaplains to invest in as many as they can.

First, churches and chaplains need to address all sins. While homosexuality may be in the forefront in contemporary times, we also need to be aware that homosexuality is not the only issue that needs to be addressed. Other issues such as adultery, pornography, and sexual abuse need attention as well. The church cannot be defined by one issue, but rather must point to the freedom from these sins that can be found in Christ.

Second, churches and chaplains need to have a greater understanding of homosexuals as individuals, not just as a group. While the Christian church may refer to groups such as the homosexual lobby, or homosexual activists, the church and chaplains need to remember ministry is done on a one-to-one basis. Homosexuals have individual faces and names and deserve to be treated as human beings. They have real struggles and emotions. Many come from pasts of abuse and trauma that need to be understood to bring about healing.

God's design from the very beginning has been for a man and a woman to be together in a monogamous, faithful relationship. Throughout the teachings of the Old Testament, the Gospels, and the rest of the New Testament, the teaching has been consistent. Sexuality is at the core of a person and any alteration of that design is against God's best plan for humanity.

Bibliography

18 U.S.C. 245 (b)(2).

Adams and Sullivan v. Howerton 673 F.2d 1036 (1982).

Akridge v. Wilkinson 178 Fed. Appx. 474 6th Cir. 2006).

Allen, John S., Hanna Damasio, Thomas J. Grabowski, Joel Bruss. and Wei Zhang. "Sexual dimorphism and Asymmetries in the Gray–White Composition of the Human Cerebrum," *NeuroImage* 18:4 (April 2003): 880–94.

Allen, Laura S., Mark F. Richey, Yee M. Chai, and Roger A. Gorski, "Sex Differences in the Corpus Callosum of the Living Human Being," *The Journal of Neuroscience* 11:4 (April 1991): 933-42.

Allen, Laura, S., Melissa Hines, James E. Shryne, and Roger A. Gorski. "Two Sexually Dimorphic Cell Groups in the Human Brain," *Journal of Neuroscience* 9:2 (February 1989): 497–506.

Allen, Laura S. and Roger A. Gorski. "Sexual Orientation and the Size of the Anterior Commissure in the Human Brain." *Proceedings of the National Academy of Sciences* 89 (1992): 7199-202.

Alpha Delta Chi v. Reed.

The American Psychiatric Association, "LGBT-Sexual Orientation." http://www.psychiatry.org/mental-health/people/lgbt-sexual-orientation, accessed December 28, 2012.

Atkinson, J. Andrew. "King Arthur in a Yankee Court: The United States Supreme Court's Use of European Law in *Lawrence v. Texas*." *ILSA Journal of International & Comparative Law* 10:1 (Fall 2003): 143-60.

Bacevich, A. J. "Military Culture and Effectiveness." *Society* 31:1 (Nov/Dec 1993): 43-47.

Bach, David L., ed., *Homosexuality, Science and the "Plain Sense" of Scripture.* Grand Rapids: Eerdmans, 2000.

Bailey, Derrick. *Homosexuality and the Western Christian Tradition.* Hamden, CT: Archon Books, 1975.

Bailey, J. Michael, Michael P. Dunne, and Nicholas G. Martin. "Genetic and Environmental Influences on Sexual Orientation and Its Correlates in an Australian Twin Sample." *Journal of Personality and Social Psychology* 78:3 (March 2000): 524-36.

Bailey, J. Michael and Richard C. Pillard. "A Genetic Study of Male Sexual Orientation." *Archives of General Psychiatry* 48 (1991): 1081–96.

Bailey, J. Michael, Richard C. Pillard, K. Dawood, Michael B. Miller, Lindsay A. Farrer, Shruti Trivedi, and Robert L. Murphy. "A family History Study of Male Sexual Orientation Using Three Independent Samples." *Behavior Genetics* 29:2 (1999): 79–86.

Bailey, J. Michael, Richard C. Pillard, Michael C. Neale and Yvonne Agyei. "Heritable Factors Influence Sexual Orientation in Women." *Archives of General Psychiatry* 50:3 (1993): 217-23.

Ball, Carlos A. *From the Closet to the Courtroom: Five LGBT Rights Lawsuits that Have Changed Our Nation.* Boston: Beacon, 2010.

Bancroft, John. "Alfred C. Kinsey and the Politics of Sex Research," *Annual Review of Sex Research* 1:15 (2004): 16–17.

Barclay, Scott, Mary Bernstein, and Anna-Maria Marshall, eds. *Queer Mobilizations: LGBT Activists Confront the Law.* New York: NYU, 2009.

Barrett, C. K. *The Gospel According to John.* 2nd Ed. Philadelphia: Westminster, 1978.

Bartlett, David. "A Biblical Perspective on Homosexuality," *Foundations: Baptist Journal of History and Theology* 20 (1977): 133-46.

Basiak, Jr., John F. "Dangerous Predictions: Referencing 'Emerging" History and Tradition in Substantive Due Process Jurisprudence in an Era of Blue State Federalism." *Widener Law Journal* 15:1 (2005): 135-74.

Bayer, Ronald. *Homosexuality and American Psychiatry: The Politics of Diagnosis.* New York: Basic Books, 1981; repr. Princeton, NJ: Princeton University, 1987.

BBC News, "Scans See Brain Differences." June 16, 2008. https://news.bbc.co.uk/2/hi/health/7456588.stm, accessed January 25, 2013.

Beauvais, Fred. "American Indians and Alcohol." http://pubs.niaaa.nih.gov/publications/arh22-4/253.pdf, accessed January 30, 2013.

Belkin, Aaron and Geoffrey Bateman, eds, *Don't Ask, Don't Tell: Debating the Gay Ban in the Military* Boulder, CO: Lynne Rienner, 2003.

Bell, Alan P. and Martin S. Weinberg. *Homosexualities.* New York: Simon & Schuster, 1978.

Beller v. Middendorf 632 F. 2d 788 (1977).

Bender, Lauretta and Alvin Eldridge Grugett. "Follow-up Report on Children Who Had Atypical Sexual Experience." *American Journal of Orthopsychiatry* 22 (1952): 825-37.

Berg v. Claytor 436 F. Supp. 76 (D.D.C. 1977).

Bernard, J. H. *A Critical and Exegetical Commentary on the Gospel According to St. John*, 2 vols. Ed. A. H. McNeile. *International Critical Commentary.* Edinburgh: T & T Clark, 1928.

Berns, Walter. "Pornography versus Democracy" *Society* (September/October 1999): 16-25.

———. "Taking Virtue Seriously" review of Harry M. Clor, *Public Morality and Liberal Society* in *The Public Interest* (Summer 1997): 126.

Bernstein v. Ocean Grove Camp Meeting Assoc., N.J. Div. on Civ. Rights, No. PN34XB-03008 (2008).

Billings, Paul and Jonathan Beckwith, "Born Gay?" *Technology Review* 96:5 (July 1993): 60-62.

Blanchard, Ray. "Fraternal Birth Order and the Maternal Immune Hypothesis of Male Homosexuality." *Hormones and Behavior* 40: (2001), 109 – 110.

———. "Controversies in Sexual Medicine—Male Homosexuality: Nature or Culture?" *Journal of Sexual Medicine* 7:10 (2010): 3245-53.

Blanchard, Ray and Anthony F. Bogaert. "Homosexuality in Men and Number of Older Brothers." *The American Journal of Psychiatry* 153:1 (January 1996): 27–31.

Blanchard, Ray, James M. Cantor, Anthony F. Bogaert, S. Marc Breedlove, and Lee Ellis. "Interaction of Fraternal Birth Order and Handedness in the Development of Male Homosexuality." *Hormones and Behavior* 49 (2006): 405–14.

Bluestone, Gloria. "Going to the Chapel and We're Going to Get Married; But Will the State Recognize the Marriage? The Constitutionality of State Marriage Laws After *Lawrence v. Texas*." *Texas Journal of Civil Liberties & Civil Rights* 10:2 (Spring 2005): 189-221.

Bonsor, Jack A. "An Objective Disorder: Homosexual Orientation and God's Eternal Law." *Horizons* 24:2 (1997): 193-214.

Borchert, Gerald L. *John* 1-11. Vol. 25A, *New American Commentary*. Nashville: Broadman & Holman, 1996.

Boswell, John. *Christianity, Social Tolerance, and Homosexuality*. Chicago: University of Chicago, 1980

Boughton, Lynne C. "Biblical Texts and Homosexuality: A Response to John Boswell," *Irish Theological Quarterly* 58 (1992): 142-43.

Boutilier v. Immigration and Naturalization Service 387 US 118 (1967).

Bowers v. Hardwick 478 US 186 (1986).

Boyarin, Daniel. "Are There Any Jews in 'The History of Sexuality'?" *Journal of the History of Sexuality* 5:3 (Jan 1995): 335-55.

Boys, Don. "Washington, Jefferson, Madison, Baptists, and the Constitution!" http://www.covenantnews.com/boys080709.htm, accessed January 10, 2013.

Brawley, Robert, ed., *Biblical Ethics and Homosexuality: Listening to Scripture*. Louisville: Westminster John Knox, 1996.

Brooks, Thomas D. "First Amendment—Penalty Enhancement for Hate Crimes: Content Regulation, Questionable State Interests and Non-Traditional Sentencing." *Journal of Criminal Law & Criminology* 84:4 (Winter/Spring 1994): 703-42.

Brown, Colin. "Love," in Colin Brown, ed. *New International Dictionary of New Testament Theology*. Grand Rapids: Zondervan, 1976, 2:538-51.

Brumley, Jeff. "'Wounded' Chaplain Leaves SBC for CBF." *Associated Baptist Press*, August 10, 2012, http://www.abpnews.com/item/7705-air-force-chaplain-who-left-sbc-for-cbf-is-deeply-wounded#.UERfJWthiSM, accessed September 3, 2012.

Bull, Christopher and John Gallagher. *Perfect Enemies: The Religious Right, the Gay Movement, and the Politics of the* 1990's. New York: Crown, 1996.

Byne, William and Bruce Parsons. "Human Sexual Orientation: The Biologic Theories Reappraised." *Archives of General Psychiatry* 50 (March 1993): 228-39.

Byne, William, Stuart Tobet, Linda A. Mattiace, Mitchell S. Lasco, Eileen Kemether, Mark A. Edgar, Susan Morgello, Monte S. Buchsbaum, and Liesl B. Jones. "The Interstitial Nuclei of the Human Anterior Hypothalamus: An Investigation of Variation with Sex, Sexual Orientation, and HIV status." *Hormones and Behavior* 40 (2001): 86-92.

Carpenter, Dale. *Flagrant Conduct: The Story of Lawrence v. Texas, How a Bedroom Arrest Decriminalized Gay Americans*. New York: W. W. Norton, 2012.

———. "The Unknown Past of *Lawrence v. Texas*." *Michigan Law Review* 102:7 (June 2004): 1464-1527.

Carson, Donald A. *The Intolerance of Tolerance*. Grand Rapids: Eerdmans, 2012.

Cenite, Mark. "Federalizing or Eliminating Online Obscenity Law as an Alternative to Contemporary Community Standards" *Communication Law & Policy* 9:1 (Winter 2004): 25-71.

Chapman, Loren, and Jean Chapman, "Test Results are What You Think They Are," in Daniel Kahneman, Paul Slovic, and Amos Tversky, eds., *Judgment Under Uncertainty: Heuristics and Biases.* Cambridge: Cambridge University, 1982, 238-48.

Childers, Brent. "An Evangelical Christian Apologizes," in Michael Gold, ed. *Crisis: 40 Stories Revealing the Personal, Social, and Religious Pain and Trauma of Growing up Gay in America.* Austin: Greenleaf, 2008, 91-95.

Chorba, Christopher. "The Danger of Federalizing Hate Crimes: Congressional Misconceptions and the Unintended Consequences of the Hate Crimes Prevention Act." *Virginia Law Review* 87:2 (April 2001): 319-80.

Christian Legal Society v. Martinez, 130 S.Ct. 795 (2009).

Ciani, Andrea Camperio, Paolo Cermelli, and Giovanni Zanzotto. "Sexually Antagonistic Selection in Human Male Homosexuality." *PloS ONE* 3:6 (June 2008): e2282.

Clor, Harry M. *Obscenity and Public Morality: Censorship in a Liberal Society.* Chicago: University of Chicago, 1969.

———. *Public Morality and Liberal Society: Essays on Decency, Law, and Pornography.* Notre Dame: University of Notre Dame, 1996.

Cohen-Bendahan, Celina C. C., Cornelieke van de Beek, and Sheri A. Berenbaum. "Prenatal Sex Hormone Effects on Child and Adult Sex-Typed Behavior: Methods and Findings." *Neuroscience and Behavioral Research Reviews* 29 (2005): 353-84.

Cohler, Bertam J. and Robert M. Galatzer-Levy. *The Course of Gay and Lesbian Lives: Social and Psychoanalytic Perspectives.* Chicago: University of Chicago, 2000.

Coker, Carter T. "Hope-Fulfilling or Effectively Chilling? Reconciling the Hate Crimes Protection Act with the First Amendment." *Vanderbilt Law Review* 64:1 (January 2011): 271-99.

Collins, Raymond. *First Corinthians.* Collegeville, MN: Liturgical, 1999.

Colucci, Frank J. "From Privacy to Liberty: Justice Kennedy's Interpretive Turn in *Lawrence v. Texas.*" Conference Paper, New England Political Science Association, 2004.

The Comstock Act 17, Statute 598.

Connick v. Myers 461 U.S. 138 (1983).

Côté, Karine, Christopher M. Earls, and Martin L. Lalumière. "Birth Order, Birth Interval, and Deviant Sexual Preferences Among Sex Offenders." *Sexual Abuse: Journal of Research and Treatment* 14 (2002): 67– 81

Crocker, Thomas P. "From Privacy to Liberty: The Fourth Amendment After *Lawrence.*" *UCLA Law Review* 57:1 (October 2009): 1-69.

Culhane, John G. "Writing On, Around, and Through *Lawrence v. Texas.*" *Creighton Law Review* 38:2 (2005): 493-506.

Cummings, Joel P. "Is Article 125, Sodomy a Dead Letter in Light of *Lawrence v. Texas* and the New Article 120?" *Army Lawyer* 428 (January 2009): 1-29.

Curtiss, Nathan R. "Unraveling *Lawrence's* Concerns About Legislated Morality: The Constitutionality of Laws Criminalizing the Sale of Obscene Devices." *Brigham Young University Law Review* 4 (2010): 1369-98.

Davies, Margaret. "New Testament Ethics and Ours," *Biblical Interpretation: A Journal of Contemporary Approaches* 3:3 (1995): 320-27.

Dawson v. Delaware 503 US 159 (1992).

Dearman, J. Andrew. "Marriage in the Old Testament," in Robert Brawley, ed. *Biblical Ethics and Homosexuality: Listening to Scripture.* Louisville: Westminster John Knox, 1996.

De Young, James B. "The Contributions of the Septuagint to Biblical Sanctions Against Homosexuality," *Journal of the Evangelical Theological Society* 34 (1991): 158-65.

Driver, S. R. *Deuteronomy, International Critical Commentary.* Edinburgh: T & T Clark, 1896.

Dronenberg v. Zech 741 f. 2d 1388 (1984).

Dubler, Aiela R. "From *McClaughlin v. Florida* to *Lawrence v. Texas*: Sexual Freedom and the Road to Marriage." *Columbia Law Review* 106:5 (June 2006): 1165-87.

Dupuis, Martin and William A. Thompson, eds. *Defending Same-Sex Marriage, Volume 3: The Freedom-to-Marry Movement: Education, Advocacy, Culture, and the Media.* Westport, CT: Praeger, 2007.

Eichrodt, Walther. *Theology of the Old Testament.* 2 vols. Trans. J. A. Baker. Philadelphia: Westminster, 1961-1967.

Eisenstadt v. Baird 405 US 438 (1972).

Elane Photography v. Willock, HRD No. 06-12-20-0685 (N.M. Human Rights Common 2008).

Eskridge, Jr., William N. *Equality Practice: Civil Unions and the Future of Gay Rights.* New York: Routledge, 2002.

Fausto-Sterling, Anne. *Sexing the Body: Gender Politics and the Construction of Sexuality.* New York: Basic Books, 2000.

Fee, Gordon. "The First Epistle to the Corinthians," in *New International Commentary of the New Testament.* Grand Rapids: Eerdmans, 1987.

Feinberg, John and Paul Feinberg. *Ethics for a Brave New World*, 2nd ed. Wheaton, IL: Crossway, 2010.

Fetner, Tina. *How the Religious Right Shaped Lesbian and Gay Activism (Social Movements, Protest, and Contention, Volume 31).* Minneapolis: University of Minnesota, 2008.

Finnis, John. "Law, Morality, and 'Sexual Orientation'" in John Corvino, ed. *Same Sex: Debating the Ethics, Science, and Culture of Homosexuality.* Lanham, MD: Rowan and Littlefield, 1997, sec. 5.

Frank, Nathaniel. *Unfriendly Fire: How the Gay Ban Undermines the Military and Weakens America.* New York: St. Martin's, 2009.

Franke, Katherine M. "The Domesticated Liberty of *Lawrence v. Texas.*" *Columbia Law Journal* 104:5 (June 2004): 1399-426

Fugelsang, Steven J. "Reconciling *Lawrence v. Texas* with 'Don't Ask, Don't Tell': The Value of the *Cook v. Gates* Intermediate-Deferential Approach." *Civil Rights Law Journal* 20:2 (2010): 237-78.

Gagnon, Robert A. J. *The Bible and Homosexual Practice: Texts and Hermeneutics.* Nashville: Abingdon, 2001.

Garcetti v. Cebdlos 547 U.S. 410 (2006).

Geldblum, Chai R. "Employment Commissioner: 'I'm having a hard time coming up with any case in which religious liberty should win." http://www.afa.net/Detail.aspx?id=2147493401, accessed 10 January, 2013.

George, Robert P. *The Clash of Orthodoxies: Law, Religion, and Morality in Crisis.* Wilmington, DE: ISI Books, 2001.

———. *Making Men Moral: Civil Liberties and Public Morality.* Oxford: Clarendon, 1993.

Germanotta, Stefani. "*Born This Way*," http://www.azlyrics.com/lyrics/ladygaga/bornthisway.html, accessed January 16, 2013.

Ginsberg, Alex. "Hate is Enough." *Brooklyn Law Review* 76:4 (Summer 2011): 1599-1633.

[GLAAD] *Media Reference Guide*, 8th ed. New York: Gay & Lesbian Alliance Against Defamation, Inc., 2010.

Gold, Michael, ed. *Crisis: 40 Stories Revealing the Personal, Social, and Religious Pain and Trauma of Growing up Gay in America.* Austin: Greenleaf, 2008.

Gooren, Louis J. "The Biology of Human Psychosexual Differentiation." *Hormone Behavior* 50:4 (2006): 589–601.

———. "Care of Transsexual Persons." *The New England Journal of Medicine* 364:13 (March 31, 2011): 1251–57.

Gorski, Roger A. "Hypothalamic imprinting by gonadal steroid hormones." *Advances in Experimental Medical Biology* 511 (2002): 57–70.

Gorski, Roger, John H. Gordon, James E. Shryne, and Arthur M. Southam. "Evidence for a Morphological Sex Difference Within the Medial Preoptic Area of the Rat." *Brain Research* 148 (1978): 333–46.

Gowan, Donald. *From Eden to Babel: A Commentary on the Book of Genesis* 1-11 (Grand Rapids: Eerdmans, 1988.

Graff, E. J. "The High Court Finally Gets It Right." *Boston Globe* (June 29, 2003), D11.

Greenberg, David. *The Construction of Homosexuality*. Chicago: University of Chicago, 1990.

Greene, Jamal. "Beyond *Lawrence*: Metaprivacy and Punishment." *Yale Law Journal* 115:8 (June 2006): 1862-928.

Greenough, Willliam T., C. S. Carter, C. Steerman, and Timothy J. DeVoogd. "Sex Differences in Dentritic Patterns in Hamster Preoptic Area." *Brain Research* 126:1 (May, 1977): 63–72.

Grenz, Stanley J. *Welcoming but Not Affirming: An Evangelical Response to Homosexuality.* Louisville: Westminster John Knox Press, 1998.

Gunton, Colin E. *The One, the Three and the Many: God, Creation and the Culture of Modernity (The 1992 Bampton Lectures).* Cambridge: Cambridge University, 1993.

———. *The Promise of Trinitarian Theology*. Edinburgh: T & T Clark, 1991.

Haenchen, Ernst. *John 2: A Commentary on the Gospel of John Chapters 7-21*. Trans. Robert W. Funk. Ed. Robert W. Funk with Ulrich Busse. *Hermeneia*. Philadelphia: Fortress, 1984.

Hagedorn, Audrey K. "'Don't Ask, Don't Tell,' the Supreme Court, and *Lawrence* the 'Laggard.'" *Indiana Law Journal* 87 (2012): 795-822.

Hagerty, Barbara Bradley. "Chaplains Worry About Careers If 'Don't Ask' Is Lifted" December 9, 2010; http://www.npr.org/2010/12/09/131918799/chaplains-worry-about-careers-if-don-t-ask-is-lifted, accessed January 31, 2011.

Haggerty, Timothy. "History Repeating Itself: Gay Men and Lesbians in the Military Before 'Don't Ask, Don't Tell'" in Aaron Belkin and Geoffrey Bateman, eds., *Don't Ask, Don't Tell: Debating the Gay Ban in the Military* (Boulder, CO: Lynne Reiner, 2003) 8-53.

Halwani, Raja, Gary Jaeger, James S. Stramel, Richard Nunan, William S. Wilkerson, and Timothy F. Murphy. "What is Gay and Lesbian Philosophy?" *Metaphilosophy* 39:4-5 (October 2008): 433-71.

Hamer, Dean, Stella Hu, Victoria L. Magnuson, Nan Hu, and Angela M.L. Pattatucci. "A Linkage Between DNA Markers on the X Chromosome and Male Sexual Orientation." *Science* 261:5119 (July 16, 1993): 321-27.

Haque, Adil Ahmad. "*Lawrence v. Texas* and the Limits of the Criminal Law." *Harvard Civil Rights-Civil Liberties Law Review* 42:1 (Winter 2007): 1-43.

Hays, Richard B. *The Moral Vision of the New Testament: Community, Cross, New Creation.* San Francisco: HarperSanFrancisco, 1996.

Hefner, Philip. "Imago Dei: The Possibility and Necessity of the Human Person," in Niels Henrick Gregersen, Willem B. Drees, and Ulf Görman, eds. *The Human Person in Science and Theology*. Grand Rapids: Eerdmans, 2000, 73-94.

Helminiak,Daniel A. "The Ethics of Sex: A Call to the Gay Community." *Pastoral Psychology* 52:3 (January 2004): 259-67.

———. *What the Bible Really Says About Homosexuality*. San Francisco: Alamo Square, 1995.

Hice, Jody. *It's Now or Never: A Call to Reclaim America.* Nashville: Westbow, 2012.

Hoffman, Brian. "'A Certain Amount of Prudishness': Nudist Magazines and the Liberalisation of American Obscenity Law, 1947-58." *Gender & History* 22:3 (November 2010): 708-32.

Hooker, Evelyn. "The Adjustment of the Male Overt Homosexual" *Journal of Projective Techniques* 21 (1957): 18-31.

———. "Male Homosexuals and Their 'Worlds,'" in Judd Marmor, ed. *Sexual Inversion.* New York: Basic Books, 1965, 83-107.

Horner, Tom. *Jonathan Loved David: Homosexuality in Biblical Times.* Philadelphia: Westminster, 1978.

House Judiciary Committee Report. "Background and Rationale for Legislation." *Congressional Digest* 86:6 (June 2007): 168-69.

Hu, Stella, Angela M.L. Pattatucci, Chavis Patterson, Lin Li, David W. Fulker, Stacey S. Cherny, Leonid Kruglyak, and Dean H. Hamer. "Linkage Between Sexual Orientation and Chromosome Xq28 in males but not in females." *Nature Genetics* 11 (1995): 248–56.

Hulstein, Matthew J. "Recognizing and Respecting the Rights of LGBT Youth in Child Custody Proceedings." *Berkeley Journal of Gender, Law & Justice* 2:2 (Summer 2012): 171-97.

Hunter, Nan D., Courtney G. Joslin, and Sharon M. McGowan. *The Rights of Lesbians, Gay Men, Bisexuals, and Transgender People: The Authoritative ACLU Guide to the Rights of Lesbians, Gay Men, Bisexuals, and Transgender People*, 4th ed. New York: NYU, 2004.

Ingram, Michael. "Participating Victims: A Study of Sexual Offenses with Boys." in Larry L. Constantine and Floyd Mansfield Martinson, eds. *Children and Sex: New Findings, New Perspectives.* Boston, Little Brown, 1981, 177-87.

Jacobs, James B. "Should Hate Be A Crime?" *Public Interest* 113 (Fall 1993): 3-14.

Jacobs, James B. and Kimberly Potter. *Hate Crimes: Criminal Law & Identity Politics (Studies in Crime and Public Policy).* New York: Oxford, 2000.

Johnson, Jeh Charles and Carter F. Ham, co-chairs, *Support Plan for Implementation: Report of the Comprehensive Review of the Issues Associated with a Repeal of "Don't Ask, Don't Tell"* Washington, DC: Department of Defense. November 30, 2010.

Jones, Gerald P. "The Study of Intergenerational Intimacy in North America: Beyond Politics and Pedophilia." *Journal of Homosexuality* 20:1-2 (1991): 275-95.

Jones, James. *Alfred Kinsey: A Public/Private Life.* New York: W. W. Norton, 1997.

Jones, Stanton and Alex W. Kwee. "Scientific Research, Homosexuality, and the Church's Moral Debate: An Update." *Journal of Psychology and Christianity* 24:4 (2005): 304-305.

Jones, Stanton and Mark A. Yarhouse. *Homosexuality: The Use of Scientific Research in the Church's Moral Debate.* Downers Grove: InterVarsity, 2000.

Julber, Eric. "You Can't Print It." *ONE* (October 1954).

Kahn, Ronald. "Originalism, the Living Constitution, and Supreme Court Decision Making in the Twenty-first Century: Explaining *Lawrence v. Texas.*" *Maryland Law Review* 67:1 (2007): 25-35.

Kaiser, Walter C. *Toward Old Testament Ethics.* Grand Rapids: Zondervan, 1983.

Kameny v. Brucker, petition for *cert.*, quoted in Murdoch and Price, 56.

Kamionkowski, S. Tamar. *Gender Reversal and Cosmic Chaos.* Sheffield: Sheffield University, 2003.

Kamisar, Yale. "Forward: Can Glucksberg Survive *Lawrence*? Another Look at the End of Life and Personal Autonomy." *Michigan Law Review* 106:8 (June 2008): 1453-78.

Karlan, Pamela S. "Forward: Loving Lawrence." *Michigan Law Review* 102:7 (June 2004): 1447-63.

Keener, Craig. *The Gospel of John: A Commentary.* 2 Vols. Peabody, MA: Hendrickson, 2003.

Kendler, Kenneth S., Laura M. Thornton, Stephen E. Gilman, and Ronald C. Kessler. "Sexual Orientation in a U.S. National Sample of Twin and Nontwin Sibling Pairs." *American Journal of Psychiatry* 157:11 (November 2000): 1843–46.

Keyishain v. Board of Regents of University of State of New York, 385 U.S. 589 (1967).

Kinsey, Alfred, Wardell Pomeroy, and Clyde Martin. *Sexual Behavior in the Human Male.* Philadelphia: W. B. Saunders Company, 1948.

Kinsey, Alfred, Wardell Pomeroy, Clyde E. Martin, and Paul H. Gebhard. *Sexual Behavior in the Human Female.* Philadelphia: W. B. Saunders Company, 1953.

The Kinsey Institute. "Facts About *Kinsey* The Film." www.kinseyinstitute.org/about/Movie-facts.html, accessed December 21, 2012.

Kirk, Marshall and Erastes Pill [Hunter Madsen]. "The Overhauling of Straight America." *Guide Magazine* (November 1987): 7-14.

Kirk, Marshall and Hunter Madsen. *After the Ball: How America Will Conquer its Fear and Hatred of Gays in the* 90's. New York: Plume, 1990.

Klar, A. J. S. "Excess of Counterclockwise Scalp Hair–Whorl Rotation in Homosexual Men." *Journal of Genetics* 83:3 (December 2004): 251-55.

Klingenschmitt, Gordon James. e-mail to supporters, dated Wednesday, January 26, 2011.

Koppelman, Andrew. "Does Obscenity Cause Moral Harm?" *Columbia Law Review* 105 (2005): 1635-79.

Kraemer, Bernd, Thomas Noll, Aba Delsignore, Gabriella Milos, Ulrich Schnyder, and Urs Hepp. "Finger Length Ratio (2D:4D) and Dimensions of Sexual Orientation." *Neuropsychobiology* 53:4 (2006): 210–14.

Kranz, Rachel and Tim Cusik. *Gay Rights: Library in a Book.* New York: Facts on File, 2000.

Kristol, Irving. "The Case for Liberal Censorship" in Victor B. Cline, ed. *Where Do You Draw the Line?: An Exploration into Media Violence, Pornography, and Censorship.* Provo, UT: Brigham Young University, 1974.

Laing, John D. *In Jesus' Name: Evangelicals and Military Chaplaincy.* Eugene, OR: Resource, 2010.

Lalumière, Martin L,. Grant T. Harris, Vernon L. Quinsey, and Marnie E. Rice. "Sexual Deviance and Number of Older Brothers Among Sexual Offenders." *Sexual Abuse: A Journal of Research and Treatment* 10.1 (1998): 5–15

Landis, Judson T. "The Experiences of 500 Children with Adult Sexual Deviation." *Psychiatric Quarterly Supplement* 30 (1956): 91-109.

Langström, Niklas, Qazi Rahman, Eva Carlstöm, and Paul Lichtenstein. "Genetic and Environmental Effects on Same-sex Sexual Behavior: A Population Study of Twins in Sweden," *Archives of Sexual Behavior* 39 (2010):75–80.

Latham, Tyger. "Scientific Homophobia: When It Comes to Homosexuality, We Have Not Always Practiced What We Preach," *Psychology Today,* April 19, 2011. http://www.psychologytoday.com/blog/therapy-matters/201104/scientific-homophobia. accessed December 28, 2012.

Lawrence, Frederick M. *Punishing Hate: Bias Crimes Under American Law.* Cambridge: Harvard, 1999.

Lawrence v. Texas 539 US 558 (2003).

Lempp, Reinhart. "Psychological Damage to Children as a Result of Sexual Offenses." *Child Abuse and Neglect* 2 (1978): 243-45.

Letter to President Barack Obama and Dr. Robert M. Gates, September 16, 2010.

LeVay, Simon. "A Difference in Hypothalamic Structure Between Heterosexual and Homosexual Men." *Science* 253:5023 (August 30, 1991): 1034-37.

———. *Gay, Straight, and the Reason Why: The Science of Sexual Orientation.* New York: Oxford, 2010.

———. "My Resume." http://www.simonlevay.com/my-resume, accessed January 4, 2013.

Lewis, Anthony. "Nudist Magazines Win Mail Rights." *New York Times.* January 14, 1958, 35.

Li, Chin-Keung. "'The Main Thing is Being Wanted': Some Case Studies on Adult Sexual Experiences with Children" *Journal of Homosexuality* 20:1-2 (1991): 129-43.

Longstaff v. Immigration and Naturalization Service 716 F.2d 1439 (1983).

Loveland, Anne C. *American Evangelicals and the U.S. Military* 1942-1993. Baton Rouge: Louisiana State, 1996.

Lund, Nelson. "*Lawrence v. Texas* and Judicial Hubris." *Michigan Law Review* 102:7 (June 2004): 1555-1614.

MacCulloch, Sophie I., Nicola S. Gray, Helen K. Phillips, John Taylor, and Malcolm J. MacCulloch. "Birth Order in Sex-Offending and Aggressive Offending Men," *Archives of Sexual Behavior* 33.5 (October 2004): 467–74.

MacDonald, Ean [pseudonym for Harry Hay], "Preliminary Concepts, International Bachelors Fraternal Orders for Peace and Social Dignity," (Los Angeles: private printing, 1950)

MacNamara, Brian S. "New York's Hate Crimes Act of 2000: Problematic and Redundant Legislation Aimed at Subjective Motivation." *Albany Law Review* 66:2 (2003): 519-45.

Macedo, Stephen. "Homosexuality and the Conservative Mind." *Georgetown Law Journal* 84 (1995): 278.

———. *Liberal Virtues: Citizenship, Virtue and Community in Liberal Constitutionalism.* Oxford: Oxford University, 1991.

Marshall, S. L. A. *Men Against Fire: The Problem of Battle Command in Future War.* New York: Morrow, 1947.

Martin, Dale. "*Arsenokoites* and *Malakos*: Meanings and Consequences," in Robert Brawley, ed. *Biblical Ethics and Homosexuality.* Louisville: Westminster John Knox, 1996, 117-36.

Matlovich v. Secretary of the Air Force 591 F.2d. 852 (1976).

McDavid, Christopher Thomas. "I Know It When I See It: Obscenity, Copyright, and the Cautionary Tale of the Lanham Act." *University of Louisville Law Review* 47:3 (Spring 2009): 561-83.

McDonald, Barry P. "If Obscenity Were to Discriminate." *Northwestern University Law Review* 103:1 (Winter 2009): 475-90.

McDonough, William. "Alasdair MacIntyre as Help for Rethinking Catholic Natural Law Estimates of Same-Sex Partnerships." *Annual of the Society of Christian Ethics* 21 (2001): 191-213.

McEwen, Alvin A. *Holy Bullies and Headless Monsters: Exposing the Lies of the Anti-gay Industry.* Bloomington, IN: Xlibris, 2007.

Medline Plus. "Congenital Adrenal Hyperplasia." http://www.nlm.nih.gov/medlineplus/ency/article/000411.htm, accessed January 9, 2013.

Mezey, Susan Gluck. *Queers in Court: Gay Rights Law and Public Policy.* Lanham: Rowman & Littlefield, 2007.

Michaels, J. Ramsey. *The Gospel of John. New International Commentary on the New Testament.* Grand Rapids: Eerdmans, 2010.

Milgrom, Jacob. "Does the Bible Prohibit Homosexuality?" *Bible Review* (Dec 1993): 11.

Miller v. California 413 US 15 (1973).

Milton, Michael A. "'So What are You Doing Here?': The Role of the Minister of the Gospel in Hospital Visitation, or A Theological Cure for the Crisis in Evangelical Pastoral Care." *Journal of the Evangelical Theological Society* 46 (2003): 449-63.

Mogul, Joey L., Andrea J. Ritchie, and Kay Whitlock. *Queer (In)Justice: The Criminalization of LGBT People in the United States.* Boston: Beacon, 2011.

Mohr, Johan W. "A Child Has Been Molested," *Medical Aspects of Human Sexuality* 2:11 (1968): 43-50.

Morris, Leon. *The Gospel According to John.* Rev. Ed. *New International Commentary on the New Testament.* Grand Rapids: Eerdmans, 1995.

Müller, Roland. *The Messenger, the Message, and the Community: Three Critical Issues for the Cross-Cultural Church Planter.* 2nd ed. Altona, Canada: CanBooks, 2010.

Murdoch, Joyce and Deb Price. *Courting Justice: Gay Men and Lesbians v. the Supreme Court.* New York: Basic, 2001.

Mustanski, Brian S., Michael G. DuPree, Caroline M. Nievergelt, Sven Bocklandt, Nicholas, J. Schork, Dean H. Hamer. "A Genomewide Scan of Male Sexual Orientation." *Human Genetics* 116 (2005): 272-78.

Myers, Carol. *Discovering Women in Context.* New York: Oxford University Press, 1988.

Naeger, Jennifer. "And Then There Were None: The Repeal of Sodomy Laws after *Lawrence v. Texas* and Its Effect on the Custody and Visitation Rights of Gay and Lesbian Parents." *St. John's Law Review* 78:2 (Spring 2004): 397-425.

Nava, Michael and Robert Dawidoff. *Created Equal: Why Gay Rights Matter to America.* New York: St. Martin's, 1994.

Nearpass, Gregory R. "The Overlooked Constitutional Objection and Practical Concerns to Penalty-Enhancement Provisions of Hate Crime Legislation." *Albany Law Review* 66:2 (2003): 547-73.

Nolland, John. *Luke* 9:21-18:34. Vol. 35B. *Word Biblical Commentary.* Dallas: Word, 1993.

"NU Cancels Human Sexuality Class." http://chicago.cbslocal.com/2011/05/09/nu-cancels-human-sexuality-class, accessed January 31, 2013.

Obama, President Barak H. "Remarks on the Enactment of the Matthew Shepard and James Byrd, Jr. Hate Crimes Prevention Act." October 28, 2009.

O'Brien, William. "Official Transcript of Proceedings before the Post Office Department." National Archives and Records Administration, College Park, Maryland, RG 21, US District Court for DC, Civil Action #74-55, *Sunshine Book Company v. Summerfield*, Box 1578, tabbed, 16W3/17/32/02.

ONE, Inc. v. Olesen 355 US 371 (1958).

Park, Mitchell F. "Defining One's Own Concept of Existence and Meaning of the Universe: The Presumption of Liberty in *Lawrence v. Texas.*" *Brigham Young University Law Review* 3 (2006): 837-87.

Perelman, Sabrina A. "A Step in the Right Direction: How *Kansas v. Limon* Indicates a Brighter Future for Gay Rights Under *Lawrence v. Texas.*" *Georgetown Journal of Gender & the Law* 7:2 (2006): 217-53.

Peterson, Meghen. "The Right Decision for the Wrong Reason." Creighton Law Review 37:3 (April 2004): 653-707.

Phelps v. Dunn 965 F.2d 93 (6th Cir. 1992).

Pickering v. Board of Education 391 U.S. 563 (1968).

Pinello, Daniel R. *Gay Rights and American Law.* New York: Cambridge, 2003.

Plumley v. Landmark Chevrolet, Inc 122 F. 3d 308, 310 (CA5 1997).

Plummer, Kenneth. "Understanding Childhood Sexualities." *Journal of Homsexuality* 20:1-2 (1991): 231-249.

Pope, Stephen J. "Scientific and Natural Law Analyses of Homosexuality." *Journal of Religious Ethics* 25:1 (Spring 1997): 89-126.

Potvin, Ernie. "Harry Hay Remembers Jim Kepner," *ONE-IGLA Bulletin* 5 (Summer 1998): 14-16.

"Prostitution and Sex Work," *Georgetown Journal of Gender & the Law* 10:2 (2009): 433-56.

Quill, Gavin F. "Motivation, Causation and Hate Crimes Sentence Enhancement: A Cautious Approach to Mind Reading and Incarceration." *Drake Law Review* 59:1 (Fall 2010): 181-216.

http://www.rainbowallianceopenfaith.homstead.com/GayAgenda.html.

Raisman, Geoffrey and Pauline Field. "Sexual Dimorphism in the Neuropil of the Preoptic Area of the Rat and Its Dependence on Neonatal Androgen." *Brain Research* 54 (1973): 1–29.

———. "Sexual Dimorphism in the Preoptic Area of the Rat." *Science* 173 (August 20, 1971): 731–33.

Reinheimer, Justin. "What *Lawrence* Should Have Said: Reconstructing an Equality Approach." *California Law Review* 96 (2008): 505-51.

Reisman, Judith A. and Edward W. Eichel. *Kinsey, Sex and Fraud: The Indoctrination of a People.* Lafayette, LA: Huntington House, 1990.

Rice, George, Carol Anderson, Neil Risch and George Ebers. "Male Homosexuality: Absence of Linkage to Microsatellite Markers at Xq28." *Science* 284 (April 1999): 248–56.

Richards, David A. J. *The Case for Gay Rights: From Bowers to Lawrence and Beyond.* Lawrence: University of Kansas, 2005.

Richlin, Amy. "Eros Underground: Greece and Rome in Gay Print Culture 1953-65." in Beert C. Verstraete and Vernon Provencal, eds. *Same-Sex Desire and Love in Greco-Roman Antiquity and in the Classical Tradition of the West.* Binghamton, NY: Harrington Park, 2005, 421-62.

Rigdon v. Perry 962 F. Supp. 150 (D.D.C. 1997).

Rimmerman, Craig A. *From Identity to Politics: The Lesbian and Gay Movements in the United States.* Philadelphia: Temple University, 2002.

Risch, Neil, Elizabeth Squires-Wheeler, and Bronya J.B.Keats. "Male Sexual Orientation and Genetic Evidence," *Science* 262 (1993): 2063–65.

Rogers, Jack. *Jesus, The Bible, and Homosexuality: Explode the Myths, Heal the Church.* Philadelphia: Westminster John Knox, 2006.

Rosen, Jeffrey. "Kennedy Curse." *New Republic* 229:3 (July 21, 2003): 15-18.

Rosenberg v. Fleuti 374 US 449 (1963).

Rosenbury, Laura A. "Sex In and Out of Intimacy." *Emory Law Journal* 59:4 (2010): 809-68.

Roth v. United States 354 US 476 (1957).

Rubin, Gayle S. "Thinking Sex: Notes for a Radical Theory of the Politics of Sexuality" in Henry Abelove, Michele Aina Barale, and David M. Halperin, eds. *The Lesbian and Gay Studies Reader.* New York: Routledge, 1993, 3-44; reprinted from Carol S. Vance, ed. *Pleasure and Danger: Exploring Female Sexuality.* London: Routledge & Kegan Paul, 1984.

Ruskoia, Teemu. "Gay Rights versus Queer Theory: What is Left of Sodomy After *Lawrence v. Texas*?" *Social Text* 23:3/4 (Fall/Winter 2005): 235-49.

Salzman, Todd A. and Michael G. Lawler. "New Natural Law Theory and Foundational Sexual Ethical Principles: A Critique and a Proposal." *Heythrop Journal* 47 (2006): 182-205.

Sandfort, Theo. *Het Seksuele Aspekt van Pedofiele Relaties: Ervaringen van Jongens.* Ultrecht: The State University, Sociological Institute, 1981. published in English as *The Sexual Aspect of Pedophile Relations: The Experience of Twenty-Five Boys.* Amsterdam: Spartacus, 1982.

———. "Pedophile Relationships in the Netherlands: Alternative Lifestyle for Children?" *Alternative Lifestyles* 5 (1983): 164-83.

San Diego v. Roe 543 U.S. 77 (2004).

Satinover, Jeffry. *Homosexuality and the Politics of Truth.* Grand Rapids: Baker, 1996.

Savic, Ivanka, Hans Berglund, and Per Lindstrom. "Brain Response to Putative Pheromones in Homosexual Men." *Proceedings of the National Academy of Science* 102 (2005): 7356–61.

Savic, Ivanka and Per Lindstrom. "PET and MRI Show Differences in Cerebral Asymmetry and Functional Connectivity Between Homo- and Heterosexual Subjects," *Proceedings of the National Academy of Sciences* 105:27 (June 16, 2008): 9403–08.

Scagliotti, John, dir., Dan Hunt, prod., Melissa Etheridge, narr., *After Stonewall* (New York: First Run Features, 1999).

Scanzoni, Letha, and Virginia Ramey Mollenkott. *Is the Homosexual My Neighbor? Another Christian View.* San Francisco: Harper and Row, 1978.

Schiller, Greta, dir., John Scagliotti, Robert Rosenberg, and Greta Schiller, prod. Rita Mae Brown, narr., *Before Stonewall: The Making of a Gay and Lesbian Community* (New York: First Run Features, 1985).

Schmidt, Gunter. "Foreword: The Debate on Pedophilia." *Journal of Homosexuality* 20:1-2 (1991): 1-4.

Schorer, Silvia and Thomas Staubli. "Saul, David, und Jonathan-eine Dreiecksgeschichte?" Ein Beitrag zum Thema 'Homosexualität,'" *Bible und Kirche* (1996): 15-22.

Schrage, Wolfgang. *The Ethics of the New Testament.* Trans. David E. Green. Philadelphia: Fortress, 1988.

Schüklenk, Udo, Edward Stein, Jacinta Kerin, and William Byne. "The Ethics of Genetic Research on Sexual Orientation," *Hastings Center Report* 27:4 (July–August, 1997): 6-13.

Schwöbel, Christoph and Colin E. Gunton, eds. *Persons, Divine and Human.* Edinburgh: T & T Clark, 1991.

Scotti, Jr., Gavin W. "Queer Eye for the Military Guy: Will 'Don't Ask, Don't Tell' Survive in the Wake of *Lawrence v. Texas*?" *St. John's Law Review* 78 (2004): 897-931.

"Sexual Privacy After *Lawrence v. Texas.*" *Georgetown Journal of Gender & the Law* 12:23 (2011): 333-65.

Shahar v. Bowers 114 F.3d 1097, 1110 (1997).

Shils, Edward and Morris Janowitz. "Cohesion and Disintegration in the Wehrmacht in World War II." *Public Opinion Quarterly* 12 (1948): 280-315.

Shilts, Randy. *Conduct Unbecoming: Gays & Lesbians in the U. S. Military.* New York: Fawcett Columbine, 1994.

Short, Thomas. "Gay Rights or Closet Virtues?" *National Review* 42:18 (September 17, 1990): 44.

Siker, Jeffrey S., ed., *Homosexuality in the Church: Both sides of the Debate.* Louisville: Westminster John Knox, 1994.

Slater, Don. "Victory! Supreme Court Upholds Homosexual Rights." *ONE* (February 1958): 17.

Snaith, Norman H. *Leviticus and Numbers, New Century Bible.* London: Nelson, 1967.

Snyder v. Phelps 563 U.S. (2011).

Somashekhar, Sandha. "Pentagon 'don't ask, don't tell' report: chaplains' views on gay strong, varied" *The Washington Post.* December 1, 2010, http://www.washingtonpost.com/wp-dyn/content/article/2010/12/01/AR2010120106 31_pf.html.

Southern Baptist Convention, "Homosexuality is not a valid alternative lifestyle. The Bible condemns it as sin," http://www.sbc.net/aboutus/pssexuality.asp, accessed Feb. 15, 2010.

Spindelman, Marc. "Surviving *Lawrence v. Texas*." *Michigan Law Review* 102 (June 2004): 1615-67.

State v. Morales 826 S.W. 2d.

Stauffer, Ethelbert. "*agapao*," in Gerhard Kittel, ed. *Theological Dictionary of the New Testament*. Trans. Geoffrey W. Bromiley. Grand Rapids: Eerdmans, 1964, 1:21-55.

Stein, Rob. "Brain Study Shows Differences Between Gays, Straights." *The Washington Post,* June 23, 2008. http://www.washingtonpost.com/wp-dyn/content/story/2008/06/22/ST2008062202006.html, accessed January 25, 2013.

Stone, Ken. "The Hermeneutics of Abomination: On Gay Men, Canaanites, and Biblical Interpretation," *Biblical Theology Bulletin* 27:2 (May 1997): 36-41.

Stouffer, Samuel, et. al. *The American Soldier.* Princeton: Princeton University, 1949.

Sullivan, Andrew. *Virtually Normal: An Argument About Homosexuality.* New York: Alfred A. Knopf, 1995.

Sullivan, Andrew, ed. *Same-Sex Marriage: Pro and Con, A Reader.* New York: Vintage, 1997, repr. 2004.

Sunshine Book Co. v. Summerfield 355 US 372 (1958).

Support to the DoD Comprehensive Review Working Group Analyzing the Impact of Repealing "Don't Ask, Don't Tell": Volume 2: Findings from the Qualitative Research Tasks. Rockville, MD: Westat, November 2010.

Swaab, Dick Frans and Eric Fliers. "A Sexually Dimorphic Nucleus in the Human Brain," *Science* 228.4703 (May 1985): 1112–15.

Swaab, Dick Frans and Michael A. Hofman, "An Enlarged Suprachiasmatic Nucleus in Homosexual Men," *Brain Research* 537 (1990): 141-48.

Swift, Michael. "Gay Revolutionary." *Gay Community News* (February 15/21, 1987).

Swiganski, Mary E., Robin Sakina Mama, and Kelly Ward, eds. *From Hate Crimes to Human Rights: A Tribute to Matthew Shepard.* Binghamton, NY: Harrington Park, 2001. Simultaneously published by Haworth Press as *Journal of Gay & Lesbian Social Services* 13:1/2 (2001).

Szasz, Thomas. *The Manufacture of Madness.* New York: Delta Books, 1970.

http://www.thegaymanifesto.com.

Thompson, Paul M., Katherine L. Narr, Rebecca E. Blanton, and Arthur W. Toga. "Mapping Structural Alterations of the Corpus Callosum During Brain Development and Degeneration," in *The Parallel Brain: The Cognitive Neuroscience of the Corpus Callosum,* Eran Zaidel and Marco Lacobni, eds. (Cambridge: Massachusetts Institute of Technology Press, 2003, 93-130.

Thorstad, David. "Man/Boy Love and the American Gay Movement." *Journal of Homosexuality* 20:1-2 (1991): 251-74.

———. "Statement to the Gay Liberation Movement on the Issue of Man/Boy Love." *Gay Community News* (January 6, 1979): 5.

Tillich, Paul. *Systematic Theology*. 3 vols. Chicago: University of Chicago, 1951-1963.

Tindall, Ralph H. "The Male Adolescent Involved with a Pederast Becomes an Adult." *Journal of Homosexuality* 3 (1978): 373-82.

Tribe, Lawrence H. "The Constitutional Inevitability of Same-Sex Marriage." *Maryland Law Review* 71:2 (2012): 471-89.

———. "*Lawrence v. Texas:* The 'Fundamental Right' That Dare Not Speak Its Name." *Harvard Law Review* 117 (2004): 1894-95.

Turner, P.D.M. "Biblical Texts Relevant to Homosexual Orientation and Practice," *Christian Scholar's Review* 26 (1997): 435-45.

United States Federal Bureau of Investigation. "Hate Crimes Based on Sexual Orientation, Gender, Gender Identity, or Disability." Congressional Digest 86:6 (June 2007): 170.

United States v. Treasury Employees 513 U.S. 454 (1995).

University of Washington, "Neuroscience for Kids: He Brains, She Brains." http://faculty.washington.edu/chudler/heshe.html, accessed December 29, 2012.

U. S. Code 10 (2011) §6031(a).

U. S. Department for Health and Human Services, "Understanding the Effects of Maltreatment on Brain Development." https://www.childwelfare.gov/pubs/issue_briefs/brain_development/how.cfm, accessed January 7, 2013.

van Camp, Julie C. "How Religion Co-opts Morality in Legal Reasoning: A Case Study of *Lawrence v. Texas*." *International Journal of Applied Philosophy* 21:2 (Fall 2007): 241-51.

van Imschoot, Paul. *Théologie de l'Ancien Testament*, 2 vols. New York: Desclée, 1954-1956.

Vance, Carol S., ed. *Pleasure and Danger: Exploring Female Sexuality*. London: Routledge & Kegan Paul, 1984.

Wainwright v. Stone 414 US 21 (1973).

Walden v. Center for Disease Control, Case No. 1:08-CV-02278-JEC (N.D. Ga. 2008).

Wallace, Jonathan D. "Constitutional Law: The First Amendment's Effects on Congressional Efforts to Protect Minors from Obscenity on the Internet." *University of Florida Journal of Law & Public Policy* 17:1 (April 2006): 189-98.

Walsh, Francis Michael. "The Return of the Naturalistic Fallacy: A Dialogue on Human Flourishing." *Heythrop Journal* 49 (2008): 370-87.

Waltke, Bruce K. *An Old Testament Theology: An Exegetical, Canonical, and Thematic Approach*. Grand Rapids: Zondervan, 2007.

Ward v. Wilbanks 2009 WL 4730457 (E.D. Mich. 2009).

Watson, John C. "Publications of a Dangerous Tendency." in Laura Castaneda and Shannon B. Campbell, eds. *News and Sexuality: Media Portraits of Diversity*. Thousand Oaks, CA: Sage Publications, 2005, 73-94.

Weeks, Ruth B. "The Sexually Exploited Child." *Southern Medical Journal* 69 (1976): 848-50;

Westfall, Bruce. "Kinsey Report," in Roland K. Harrison, ed. *Encyclopedia of Biblical and Christian Ethics*. Nashville: Thomas Nelson, rev. 1992: 140.

Whitman, Frederick L., Milton Diamond, James Martin. "Homosexual Orientation in Twins: A Report of 61 pairs and three Triplet Sets." *Archives of Sexual Behavior* 22:3 (1993): 187-206.

Williams, Walter L. and Yolanda Retter, eds. *Gay and Lesbian Rights in the United States: A Documentary History (Primary Documents in American History and Contemporary Issues)*. Westport, CT: Greenwood, 2003.

Wilson, Glenn D. and David N. Cox. *The Child-Lovers: A Study of Paedophiles in Society*. London: Peter Owen, 1983.

Wink, Walter. "Homosexuality and the Bible," in Walter Wink, ed. *Homosexuality and Christian Faith: Questions for the Churches*. Minneapolis: Fortress, 1999, 33-49.

Wisconsin v. Mitchell 169 Wis. 2d. 153 (1991) at 163; 485 N. W. 2d 807 (1992).
Wisconsin v. Mitchell 508 US 476 (1993).
Witacre, Rodney. *John.* Vol 4. *IVP New Testament Commentary. Downers Grove: InterVarsity,* 1999.
Wright, David F. "Homosexuality: The Relevance of the Bible," *The Evangelical Quarterly* (Oct-Dec 1989): 291-300.
Yates, Gary J. "How Many People are Lesbian, Gay, Bisexual, and Transgender?" http://williamsinstitute.law.ucla.edu/wp-content/uploads/Gates-How-Many-People-LGBT-Apr-2011.pdf, accessed January 3, 2013.
Yokota, Y., Y. Kawamura, and Y. Kameya. "Callosal Shapes at the Midsagittal Plane: MRI Differences of Normal Males, Normal Females, and GID," Conference Proceedings of the 2005 IEEE Engineering in Medicine and Biology 27th Annual Conference, Shanghai, China, September 1-4, 2005. 3:3055-58.
Zaidel, Eran and Marco Lacobni, eds. *The Parallel Brain: The Cognitive Neuroscience of the Corpus Callosum.* Cambridge: MIT, 2003.

34219246R00133

Made in the USA
Lexington, KY
20 March 2019